Mastering Concurrency in Python

Create faster programs using concurrency, asynchronous,
multithreading, and parallel programming

Quan Nguyen

BIRMINGHAM - MUMBAI

Mastering Concurrency in Python

Commissioning Editor: Richa Tripathi
Acquisition Editor: Shahnish Khan
Content Development Editor: Zeeyan Pinheiro
Technical Editor: Romy Dias
Copy Editor: Safis Editing
Project Coordinator: Vaidehi Sawant
Proofreader: Safis Editing
Indexer: Rekha Nair
Graphics: Alishon Mendonsa
Production Coordinator: Aparna Bhagat

First published: November 2018

Production reference: 1231118

Published by Packt Publishing Ltd.
Livery Place
35 Livery Street
Birmingham
B3 2PB, UK.

ISBN 978-1-78934-305-2

www.packtpub.com

To Tiffany, my incredible mentor and friend. Your guidance and friendship made all of this possible

– Quan Nguyen

`mapt.io`

Mapt is an online digital library that gives you full access to over 5,000 books and videos, as well as industry leading tools to help you plan your personal development and advance your career. For more information, please visit our website.

Why subscribe?

- Spend less time learning and more time coding with practical eBooks and Videos from over 4,000 industry professionals

- Improve your learning with Skill Plans built especially for you

- Get a free eBook or video every month

- Mapt is fully searchable

- Copy and paste, print, and bookmark content

Packt.com

Did you know that Packt offers eBook versions of every book published, with PDF and ePub files available? You can upgrade to the eBook version at `www.packt.com` and as a print book customer, you are entitled to a discount on the eBook copy. Get in touch with us at `customercare@packtpub.com` for more details.

At `www.packt.com`, you can also read a collection of free technical articles, sign up for a range of free newsletters, and receive exclusive discounts and offers on Packt books and eBooks.

Contributors

About the author

Quan Nguyen is a Python enthusiast and data scientist. He is currently a data analysis engineer at Micron Technology, Inc. With a strong background in mathematics and statistics, Quan is interested in the fields of scientific computing and machine learning. With data analysis being his focus, Quan also enjoys incorporating technology automation into everyday tasks through programming.

Quan's passion for Python programming has led him to be heavily involved in the Python community. He started as a primary contributor for the book *Python for Scientists and Engineers* and various open source projects on GitHub. Quan is also a writer for the Python Software Foundation and an occasional content contributor for DataScience.com (part of Oracle).

I'm grateful to my parents for their unwavering support. Special thanks to my sister, who somehow always managed to remind me of the truly important things in life. To aunt Y and uncle Nam: thank you for helping me in ways I never knew I needed.

A big thanks to my friends at Sigma Nu for always pushing me forward. To Karan, who started this amazing journey. Thank you, Zeeyan and Romy, for your dedication. To technical reviewers, for your insightful feedback.

About the reviewers

Romain Picard is currently a data science engineer. He has been working in the digital TV and telecommunications industry for 20 years. His daily work consists of data manipulation, machine learning model training, and model deployment. Most of these tasks are based on Python code.

He was previously a media software architect and a software developer. In these previous positions, he designed and developed TV and OTT players that have been used in millions of set-top boxes. Romain is especially interested in algorithms, and is constantly hunting for the most effective algorithm for each given use case.

Yogendra Sharma is a developer with experience of the architecture, design, and development of scalable and distributed applications. He was awarded a bachelor's degree from Rajasthan Technical University in computer science. With a core interest in microservices and Spring, he also has hands-on experience with technologies such as AWS Cloud, Python, J2EE, Node.js, JavaScript, Angular, MongoDB, and Docker. Currently, he works as an IoT and cloud architect at Intelizign Engineering Services, Pune.

Simone Marzola is a software engineer and technical lead with 10 years of experience. He is passionate about Python and machine learning, which have led him to be an active contributor in open source communities such as Mozilla Services and the Pylons Project, as well as involvement in European conferences as a speaker. Simone has been a lecturer on the BIG DIVE data science and machine learning course. He is currently a CTO and Scrum Master at Oval Money.

Packt is searching for authors like you

If you're interested in becoming an author for Packt, please visit `authors.packtpub.com` and apply today. We have worked with thousands of developers and tech professionals, just like you, to help them share their insight with the global tech community. You can make a general application, apply for a specific hot topic that we are recruiting an author for, or submit your own idea.

Table of Contents

Preface

Concurrency can be notoriously difficult to get right, but fortunately, the Python programming language makes working with concurrency tractable and easy. This book shows how Python can be used to program high-performance, robust, concurrent programs with its unique form of programming.

Designed for any curious developer with an interest in building fast, non-blocking, and resource-thrifty systems applications, this book will cover the best practices and patterns to help you incorporate concurrency into your systems. Additionally, emerging topics in Python concurrent programming will be discussed, including the new AsyncIO syntax, the widely accepted view that "locks don't lock anything," the use of atomic message queues, concurrent application architecture, and best practices.

We will tackle complex concurrency concepts and models via hands-on and engaging code examples. Having read this book, you will have gained a deep understanding of the principal components in the Python concurrency ecosystem, as well as a practical appreciation of different approaches to a real-life concurrency problem.

Who this book is for

If you're a developer familiar who's and you Python who want to learn to build high-performance applications that scale by leveraging single-core, multi-core, or distributed concurrency, then this book is for you.

What this book covers

Chapter 1, *Advanced Introduction to Concurrent and Parallel Programming*, introduces you to the concept of concurrency, and demonstrates an instance in which concurrent programming can improve significantly the speed of a Python program.

Chapter 2, *Amdahl's Law*, takes a theoretical approach and discusses the limitations of concurrency in improving the speed of applications. We will take a look at what concurrency truly provides and how we can best incorporate it.

`Chapter 3`, *Working with Threads in Python*, introduces the formal definition of threading and covers a different approach to implementing threading in a Python program. In this chapter, we will also discuss a major element in concurrent programming—the concept of synchronization.

`Chapter 4`, *Using the with Statement in Threads*, combines the concept of context management with threading in the overall context of concurrent programming in Python. We will be introduced to the main idea behind context management and how it is used in various programming practices, including threading.

`Chapter 5`, *Concurrent Web Requests*, covers one of the main applications of concurrent programming: web scraping. It also covers the concept of web scraping, along with other relevant elements, before discussing how threading can be applied to web scraping programs in order to achieve significant speedup.

`Chapter 6`, *Working with Processes in Python*, shows the formal definition of multiprocessing and how Python supports it. We will also learn more about the key differences between threading and multiprocessing, which are often confused with one another.

`Chapter 7`, *Reduction Operators in Processes*, pairs the concepts of reduction operations and multiprocessing together as a concurrent programming practice. This chapter will go over the theoretical foundation of reduction operations and how it is relevant to multiprocessing as well as programming in general.

`Chapter 8`, *Concurrent Image Processing*, goes into a specific application of concurrency: image processing. The basic ideas behind image processing, in addition to some of the most common processing techniques, are discussed. We will, of course, see how concurrency, specifically multiprocessing, can speed up the task of image processing.

`Chapter 9`, *Introduction to Asynchronous Programming*, considers the formal concept of asynchronous programming as one of the three major concurrent programming models aside from threading and multiprocessing. We will learn how asynchronous programming is fundamentally different from the two mentioned, but can still speedup concurrent applications.

`Chapter 10`, *Implementing Asynchronous Programming in Python*, goes in depth into the API that Python provides to facilitate asynchronous programming. Specifically, we will learn about the `asyncio` module, which is the main tool for implementing asynchronous programming in Python, and the general structure of an asynchronous application.

Chapter 11, *Building Communication Channels with asyncio*, combines the knowledge obtained regarding asynchronous programming covered in previous chapters with the topic of network communication. Specifically, we will look into using the `aiohttp` module as a tool to make asynchronous HTTP requests to web servers, as well as the `aiofile` module that implements asynchronous file reading/writing.

Chapter 12, *Deadlocks*, introduces the first of the problems that are commonly faced in concurrent programming. We will learn about the classical dining philosophers problem as an example of how deadlocks can cause concurrent programs to stop functioning. This chapter will also cover a number of potential approaches to deadlocks as well as relevant concepts, such as livelocks and distributed deadlocks.

Chapter 13, *Starvation*, considers another common problem in concurrent applications. The chapter uses the narrative of the classical readers-writers problem to explain the concept of starvation and its causes. We will, of course, also discuss potential solutions to these problems via hands-on examples in Python.

Chapter 14, *Race Conditions*, addresses arguably the most well-known concurrency problem: race conditions. We will also discuss the concept of a critical section, which is an essential element in the context of race conditions specifically, and concurrent programming in general. The chapter will then cover mutual exclusion as a potential solution for this problem.

Chapter 15, *The Global Interpreter Lock*, introduces the infamous GIL, which is considered the biggest challenge in concurrent programming in Python. We will learn about the reason behind GIL's implementation and the problems that it raises. This chapter concludes with some thoughts regarding how Python programmers and developers should think about and interact with the GIL.

Chapter 16, *Designing Lock-Based and Mutex-Free Concurrent Data Structures*, analyzes the process of designing two common concurrent data structures involving locks as a synchronization mechanism: lock-based and mutex-free. Several advanced analyses of the implementation of the data structures, as well as the performance thereof, are incorporated into the chapter so that readers will develop a critical mindset when it comes to designing concurrent applications.

Chapter 17, *Memory Models and Operations on Atomic Types*, includes theoretical topics that involve the underlying structure of the Python language and how programmers can take advantage of that in their concurrent applications. The concept of atomic operations is also introduced to readers in this chapter.

Chapter 18, *Building a Server from Scratch*, walks readers through the process of building a non-blocking server on a low level. We will learn about network programming functionalities that the socket module in Python provides and how we can use them to implement a functioning server. We will also apply the general structure of an asynchronous program discussed earlier in the book to convert a blocking server into a non-blocking one.

Chapter 19, *Testing, Debugging, and Scheduling Concurrent Applications*, covers higher-level uses of concurrent programs. The chapter will first cover how concurrency can be applied to the task of scheduling Python applications via the APScheduler module. We will then discuss the complexities that arise from concurrency in the topics of testing and debugging Python programs.

To get the most out of this book

Readers of this book should know how to execute Python programs in a development environment, or simply from a command prompt. They should also be familiar with general syntax and practices in Python programming (variables, functions, importing packages, and so on). Some basic computer science knowledge of elements such as pixels, the execution stack, and bytecode instructions is assumed at various points throughout this book.

The final section of Chapter 1, *Advanced Introduction to Concurrent and Parallel Programming*, covers the process of getting your Python environment set up. Chapters in this book might discuss the use of external libraries or tools that have to be installed via a package manager such as pip and Anaconda, and specific instructions on how to install those libraries are included in their corresponding chapters.

Download the example code files

You can download the example code files for this book from your account at www.packt.com. If you purchased this book elsewhere, you can visit www.packt.com/support and register to have the files emailed directly to you.

You can download the code files by following these steps:

1. Log in or register at www.packt.com.
2. Select the **SUPPORT** tab.
3. Click on **Code Downloads & Errata**.
4. Enter the name of the book in the **Search** box and follow the onscreen instructions.

Once the file is downloaded, please make sure that you unzip or extract the folder using the latest version of:

- WinRAR/7-Zip for Windows
- Zipeg/iZip/UnRarX for Mac
- 7-Zip/PeaZip for Linux

The code bundle for the book is also hosted on GitHub at `https://github.com/PacktPublishing/Mastering-Concurrency-in-Python`. In case there's an update to the code, it will be updated on the existing GitHub repository.

We also have other code bundles from our rich catalog of books and videos available at `https://github.com/PacktPublishing/`. Check them out!

Download the color images

We also provide a PDF file that has color images of the screenshots/diagrams used in this book. You can download it here: `https://www.packtpub.com/sites/default/files/downloads/9781789343052_ColorImages.pdf`.

Code in Action

Visit the following link to check out videos of the code being run: `http://bit.ly/2BsvQj6`

Conventions used

There are a number of text conventions used throughout this book.

`CodeInText`: Indicates code words in text, database table names, folder names, filenames, file extensions, pathnames, dummy URLs, user input, and Twitter handles. Here is an example: "The `asyncio` module provides a number of different transport classes."

A block of code is set as follows:

```
async def main(url):
    async with aiohttp.ClientSession() as session:
        await download_html(session, url)
```

When we wish to draw your attention to a particular part of a code block, the relevant lines or items are set in bold:

```
urls = [
    'http://packtpub.com',
    'http://python.org',
    'http://docs.python.org/3/library/asyncio',
    'http://aiohttp.readthedocs.io',
    'http://google.com'
]
```

Any command-line input or output is written as follows:

```
> python3 example5.py
Took 0.72 seconds.
```

Bold: Indicates a new term, an important word, or words that you see on screen. For example, words in menus or dialog boxes appear in the text like this. Here is an example: "To download the repository, simply click on the **Clone or download** button in the top-right corner of your window."

Warnings or important notes appear like this.

Tips and tricks appear like this.

Get in touch

Feedback from our readers is always welcome.

General feedback: If you have questions about any aspect of this book, mention the book title in the subject of your message and email us at customercare@packtpub.com.

Errata: Although we have taken every care to ensure the accuracy of our content, mistakes do happen. If you have found a mistake in this book, we would be grateful if you would report this to us. Please visit www.packt.com/submit-errata, selecting your book, clicking on the Errata Submission Form link, and entering the details.

Piracy: If you come across any illegal copies of our works in any form on the internet, we would be grateful if you would provide us with the location address or website name. Please contact us at `copyright@packt.com` with a link to the material.

If you are interested in becoming an author: If there is a topic that you have expertise in, and you are interested in either writing or contributing to a book, please visit `authors.packtpub.com`.

Reviews

Please leave a review. Once you have read and used this book, why not leave a review on the site that you purchased it from? Potential readers can then see and use your unbiased opinion to make purchase decisions, we at Packt can understand what you think about our products, and our authors can see your feedback on their book. Thank you!

For more information about Packt, please visit `packt.com`.

1
Advanced Introduction to Concurrent and Parallel Programming

This first chapter of *Mastering Concurrency in Python* will provide an overview of what concurrent programming is (in contrast to sequential programming). We will briefly discuss the differences between a program that can be made concurrent and one that cannot. We will go over the history of concurrent engineering and programming, and we will provide a number of examples of how concurrent programming is used in the present day. Finally, we will give a brief introduction to the approach that will be taken in this book, including an outline of the chapter structure and detailed instructions for how to download the code and create a working Python environment.

The following topics will be covered in this chapter:

- The concept of concurrency
- Why some programs cannot be made concurrent, and how to differentiate them from programs that can
- The history of concurrency in computer science: how it is used in the industry today, and what can be expected in the future
- The specific topics that will be covered in each section/chapter of the book
- How to set up a Python environment, and how to check out/download code from GitHub

Technical requirements

Check out the following video to see the Code in Action: `http://bit.ly/2TAMAeR`

What is concurrency?

It is estimated that the amount of data that needs to be processed by computer programs doubles every two years. The **International Data Corporation** (**IDC**), for example, estimates that, by 2020, there will be 5,200 GB of data for every person on earth. With this staggering volume of data come insatiable demands for computing power, and, while numerous computing techniques are being developed and utilized every day, concurrent programming remains one of the most prominent ways to effectively and accurately process data.

While some might be intimidated when the word concurrency appears, the notion behind it is quite intuitive, and it is very common, even in a non-programming context. However, this is not to say that concurrent programs are as simple as sequential ones; they are indeed more difficult to write and understand. Yet, once a correct and effective concurrent structure is achieved, significant improvement in execution time will follow, as you will see later on.

Concurrent versus sequential

Perhaps the most obvious way to understand concurrent programming is to compare it to sequential programming. While a sequential program is in one place at a time, in a concurrent program, different components are in independent, or semi-independent, states. This means that components in different states can be executed independently, and therefore at the same time (as the execution of one component does not depend on the result of another). The following diagram illustrates the basic differences between these two types:

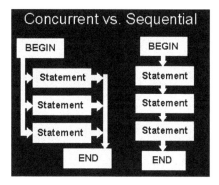

Difference between concurrent and sequential programs

One immediate advantage of concurrency is an improvement in execution time. Again, since some tasks are independent and can therefore be completed at the same time, less time is required for the computer to execute the whole program.

Example 1 – checking whether a non-negative number is prime

Let's consider a quick example. Suppose that we have a simple function that checks whether a non-negative number is prime, as follows:

```python
# Chapter01/example1.py

from math import sqrt

def is_prime(x):
    if x < 2:
    return False

if x == 2:
    return True

if x % 2 == 0:
    return False

limit = int(sqrt(x)) + 1
    for i in range(3, limit, 2):
        if x % i == 0:
            return False

return True
```

Also, suppose that we have a list of significantly large integers (10^{13} to $10^{13} + 500$), and we want to check whether each of them is prime by using the preceding function:

```
input = [i for i in range(10 ** 13, 10 ** 13 + 500)]
```

A sequential approach would be to simply pass one number after another to the `is_prime()` function, as follows:

```
# Chapter01/example1.py

from timeit import default_timer as timer

# sequential
start = timer()
result = []
for i in input:
    if is_prime(i):
        result.append(i)
print('Result 1:', result)
print('Took: %.2f seconds.' % (timer() - start))
```

Copy the code or download it from the GitHub repository and run it (using the `python example1.py` command). The first section of your output will be something similar to the following:

```
> python example1.py
Result 1: [10000000000037, 10000000000051, 10000000000099, 10000000000129,
10000000000183, 10000000000259, 10000000000267, 10000000000273,
10000000000279, 10000000000283, 10000000000313, 10000000000343,
10000000000391, 10000000000411, 10000000000433, 10000000000453]
Took: 3.41 seconds.
```

You can see that the program took around `3.41` seconds to process all of the numbers; we will come back to this number soon. For now, it will also be beneficial for us to check how hard the computer was working while running the program. Open an Activity Monitor application in your operating system, and run the Python script again; the following screenshot shows my results:

System:	6.63%	CPU LOAD	Threads:	1439
User:	10.46%		Processes:	371
Idle:	82.91%			

Activity Monitor showing computer performance

Evidently, the computer was not working too hard, as it was nearly 83% idle.

Now, let's see if concurrency can actually help us to improve our program. The `is_prime()` function contains a lot of heavy computation, and therefore it is a good candidate for concurrent programming. Since the process of passing one number to the `is_prime()` function is independent from passing another, we could potentially apply concurrency to our program, as follows:

```
# Chapter01/example1.py

# concurrent
start = timer()
result = []
with concurrent.futures.ProcessPoolExecutor(max_workers=20) as executor:
    futures = [executor.submit(is_prime, i) for i in input]

    for i, future in enumerate(concurrent.futures.as_completed(futures)):
        if future.result():
            result.append(input[i])

print('Result 2:', result)
print('Took: %.2f seconds.' % (timer() - start))
```

Roughly speaking, we are splitting the tasks into different, smaller chunks, and running them at the same time. Don't worry about the specifics of the code for now, as we will discuss this use of a pool of processes in greater detail later on.

When I executed the function, the execution time was noticeably better, and the computer also used more of its resources, being only 37% idle:

```
> python example1.py
Result 2: [10000000000183, 10000000000037, 10000000000129, 10000000000273,
10000000000259, 10000000000343, 10000000000051, 10000000000267,
10000000000279, 10000000000099, 10000000000283, 10000000000313,
10000000000391, 10000000000433, 10000000000411, 10000000000453]
Took: 2.33 seconds
```

The output of the Activity Monitor application will look something like the following:

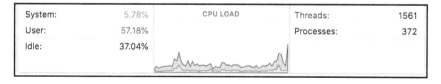

Activity Monitor showing computer performance

Concurrent versus parallel

At this point, if you have had some experience in parallel programming, you might be wondering whether concurrency is any different from parallelism. The key difference between concurrent and parallel programming is that, while in parallel programs there are a number of processing flows (mainly CPUs and cores) working independently all at once, there might be different processing flows (mostly threads) accessing and using **a shared resource** at the same time in concurrent programs.

Since this shared resource can be read and overwritten by any of the different processing flows, some form of coordination is required at times, when the tasks that need to be executed are not entirely independent from one another. In other words, it is important for some tasks to be executed after the others, to ensure that the programs will produce the correct results.

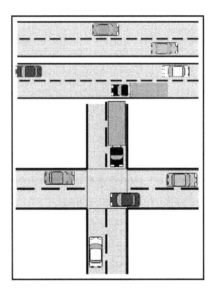

Difference between concurrency and parallelism

The preceding figure illustrates the difference between concurrency and parallelism: while in the upper section, parallel activities (in this case, cars) that do not interact with each other can run at the same time, in the lower section, some tasks have to wait for others to finish before they can be executed.

We will look at more examples of these distinctions later on.

A quick metaphor

Concurrency is a quite difficult concept to fully grasp immediately, so let's consider a quick metaphor, in order to make concurrency and its differences from parallelism easier to understand.

Although some neuroscientists might disagree, let's briefly assume that different parts of the human brain are responsible for performing separate, exclusive body part actions and activities. For example, the left hemisphere of the brain controls the right side of the body, and hence, the right hand (and vice versa); or, one part of the brain might be responsible for writing, while another solely processes speaking.

Now, let's consider the first example, specifically. If you want to move your left hand, the right side of your brain (and only the right side) has to process that command to move, which means that the left side of your brain is *free* to process other information. So, it is possible to move and use the left and right hands at the same time, in order to do different things. Similarly, it is possible to be writing *and* talking at the same time.

That is parallelism: where different processes don't interact with, and are independent of, each other. Remember that concurrency is not quite like parallelism. Even though there are instances where processes are executed together, concurrency also involves sharing the same resources. If parallelism is similar to using your left and right hands for independent tasks at the same time, concurrency can be associated with juggling, where the two hands perform different tasks simultaneously, but they also interact with the same object (in this case, the juggling balls), and some form of coordination between the two hands is therefore required.

Not everything should be made concurrent

Not all programs are created equal: some can be made parallel or concurrent relatively easily, while others are **inherently sequential**, and thus cannot be executed concurrently, or in parallel. An extreme example of the former is **embarrassingly parallel** programs, which can be divided into different parallel tasks, between which there is little or no dependency or need for communication.

Embarrassingly parallel

A common example of an embarrassingly parallel program is the 3D video rendering handled by a graphics processing unit, where each frame or pixel can be processed with no interdependency. Password cracking is another embarrassingly parallel task that can easily be distributed on CPU cores. In a later chapter, we will tackle a number of similar problems, including image processing and web scraping, which can be made concurrent/parallel intuitively, resulting in significantly improved execution times.

Inherently sequential

In opposition to embarrassingly parallel tasks, the execution of some tasks depends heavily on the results of others. In other words, those tasks are not independent, and thus, cannot be made parallel or concurrent. Furthermore, if we were to try to implement concurrency into those programs, it could cost us more execution time to produce the same results. Let's go back to our prime-checking example from earlier; the following is the output that we saw:

```
> python example1.py
Result 1: [10000000000037, 10000000000051, 10000000000099, 10000000000129,
10000000000183, 10000000000259, 10000000000267, 10000000000273,
10000000000279, 10000000000283, 10000000000313, 10000000000343,
10000000000391, 10000000000411, 10000000000433, 10000000000453]
Took: 3.41 seconds.
Result 2: [10000000000183, 10000000000037, 10000000000129, 10000000000273,
10000000000259, 10000000000343, 10000000000051, 10000000000267,
10000000000279, 10000000000099, 10000000000283, 10000000000313,
10000000000391, 10000000000433, 10000000000411, 10000000000453]
Took: 2.33 seconds.
```

Pay close attention, and you will see that the two results from the two methods are not identical; the primes in the second result list are **out of order**. (Recall that, in the second method, to apply concurrency we specified splitting the tasks into different groups to be executed simultaneously, and the order of the results we obtained is the order in which each task finished being executed.) This is a direct result of using concurrency in our second method: we split the tasks to be executed by the program into different groups, and our program processed the tasks in these groups at the same time.

Since tasks across different groups were executed simultaneously, there were tasks that were behind other tasks in the input list, and yet were executed before those other tasks. For example, the number `10000000000183` was behind the number `10000000000129` in our input list, but was processed prior to, and therefore in front of, the number `10000000000129` in our output list. In fact, if you execute the program again and again, the second result will vary in almost every run.

Evidently, this situation is not desirable if the result we'd like to obtain needs to be in the order of the input we originally had. Of course, in this example, we can simply modify the result by using some form of sorting, but it will cost us extra execution time in the end, which might make it even more expensive than the original sequential approach.

A concept that is commonly used to illustrate the innate sequentiality of some tasks is pregnancy: the number of women will never reduce the length of pregnancy. As opposed to parallel or concurrent tasks, where an increase in the number of processing entities will improve the execution time, adding more processors in inherently sequential tasks will not. Famous examples of inherent sequentiality include iterative algorithms: Newton's method, iterative solutions to the three-body problem, or iterative numerical approximation methods.

Example 2 – inherently sequential tasks

Let us consider a quick example:

Computing $f^{1000}(3)$, with $f(x) = x^2 - x + 1$, and $f^{n+1}(x) = f(f^n(x))$.

With complicated functions like f (where it is relatively difficult to find a general form of $f^n(x)$), the only obviously reasonable way to compute $f^{1000}(3)$ or similar values is to iteratively compute $f^2(3) = f(f(3))$, $f^3(3) = f(f^2(3))$, ... , $f^{999}(3) = f(f^{998}(3))$, and, finally, $f^{1000}(3) = f(f^{999}(3))$.

Since it will take significant time to actually compute $f^{1000}(3)$, even when using a computer, we will only consider $f^{20}(3)$ in our code (my laptop actually started heating up after $f^{25}(3)$):

```
# Chapter01/example2.py

def f(x):
    return x * x - x + 1

# sequential
def f(x):
    return x * x - x + 1

start = timer()
```

```
result = 3
for i in range(20):
    result = f(result)

print('Result is very large. Only printing the last 5 digits:', result %
100000)
print('Sequential took: %.2f seconds.' % (timer() - start))
```

Run it (or use `python example2.py`); the following code shows the output I received:

```
> python example2.py
Result is very large. Only printing the last 5 digits: 35443
Sequential took: 0.10 seconds.
```

Now, if we were to attempt to apply concurrency to this script, the only possible way would be through a `for` loop. One solution might be as follows:

```
# Chapter01/example2.py

# concurrent
def concurrent_f(x):
    global result
    result = f(result)

result = 3

with concurrent.futures.ThreadPoolExecutor(max_workers=20) as exector:
    futures = [exector.submit(concurrent_f, i) for i in range(20)]

    _ = concurrent.futures.as_completed(futures)

print('Result is very large. Only printing the last 5 digits:', result %
100000)
print('Concurrent took: %.2f seconds.' % (timer() - start))
```

The output I received is shown as follows:

```
> python example2.py
Result is very large. Only printing the last 5 digits: 35443
Concurrent took: 0.19 seconds.
```

Even though both methods produced the same result, the concurrent method took almost twice as long as the sequential method. This is due to the fact that every time a new thread (from `ThreadPoolExecutor`) was spawned, the function `conconcurrent_f()`, inside that thread, needed to wait for the variable `result` to be processed by the previous thread completely, and the program as a whole was thus executed in a sequential manner, nonetheless.

So, while there was no actual concurrency involved in the second method, the overhead cost of spawning new threads contributed to the significantly worse execution time. This is one example of inherently sequential tasks, where concurrency or parallelism should not be applied to attempt an improvement in execution time.

I/O bound

Another way to think about sequentiality is the concept (in computer science) of a condition called I/O bound, in which the time it takes to complete a computation is mainly determined by the time spent waiting for **input/output** (**I/O**) operations to be completed. This condition arises when the rate at which data is requested is slower than the rate at which it is consumed, or, in short, more time is spent requesting data than processing it.

In an I/O bound state, the CPU must stall its operation, waiting for data to be processed. This means that, even if the CPU gets faster at processing data, processes tend to not increase in speed in proportion to the increased CPU speed, since they get more I/O-bound. With faster computation speed being the primary goal of new computer and processor designs, I/O bound states are becoming undesirable, yet more and more common, in programs.

As you have seen, there are a number of situations in which the application of concurrent programming results in decreased processing speed, and they should thus be avoided. It is therefore important for us to not see concurrency as a golden ticket that can produce unconditionally better execution times, and to understand the differences between the structures of programs that benefit from concurrency and programs that do not.

The history, present, and future of concurrency

In the following sub-topics, we will discuss the past, present, and future of concurrency.

The field of concurrent programming has enjoyed significant popularity since the early days of computer science. In this section, we will discuss how concurrent programming started and evolved throughout its history, its current usage in the industry, and some predictions regarding how concurrency will be used in the future.

The history of concurrency

The concept of concurrency has been around for quite some time. The idea developed from early work on railroads and telegraphy in the nineteenth and early twentieth centuries, and some terms have even survived to this day (such as **semaphore**, which indicates a variable that controls access to a shared resource in concurrent programs). Concurrency was first applied to address the question of how to handle multiple trains on the same railroad system, in order to avoid collisions and maximize efficiency, and how to handle multiple transmissions over a given set of wires in early telegraphy.

A significant portion of the theoretical groundwork for concurrent programming was actually laid in the 1960s. The early algorithmic language ALGOL 68, which was first developed in 1959, includes features that support concurrent programming. The academic study of concurrency officially started with a seminal paper in 1965 from Edsger Dijkstra, who was a pioneer in computer science, best known for the path-finding algorithm that was named after him.

That seminal paper is considered the first paper in the field of concurrent programming, in which Dijkstra identified and solved the mutual exclusion problem. Mutual exclusion, which is a property of concurrency control that prevents race conditions (which we will discuss later on), went on to become one of the most discussed topics in concurrency.

Yet, there was no considerable interest after that. From around 1970 to early 2000, processors were said to double in executing speed every 18 months. During this period, programmers did not need to concern themselves with concurrent programming, as all they had to do to have their programs run faster was wait. However, in the early 2000s, a paradigm shift in the processor business took place; instead of making increasingly big and fast processors for computers, manufacturers started focusing on smaller, slower processors, which were put together in groups. This was when computers started to have multicore processors.

Nowadays, an average computer has more than one core. So, if a programmer writes all of their programs to be non-concurrent in any way, they will find that their programs utilize only one core or one thread to process data, while the rest of the CPU sits idle, doing nothing (as we saw in the *Example 1 – Checking whether a non-negative number is prime* section). This is one reason for the recent push in concurrent programming.

Another reason for the increasing popularity of concurrency is the growing field of graphical, multimedia, and web-based application development, in which the application of concurrency is widely used to solve complex and meaningful problems. For example, concurrency is a major player in web development: each new request made by a user typically comes in as its own process (this is called multiprocessing; see Chapter 6, *Working with Processes in Python*) or asynchronously coordinated with other requests (this is called asynchronous programming; see Chapter 9, *Introduction to Asynchronous Programming*); if any of those requests need to access a shared resource (a database, for example) where data can be changed, concurrency should be taken into consideration.

The present

Considering the present day, where an explosive growth the internet and data sharing happens every second, concurrency is more important than ever. The current use of concurrent programming emphasizes correctness, performance, and robustness.

Some concurrent systems, such as operating systems or database management systems, are generally designed to operate indefinitely, including automatic recovery from failure, and not terminate unexpectedly. As mentioned previously, concurrent systems use shared resources, and thus they require some form of **semaphore** in their implementation, to control and coordinate access to those resources.

Concurrent programming is quite ubiquitous in the field of software development. Following are a few examples where concurrency is present:

- Concurrency plays an important role in most common programming languages: C++, C#, Erlang, Go, Java, Julia, JavaScript, Perl, Python, Ruby, Scala, and so on.
- Again, since almost every computer today has more than one core in its CPU, desktop applications need to be able to take advantage of that computing power, in order to provide truly well-designed software.

Multicore processors used in MacBook Pro computers

- The iPhone 4S, which was released in 2011, has a dual-core CPU, so mobile development also has to stay connected to concurrent applications.
- As for video games, two of the biggest players on the current market are the Xbox 360, which is a multi-CPU system, and Sony's PS3, which is essentially a multicore system.
- Even the current iteration of the $35 Raspberry Pi is built around a quad-core system.
- It is estimated that on average, Google processes over 40,000 search queries every second, which equates to over 3.5 billion searches per day, and 1.2 trillion searches per year, worldwide. Apart from having massive machines with incredible processing power, concurrency is the best way to handle that amount of data requests.

A large percentage of today's data and applications are stored in the cloud. Since computing instances on the cloud are relatively small in size, almost every web application is therefore forced to be concurrent, processing different small jobs simultaneously. As it gains more customers and has to process more requests, a well-designed web application can simply utilize more servers while keeping the same logic; this corresponds to the property of robustness that we mentioned earlier.

Even in the increasingly popular fields of artificial intelligence and data science, major advances have been made, in part due to the availability of high-end graphics cards (GPUs), which are used as parallel computing engines. In every notable competition on the biggest data science website (`https://www.kaggle.com/`), almost all prize-winning solutions feature some form of GPU usage during the training process. With the sheer amount of data that big data models have to comb through, concurrency provides an effective solution. Some AI algorithms are even designed to break their input data down into smaller portions and process them independently, which is a perfect opportunity to apply concurrency in order to achieve better model-training time.

The future

In this day and age, computer/internet users expect instant output, no matter what applications they are using, and developers often find themselves struggling with the problem of providing better speed for their applications. In terms of usage, concurrency will continue to be one of the main players in the field of programming, providing unique and innovative solutions to those problems. As mentioned earlier, whether it be video game design, mobile apps, desktop software, or web development, concurrency is, and will be, omnipresent in the near future.

Given the need for concurrency support in applications, some might argue that concurrent programming will also become more standard in academia. Even though specific topics in concurrency and parallelism are being covered in computer science courses, in-depth, complex subjects on concurrent programming (both theoretical and applied subjects) will be implemented in undergraduate and graduate courses, to better prepare students for the industry, where concurrency is being used every day. Computer science courses on building concurrent systems, studying data flows, and analyzing concurrent and parallel structures will only be the beginning.

Others might have a more skeptical view of the future of concurrent programming. Some say that concurrency is really about dependency analysis: a sub-field of compiler theory that analyzes execution-order constraints between statements/instructions, and determines whether it is safe for a program to **reorder** or **parallelize** its statements. Furthermore, since only a very small number of programmers truly understand concurrency and all of its intricacies, there will be a push for compilers, along with support from the operating system, to take on the responsibility of actually implementing concurrency into the programs they compile on their own.

Specifically, in the future programmers will not have to concern themselves with the concepts and problems of concurrent programming, nor should they. An algorithm implemented on the compiler-level should look at the program being compiled, analyze the statements and instructions, produce a dependency graph to determine the optimal order of execution for those statements and instructions, and apply concurrency/parallelism where it is appropriate and efficient. In short, the combination of the low number of programmers understanding and being able to effectively work with concurrent systems and the possibility of automating the design of concurrency will lead to a decrease in interest in concurrent programming.

In the end, only time will tell what the future holds for concurrent programming. We programmers can only look at how concurrency is currently being used in the real world, and determine whether it is worth learning or not: which, as we have seen in this case, it is. Furthermore, even though there are strong connections between designing concurrent programs and dependency analysis, I personally see concurrent programming as a more intricate and involved process, which might be very difficult to achieve through automation.

Concurrent programming is indeed extremely complicated and very hard to get right, but that also means the knowledge gained through the process will be beneficial and useful to any programmer, and I see that as a good enough reason to learn about concurrency. The ability to analyze the problems of program speedup, restructure your programs into different independent tasks, and coordinate those tasks to use the same resources, are the main skills that programmers build while working with concurrency, and knowledge of these topics will help them with other programming problems, as well.

A brief overview of mastering concurrency in Python

Python is one of the most popular programming languages out there, and for good reason. The language comes with numerous libraries and frameworks that facilitate high-performance computing, whether it be software development, web development, data analysis, or machine learning. Yet, there have been discussions among developers criticizing Python, which often revolve around the **Global Interpreter Lock (GIL)** and the difficulty of implementing concurrent and parallel programs that it leads to.

While concurrency and parallelism do behave differently in Python than in other common programming languages, it is still possible for programmers to implement Python programs that run concurrently or in parallel, and achieve significant speedup for their programs.

Mastering Concurrency in Python will serve as a comprehensive introduction to various advanced concepts in concurrent engineering and programming in Python. This book will also provide a detailed overview of how concurrency and parallelism are being used in real-world applications. It is a perfect blend of theoretical analyses and practical examples, which will give you a full understanding of the theories and techniques regarding concurrent programming in Python.

This book will be divided into six main sections. It will start with the idea behind concurrency and concurrent programming—the history, how it is being used in the industry today, and finally, a mathematical analysis of the speedup that concurrency can potentially provide. Additionally, the last section in this chapter (which is our next section) will cover instructions for how to follow the coding examples in this book, including setting up a Python environment on your own computer, downloading/cloning the code included in this book from GitHub, and running each example from your computer.

The next three sections will cover three of the main implementation approaches in concurrent programming: threads, processes, and asynchronous I/O, respectively. These sections will include theoretical concepts and principles for each of these approaches, the syntax and various functionalities that the Python language provides to support them, discussions of best practices for their advanced usage, and hands-on projects that directly apply these concepts to solve real-world problems.

Section five will introduce readers to some of the most common problems that engineers and programmers face in concurrent programming: deadlock, starvation, and race conditions. Readers will learn about the theoretical foundations and causes for each problem, analyze and replicate each of them in Python, and finally implement potential solutions. The last chapter in this section will discuss the aforementioned GIL, which is specific to the Python language. It will cover the GIL's integral role in the Python ecosystem, some challenges that the GIL poses for concurrent programming, and how to implement effective workarounds.

In the last section of the book, we will be working on various advanced applications of concurrent Python programming. These applications will include the design of lock-free and lock-based concurrent data structures, memory models and operations on atomic types, and how to build a server that supports concurrent request processing from scratch. The section will also cover the the best practices when testing, debugging, and scheduling concurrent Python applications.

Throughout this book, you will be building essential skills for working with concurrent programs, just through following the discussions, the example code, and the hands-on projects. You will understand the fundamentals of the most important concepts in concurrent programming, how to implement them in Python programs, and how to apply that knowledge to advanced applications. By the end of *Mastering Concurrency in Python*, you will have a unique combination of extensive theoretical knowledge regarding concurrency, and practical know-how of the various applications of concurrency in the Python language.

Why Python?

As mentioned previously, one of the difficulties that developers face while working with concurrency in the Python programming language (specifically, CPython—a reference implementation of Python written in C) is its GIL. The GIL is a mutex that protects access to Python objects, preventing multiple threads from executing Python byte codes at once. This lock is necessary mainly because CPython's memory management is not thread-safe. CPython uses reference counting to implement its memory management. This results in the fact that multiple threads can access and execute Python code simultaneously; this situation is undesirable, as it can cause an incorrect handling of data, and we say that this type of memory management is not thread-safe. To address this problem, the GIL is, as the name suggests, a lock that allows only one thread to access Python code and objects. However, this also means that, to implement multithreading programs in CPython, developers need to be aware of the GIL and work around it. That is why many have problems with implementing concurrent systems in Python.

So, why use Python for concurrency at all? Even though the GIL prevents multithreaded CPython programs from taking full advantage of multiprocessor systems in certain situations, most blocking or long-running operations, such as I/O, image processing, and NumPy number crunching, happen outside the GIL. Therefore, the GIL only becomes a potential bottleneck for multithreaded programs that spend significant time inside the GIL. As you will see in future chapters, multithreading is only a form of concurrent programming, and, while the GIL poses some challenges for multithreaded CPython programs that allow more than one thread to access shared resources, other forms of concurrent programming do not have this problem. For example, multiprocessing applications that do not share any common resources among processes, such as I/O, image processing, or NumPy number crunching, can work seamlessly with the GIL. We will discuss the GIL and its place in the Python ecosystem in greater depth in Chapter 15, *The Global Interpret Lock*.

Aside from that, Python has been gaining increasing popularity from the programming community. Due to its user-friendly syntax and overall readability, more and more people have found it relatively straightforward to use Python in their development, whether it is beginners learning a new programming language, intermediate users looking for the advanced functionalities of Python, or experienced programmers using Python to solve complex problems. It is estimated that the development of Python code can be up to 10 times faster than C/C++ code.

The large number of developers using Python has resulted in a strong, ever-growing support community. Libraries and packages in Python are being developed and released every day, tackling different problems and technologies. Currently, the Python language supports an incredibly wide range of programming—namely, software development, desktop GUIs, video game design, web and internet development, and scientific and numeric computing. In recent years, Python has also been growing as one of the top tools in data science, big data, and machine learning, competing with the long-time player in the field, R.

The sheer number of development tools available in Python has encouraged more developers to start programming with Python, making Python even more popular and easy to use; I call this *the vicious circle of Python*. David Robinson, chief data scientist at DataCamp, wrote a blog (https://stackoverflow.blog/2017/09/06/incredible-growth-python/) about the incredible growth of Python, and called it the most popular programming language.

However, Python is slow, or at least slower than other popular programming languages. This is due to the fact that Python is a dynamically typed, interpreted language, where values are stored not in dense buffers, but in scattered objects. This is a direct result of Python's readability and user-friendliness. Luckily, there are various options regarding how to make your Python program run faster, and concurrency is one of the most complex of them; that is what we are going to master throughout this book.

Setting up your Python environment

Before we move any further, let's go through a number of specifications regarding how to set up the necessary tools that you will be using throughout this book. In particular, we will discuss the process of obtaining a Python distribution for your system and an appropriate development environment, as well as how to download the code used in the examples included in the chapters of this book.

General setup

Let's look at the process of obtaining a Python distribution for your system and an appropriate development environment:

- Any developer can obtain their own Python distribution from `https://www.python.org/downloads/`.
- Even though both Python 2 and Python 3 are being supported and maintained, throughout this book we will be using Python 3.
- The choice of an **integrated development environment** (**IDE**) is flexible for this book. Although it is technically possible to develop Python applications using a minimal text editor, such as Notepad or TextEdit, it is usually much easier to read and write code with IDEs designed specifically for Python. These include IDLE (`https://docs.python.org/3/library/idle.html`), PyCharm (`https://www.jetbrains.com/pycharm/`), Sublime Text (`https://www.sublimetext.com/`), and Atom (`https://atom.io/`).

Downloading example code

To obtain the code used throughout this book, you can download a repository from GitHub, which includes all of the example and project code covered in this book:

- First, visit https://github.com/PacktPublishing/Mastering-Concurrency-in-Python.
- To download the repository, simply click on the **Clone or download** button in the top right corner of your window. Choose **Download ZIP** to download the compressed repository to your computer:

Click on Download ZIP to download the repository

- Uncompress the downloaded file to create the folder that we are looking for. The folder should have the name Mastering-Concurrency-in-Python.

Separate folders, titled ChapterXX, are inside the folder, indicating the chapter that covers the code in that folder. For example, the Chapter03 folder contains the example and project code covered in Chapter 3, *Working with Threads in Python*. In each subfolder, there are various Python scripts; as you go through each code example in the book, you will know which script to run at a specific point in each chapter.

Summary

You have now been introduced to the concept of concurrent and parallel programming. It is about designing and structuring programming commands and instructions, so that different sections of the program can be executed in an efficient order, while sharing the same resources. Since time is saved when some commands and instructions are executed at the same time, concurrent programming provides significant improvements in program execution time, as compared to traditional sequential programming.

However, various factors need to be taken into consideration while designing a concurrent program. While there are specific tasks that can easily be broken down into independent sections that can be executed in parallel (embarrassingly parallel tasks), others require different forms of coordination between the program commands, so that shared resources are used correctly and efficiently. There are also inherently sequential tasks, in which no concurrency and parallelism can be applied to achieve program speedup. You should know the fundamental differences between these tasks, so that you can design your concurrent programs appropriately.

Recently, there was a paradigm shift that facilitated the implementation of concurrency into most aspects of the programming world. Now, concurrency can be found almost everywhere: desktop and mobile applications, video games, web and internet development, AI, and so on. Concurrency is still growing, and it is expected to keep growing in the future. It is therefore crucial for any experienced programmer to understand concurrency and its relevant concepts, and to know how to integrate those concepts into their applications.

Python, on the other hand, is one of the most (if not the most) popular programming languages. It provides powerful options in most sub-fields of programming. The combination of concurrency and Python is therefore one of the topics most worth learning and mastering in programming.

In the next chapter, on Amdahl's Law, we will discuss how significant the improvements in speedup that concurrency provides for our programs are. We will analyze the formula for Amdahl's Law, discussing its implications and considering Python examples.

Questions

- What is the idea behind concurrency, and why is it useful?
- What are the differences between concurrent programming and sequential programming?
- What are the differences between concurrent programming and parallel programming?
- Can every program be made concurrent or parallel?
- What are embarrassingly parallel tasks?
- What are inherently sequential tasks?
- What does I/O bound mean?
- How is concurrent processing currently being used in the real world?

Further reading

For more information you can refer to the following links:

- *Python Parallel Programming Cookbook*, by Giancarlo Zaccone, Packt Publishing Ltd, 2015
- *Learning Concurrency in Python: Build highly efficient, robust, and concurrent applications* (2017), by Forbes, Elliot
- "The historical roots of concurrent engineering fundamentals." *IEEE Transactions on Engineering Management* 44.1 (1997): 67-78, by Robert P. Smith
- *Programming language pragmatics*, Morgan Kaufmann, 2000, by Michael Lee Scott

2
Amdahl's Law

Often used in discussions revolving around concurrent programs, Amdahl's Law explains the theoretical speedup of the execution of a program that can be expected when using concurrency. In this chapter, we will discuss the concept of Amdahl's Law, and we will analyze its formula, which estimates the potential speedup of a program and replicates it in Python code. This chapter will also briefly cover the relationship between Amdahl's Law and the law of diminishing returns.

The following topics will be covered in this chapter:

- Amdahl's Law
- Amdahl's Law: its formula and interpretation
- The relationship between Amdahl's Law and the law of diminishing returns
- Simulation in Python, and the practical applications of Amdahl's Law

Technical requirements

The following is a list of prerequisites for this chapter:

- Ensure that you have Python 3 installed on your computer
- Download the GitHub repository at `https://github.com/PacktPublishing/Mastering-Concurrency-in-Python`
- During this chapter, we will be working with the subfolder named `Chapter02`
- Check out the following video to see the Code in Action: `http://bit.ly/2DWaOeQ`

Amdahl's Law

How do you find a balance between parallelizing a sequential program (by increasing the number of processors) and optimizing the execution speed of the sequential program itself? For example, which is the better option: Having four processors running a given program for 40% of its execution, or using only two processors executing the same program, but for twice as long? This type of trade-off, which is commonly found in concurrent programming, can be strategically analyzed and answered by applying Amdahl's Law.

Additionally, while concurrency and parallelism can be a powerful tool that provides significant improvements in program execution time, they are not a silver bullet that can speed up any non-sequential architecture infinitely and unconditionally. It is therefore important for developers and programmers to know and understand the limits of the speed improvements that concurrency and parallelism offer to their programs, and Amdahl's Law addresses those concerns.

Terminology

Amdahl's Law provides a mathematical formula that calculates the potential improvement in speed of a concurrent program by increasing its resources (specifically, the number of available processors). Before we can get into the theory behind Amdahl's Law, first, we must clarify some terminology, as follows:

- Amdahl's Law solely discusses the potential speedup in latency resulting from executing a task in **parallel**. While concurrency is not directly discussed here, the results from Amdahl's Law concerning parallelism will nonetheless give us an estimation regarding concurrent programs.
- The **speed** of a program denotes the time it takes for the program to execute in full. This can be measured in any increment of time.
- **Speedup** is the time that measures the benefit of executing a computation in parallel. It is defined as the time it takes a program to execute in serial (with one processor), divided by the time it takes to execute in parallel (with multiple processors). The formula for speedup is as follows:

$$S = \frac{T(1)}{T(j)}$$

In the preceding formula, $T(j)$ is the time it takes to execute the program when using j processors.

Formula and interpretation

Before we get into the formula for Amdahl's Law and its implications, let's explore the concept of speedup, through some brief analysis. Let's assume that there are N workers working on a given job that is fully parallelizable—that is, the job can be perfectly divided into N equal sections. This means that N workers working together to complete the job will only take $1/N$ of the time it takes one worker to complete the same job.

However, most computer programs are not 100% parallelizable: some parts of a program might be inherently sequential, while others are broken up into parallel tasks.

The formula for Amdahl's Law

Now, let B denote the fraction of the program that is strictly serial, and consider the following:

- $B * T(1)$ is the time it takes to execute the parts of the program that are inherently sequential.
- $T(1) - B * T(1) = (1 - B) * T(1)$ is the time it takes to execute the parts of the program that are parallelizable, with one processor:
  - Then, $(1 - B) * T(1) / N$ is the time it takes to execute these parts with N processors
- So, $B * T(1) + (1 - B) * T(1) / N$ is the total time it takes to execute the whole program with N processors.

Coming back to the formula for the speedup quantity, we have the following:

$$S = \frac{T(1)}{T(j)} = \frac{T(1)}{B.T(1) + \frac{(1-B).T(1)}{j}} = \frac{1}{B + \frac{1-B}{j}}$$

This formula is actually a form of Amdahl's Law, used to estimate the speedup in a parallel program.

A quick example

Let's assume that we have a computer program, and the following applies to it:

- 40% of it is subject to parallelism, so $B = 1 - 40\% = 0.6$
- Its parallelizable parts will be processed by four processors, so $j = 4$

Amdahl's Law states that the overall speedup of applying the improvement will be as follows:

$$S = \frac{1}{B + \frac{1-B}{j}} = \frac{1}{0.6 + \frac{1-0.6}{4}} = \frac{10}{7} \approx 1.43$$

Implications

The following is a quote from Gene Amdahl, in 1967:

> *"For over a decade prophets have voiced the contention that the organization of a single computer has reached its limits and that truly significantly advances can be made only by interconnection of a multiplicity of computers in such a manner as to permit cooperative solution... The nature of this overhead (in parallelism) appears to be sequential so that it is unlikely to be amenable to parallel processing techniques. Overhead alone would then place an upper limit on throughput of five to seven times the sequential processing rate, even if the housekeeping were done in a separate processor... At any point in time it is difficult to foresee how the previous bottlenecks in a sequential computer will be effectively overcome."*

Through the quote, Amdahl indicated that whatever concurrent and parallel techniques are implemented in a program, the sequential nature of the overhead portion required in the program always sets an upper boundary on how much speedup the program will gain. This is one of the implications that Amdahl's Law further suggests. Consider the following example:

$$\frac{1-B}{j} > \frac{1-B}{j+1} \implies \frac{1}{B + \frac{1-B}{j}} < \frac{1}{B + \frac{1-B}{j+1}} \implies S_j < S_{j+1}$$

S_n denotes the speedup gained from n processors

This shows that, as the number of resources (specifically, the number of available processors) increases, the speedup of the execution of the whole task also increases. However, this does not mean that we should always implement concurrency and parallelism with as many system processors as possible, to achieve the highest performance. In fact, from the formula, we can also gather that the speedup achieved from incrementing the number of processors decreases. In other words, as we add more processors for our concurrent program, we will obtain less and less improvement in execution time.

Furthermore, as mentioned previously, another implication that Amdahl's Law suggests concerns the upper limit of the execution time improvement:

$$\begin{cases} S \le \frac{1}{B} \\ \lim_{j \to \infty} S = \frac{1}{B} \end{cases}$$

$\frac{1}{B}$ is the cap of how much improvement concurrency and parallelism can offer your program. This is to say that, no matter how many available resources your system has, it is impossible to obtain a speedup larger than $\frac{1}{B}$ through concurrency, and this limit is dictated by the sequential overhead portion of the program (B is the fraction of the program that is strictly serial).

Amdahl's Law's relationship to the law of diminishing returns

Amdahl's Law is often conflated with the law of diminishing returns, which is a rather popular concept in economics. However, the law of diminishing returns is only a special case of applying Amdahl's Law, depending on the order of improvement. If the order of separate tasks in the program is chosen to be improved in an **optimal** way, a monotonically decreasing improvement in execution time will be observed, demonstrating diminishing returns. An optimal method indicates first applying those improvements that will result in the greatest speedups, and leaving those improvements yielding smaller speedups for later.

Now, if we were to reverse this sequence for choosing resources, in which we improve less optimal components of our program before more optimal components, the speedup achieved through the improvement would increase throughout the process. Furthermore, it is actually more beneficial for us to implement system improvements in this **reverse-optimal** order in reality, as the more optimal components are usually more complex, and take more time to improve.

Another similarity between Amdahl's Law and the law of diminishing returns concerns the improvement in speedup obtained through adding more processors to a system. Specifically, as a new processor is added to the system to process a fixed-size task, it will offer less usable computation power than the previous processor. As we discussed in the last section, the improvement in this situation strictly decreases as the number of processors increases, and the total throughout approaches the upper boundary of *1/B*.

It is important to note that this analysis does not take into account other potential bottlenecks, such as memory bandwidth and I/O bandwidth. In fact, if these resources do not scale with the number of processors, then simply adding processors results in even lower returns.

How to simulate in Python

In this section, we will look at the results of Amdahl's Law through a Python program. Still considering the task of determining whether an integer is a prime number, as discussed in Chapter 1, *Advanced Introduction to Concurrent and Parallel Programming,* we will see what actual speedup is achieved through concurrency. If you already have the code for the book downloaded from the GitHub page, we are looking at the Chapter02/example1.py file.

As a refresher, the function that checks for prime numbers is as follows:

```python
# Chapter02/example1.py

from math import sqrt

def is_prime(x):
    if x < 2:
        return False

    if x == 2:
        return x

    if x % 2 == 0:
        return False

    limit = int(sqrt(x)) + 1
    for i in range(3, limit, 2):
        if x % i == 0:
            return False

    return x
```

The next part of the code is a function that takes in an integer that indicates the number of processors (workers) that we will be utilizing to concurrently solve the problem (in this case, it is used to determine which numbers in a list are prime numbers):

```
# Chapter02/example1.py

import concurrent.futures

from timeit import default_timer as timer

def concurrent_solve(n_workers):
    print('Number of workers: %i.' % n_workers)

    start = timer()
    result = []

    with concurrent.futures.ProcessPoolExecutor(
      max_workers=n_workers) as executor:

        futures = [executor.submit(is_prime, i) for i in input]
        completed_futures = concurrent.futures.as_completed(futures)

        sub_start = timer()

        for i, future in enumerate(completed_futures):
            if future.result():
                result.append(future.result())

        sub_duration = timer() - sub_start

    duration = timer() - start
    print('Sub took: %.4f seconds.' % sub_duration)
    print('Took: %.4f seconds.' % duration)
```

Notice that the variables `sub_start` and `sub_duration` measure the portion of the task that is being solved concurrently, which, in our earlier analysis, is denoted as *1 - B*. As for the input, we will be looking at numbers between 10^{13} and $10^{13} + 1000$:

```
input = [i for i in range(10 ** 13, 10 ** 13 + 1000)]
```

Lastly, we will be looping from one to the maximum number of processors available in our system, and we will pass that number to the preceding `concurrent_solve()` function. As a quick tip, to obtain the number of available processors from your computer, call `multiprocessing.cpu_count()`, as follows:

```
for n_workers in range(1, multiprocessing.cpu_count() + 1):
    concurrent_solve(n_workers)
    print('_' * 20)
```

You can run the whole program by entering the command `python example1.py`. Since my laptop has four cores, the following is my output after running the program:

```
Number of workers: 1.
Sub took: 7.5721 seconds.
Took: 7.6659 seconds.
_____
Number of workers: 2.
Sub took: 4.0410 seconds.
Took: 4.1153 seconds.
_____
Number of workers: 3.
Sub took: 3.8949 seconds.
Took: 4.0063 seconds.
_____
Number of workers: 4.
Sub took: 3.9285 seconds.
Took: 4.0545 seconds.
_____
```

A few things to note are as follows:

- First, in each iteration, the subsection of the task was almost as long as the whole program. In other words, the concurrent computation formed the majority of the program during each iteration. This is quite understandable, since there is hardly any other heavy computation in the program, aside from prime checking.
- Secondly, and arguably more interestingly, we can see that, while considerable improvements were gained after increasing the number of processors from 1 to 2 (`7.6659 seconds` to `4.1153 seconds`), hardly any speedup was achieved during the third iteration. It took longer during the forth iteration than the third, but this was most likely overhead processing. This is consistent with our earlier discussions regarding the similarity between Amdahl's Law and the law of diminishing returns, when considering the number of processors.

- We can also refer to a speedup curve to visualize this phenomenon. A speedup curve is simply a graph with the *x* axis showing the number of processors, compared to the *y* axis showing the speedup achieved. In a perfect scenario, where $S = j$ (that is, the speedup achieved is equal to the number of processors used), the speedup curve would be a straight, 45-degree line. Amdahl's Law shows that the speedup curve produced by any program will remain below that line, and will begin to flatten out as efficiency reduced. In the preceding program, this was during the transition from two to three processors:

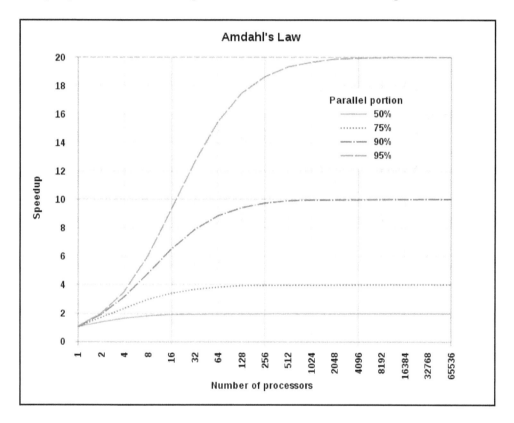

Speedup curves with different parallel portions

Practical applications of Amdahl's Law

As we have discussed, by analyzing the sequential and parallelizable portion of a given program or system with Amdahl's Law, we can determine, or at least estimate, the upper limit of any potential improvements in speed resulting from parallel computing. Upon obtaining this estimation, we can then make an informed decision on whether an improved execution time is worth an increase in processing power.

From our examples, we can see that Amdahl's Law is applied when you have a concurrent program that is a mixture of both sequentially and executed-in-parallels instructions. By performing analysis using Amdahl's Law, we can determine the speedup through each incrementation of the number of cores available to perform the execution, as well as how close that incrementation is to helping the program achieve the best possible speedup from parallelization.

Now, let's come back to the initial problem that we raised at the beginning of the chapter: the trade-off between an increase in the number of processors versus an increase in how long parallelism can be applied. Let's suppose that you are in charge of developing a concurrent program that currently has 40 percent of its instructions parallelizable. This means that multiple processors can be running simultaneously for 40 percent of the program execution. Now you have been tasked with increasing the speed of this program by implementing either of the following two choices:

- Having four processors implemented to execute the program instructions
- Having two processors implemented, in addition to increasing the parallelizable portion of the program to 80 percent

How can we analytically compare these two choices, in order to determine the one that will produce the best speed for our program? Luckily, Amdahl's Law can assist us during this process:

- For the first option, the speedup that can be obtained is as follows:

$$S = \frac{1}{B + \frac{1-B}{j}} = \frac{1}{1 - 0.4 + \frac{0.4}{4}} = \frac{10}{7} \approx 1.43$$

- For the second option, the speedup is as follows:

$$S = \frac{1}{B + \frac{1-B}{j}} = \frac{1}{1 - 0.8 + \frac{0.8}{2}} = \frac{10}{6} \approx 1.67$$

As you can see, the second option (which has fewer processors than the first) is actually the better choice to speed up our specific program. This is another example of Amdahl's Law, illustrating that sometimes simply increasing the number of available processors is, in fact, undesirable in terms of improving the speed of a program. Similar trade-offs, with potentially different specifications, can also be analyzed this way.

As a final note, it is important for us to know that, while Amdahl's Law offers an estimation of potential speedup in an unambiguous way, the law itself makes a number of underlying assumptions and does not take into account some potentially important factors, such as the overhead of parallelism or the speed of memory. For this reason, the formula of Amdahl's Law simplifies various considerations that might be common in practice.

So, how should programmers of concurrent programs think about and use Amdahl's Law? We should keep in mind that the results of Amdahl's Law are simply estimates that can provide us with an idea about where, and by how much, we can further optimize a concurrent system, specifically by increasing the number of available processors. In the end, only actual measurements can precisely answer our questions about how much speedup our concurrent programs will achieve in practice. With that said, Amdahl's Law can still help us to effectively identify good theoretical strategies for improving computing speed using concurrency and parallelism.

Summary

Amdahl's Law offers us a method to estimate the potential speedup in execution time of a task that we can expect from a system when its resources are improved. It illustrates that, as the resources of the system are improved, so is the execution time. However, the differential speedup when incrementing the resources strictly decreases, and the throughput speedup is limited by the sequential overhead of its program.

You also saw that in specific situations (namely, when only the number of processors increases), Amdahl's Law resembles the law of diminishing returns. Specifically, as the number of processors increases, the efficiency gained through the improvement decreases, and the speedup curve flattens out.

Lastly, this chapter showed that improvement through concurrency and parallelism is not always desirable, and detailed specifications are needed for an effective and efficient concurrent program.

With more knowledge of the extent to which concurrency can help to speed up our programs, we will now start to discuss the specific tools that Python provides to implement concurrency. Specifically, we will consider one of the main players in concurrent programming, threads, in the next chapter, including their application in Python programming.

Questions

- What is Amdahl's Law? What problem does Amdahl's Law try to solve?
- Explain the formula of Amdahl's Law, along with its components.
- According to Amdahl's Law, will speedup increase indefinitely as the resources of the system improve?
- What is the relationship between Amdahl's Law and the law of diminishing returns?

Further reading

For more information you can refer to the following links:

- *Amdahl's Law* (https://home.wlu.edu/~whaleyt/classes/parallel/topics/amdahl.html), by Aaron Michalove
- *Uses and abuses of Amdahl's Law*, Journal of Computing Sciences in Colleges 17.2 (2001): 288-293, S. Krishnaprasad
- *Learning Concurrency in Python: Build highly efficient, robust, and concurrent applications* (2017), Elliot Forbes

Working with Threads in Python 3

In Chapter 1, *Advanced Introduction to Concurrent and Parallel Programming*, you saw an example of threads being used in concurrent and parallel programming. In this chapter, you will be introduced to the formal definition of a thread, as well as the threading module in Python. We will cover a number of ways to work with threads in a Python program, including activities such as creating new threads, synchronizing threads, and working with multithreaded priority queues, via specific examples. We will also discuss the concept of a lock in thread synchronization, and we will implement a lock-based multithreaded application, in order to better understand the benefits of thread synchronization.

The following topics will be covered in this chapter:

- The concept of a thread in the context of concurrent programming in computer science
- The basic API of the threading module in Python
- How to create a new thread via the threading module
- The concept of a lock and how to use different locking mechanisms to synchronize threads
- The concept of a queue in the context of concurrent programming, and how to use the Queue module to work with queue objects in Python

Technical requirements

The following is a list of prerequisites for this chapter:

- Ensure that you have Python 3 installed on your computer
- Download the GitHub repository at `https://github.com/PacktPublishing/Mastering-Concurrency-in-Python`
- During this chapter, we will be working with the subfolder titled `Chapter03`
- Check out the following video to see the Code in Action: `http://bit.ly/2SeD2oz`

The concept of a thread

In the field of computer science, a **thread of execution** is the smallest unit of programming commands (code) that a scheduler (usually as part of an operating system) can process and manage. Depending on the operating system, the implementation of threads and processes (which we will cover in future chapters) varies, but a thread is typically an element (a component) of a process.

Threads versus processes

More than one thread can be implemented within the same process, most often executing concurrently and accessing/sharing the same resources, such as memory; separate processes do not do this. Threads in the same process share the latter's instructions (its code) and context (the values that its variables reference at any given moment).

The key difference between the two concepts is that a thread is typically a component of a process. Therefore, one process can include multiple threads, which can be executing simultaneously. Threads also usually allow for shared resources, such as memory and data, while it is fairly rare for processes to do so. In short, a thread is an independent component of computation that is similar to a process, but the threads within a process can share the address space, and hence the data, of that process:

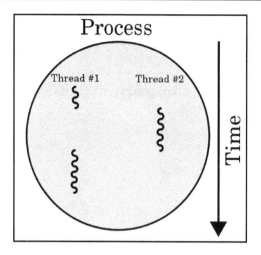

A process with two threads of execution running on one processor

Threads were reportedly first used for a variable number of tasks in OS/360 multiprogramming, which is a discontinued batch processing system that was developed by IBM in 1967. At the time, threads were called tasks by the developers, while the term thread became popular later on and has been attributed to Victor A. Vyssotsky, a mathematician and computer scientist who was the founding director of Digital's Cambridge Research Lab.

Multithreading

In computer science, single-threading is similar to traditional sequential processing, executing a single command at any given time. On the other hand, **multithreading** implements more than one thread to exist and execute in a single process, simultaneously. By allowing multiple threads to access shared resources/contexts and be executed independently, this programming technique can help applications to gain speed in the execution of independent tasks.

Multithreading can primarily be achieved in two ways. In single-processor systems, multithreading is typically implemented via **time slicing**, a technique that allows the CPU to switch between different software running on different threads. In time slicing, the CPU switches its execution so quickly and so often that users usually perceive that the software is running in parallel (for example, when you open two different software at the same time on a single-processor computer):

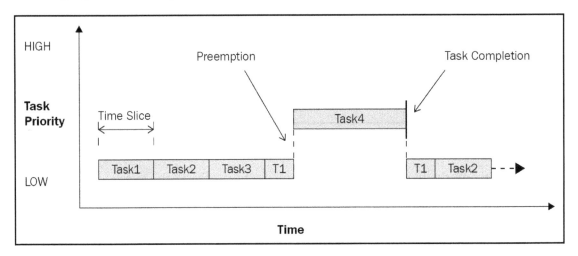

An example of a time slicing technique called round-robin scheduling

As opposed to single-processor systems, systems with multiple processors or cores can easily implement multithreading, by executing each thread in a separate process or core, simultaneously. Additionally, time slicing is an option, as these multiprocess or multicore systems can have only one processor/core to switch between tasks—although this is generally not a good practice.

Multithreaded applications have a number of advantages, as compared to traditional sequential applications; some of them are listed as follows:

- **Faster execution time**: One of the main advantages of concurrency through multithreading is the speedup that is achieved. Separate threads in the same program can be executed concurrently or in parallel, if they are sufficiently independent of one another.

- **Responsiveness**: A single-threaded program can only process one piece of input at a time; therefore, if the main execution thread blocks on a long-running task (that is, a piece of input that requires heavy computation and processing), the whole program will not be able to continue with other input, and hence, it will appear to be frozen. By using separate threads to perform computation and remain running to take in different user input simultaneously, a multithreaded program can provide better responsiveness.
- **Efficiency in resource consumption**: As we mentioned previously, multiple threads within the same process can share and access the same resources. Consequently, multithreaded programs can serve and process many client requests for data concurrently, using significantly fewer resources than would be needed when using single-threaded or multiprocess programs. This also leads to quicker communication between threads.

That being said, multithreaded programs also have their disadvantages, as follows:

- **Crashes**: Even though a process can contain multiple threads, a single illegal operation within one thread can negatively affect the processing of all of the other threads in the process, and can crash the entire program as a result.
- **Synchronization**: Even though sharing the same resources can be an advantage over traditional sequential programming or multiprocessing programs, careful consideration is also needed for the shared resources. Usually, threads must be coordinated in a deliberate and systematic manner, so that shared data is computed and manipulated correctly. Unintuitive problems that can be caused by careless thread coordination include deadlocks, livelocks, and race conditions, all of which will be discussed in future chapters.

An example in Python

To illustrate the concept of running multiple threads in the same process, let's look at a quick example in Python. If you have already downloaded the code for this book from the GitHub page, go ahead and navigate to the `Chapter03` folder. Let's take a look at the `Chapter03/my_thread.py` file, as follows:

```
# Chapter03/my_thread.py

import threading
import time


class MyThread(threading.Thread):
    def __init__(self, name, delay):
```

```
        threading.Thread.__init__(self)
        self.name = name
        self.delay = delay

    def run(self):
        print('Starting thread %s.' % self.name)
        thread_count_down(self.name, self.delay)
        print('Finished thread %s.' % self.name)

def thread_count_down(name, delay):
    counter = 5

    while counter:
        time.sleep(delay)
        print('Thread %s counting down: %i...' % (name, counter))
        counter -= 1
```

In this file, we are using the threading module from Python as the foundation of the
MyThread class. Each object of this class has a name and delay parameter. The function
run(), which is called as soon as a new thread is initialized and started, prints out a
starting message, and, in turn, calls the thread_count_down() function. This function
counts down from the number 5 to the number 0, while sleeping between iterations for a
number of seconds, specified by the delay parameter.

The point of this example is to show the concurrent nature of running more than one thread
in the same program (or process) by starting more than one object of the MyThread class at
the same time. We know that, as soon as each thread is started, a time-based countdown for
that thread will also start. In a traditional sequential program, separate countdowns will be
executed separately, in order (that is, a new countdown will not start until the current one
finishes). As you will see, the separate countdowns for separate threads are executed
concurrently.

Let's look at the Chapter3/example1.py file, as follows:

```
# Chapter03/example1.py

from my_thread import MyThread


thread1 = MyThread('A', 0.5)
thread2 = MyThread('B', 0.5)

thread1.start()
thread2.start()

thread1.join()
```

```
thread2.join()
```

```
print('Finished.')
```

Here, we are initializing and starting two threads together, each of which has 0.5 seconds as its delay parameter. Run the script using your Python interpreter. You should get the following output:

```
> python example1.py
Starting thread A.
Starting thread B.
Thread A counting down: 5...
Thread B counting down: 5...
Thread B counting down: 4...
Thread A counting down: 4...
Thread B counting down: 3...
Thread A counting down: 3...
Thread B counting down: 2...
Thread A counting down: 2...
Thread B counting down: 1...
Thread A counting down: 1...
Finished thread B.
Finished thread A.
Finished.
```

Just as we expected, the output tells us that the two countdowns for the threads were executed concurrently; instead of finishing the first thread's countdown and then starting the second thread's countdown, the program ran the two countdowns at almost the same time. Without including some overhead and miscellaneous declarations, this threading technique allows almost double improvement in speed for the preceding program.

There is one additional thing that should be taken note of in the preceding output. After the first countdown for number 5, we can see that the countdown of thread B actually got ahead of thread A in execution, even though we know that thread A was initialized and started before thread B. This change actually allowed thread B to finish before thread A. This phenomenon is a direct result of concurrency via multithreading; since the two threads were initialized and started almost simultaneously, it was quite likely for one thread to get ahead of the other in execution.

If you were to execute this script many times, it would be quite likely for you to get varying output, in terms of the order of execution and the completion of the countdowns. The following are two pieces of output that I obtained by executing the script again and again. The first output shows a uniform and unchanging order of execution and completion, in which the two countdowns were executed hand in hand. The second shows a case in which thread A was executed significantly faster than thread B; it even finished before thread B counted to number 1. This variation of output further illustrates the fact that the threads were treated and executed by Python equally.

The following code shows one possible output of the program:

```
> python example1.py
Starting thread A.
Starting thread B.
Thread A counting down: 5...
Thread B counting down: 5...
Thread A counting down: 4...
Thread B counting down: 4...
Thread A counting down: 3...
Thread B counting down: 3...
Thread A counting down: 2...
Thread B counting down: 2...
Thread A counting down: 1...
Thread B counting down: 1...
Finished thread A.
Finished thread B.
Finished.
```

The following is another possible output:

```
> python example1.py
Starting thread A.
Starting thread B.
Thread A counting down: 5...
Thread B counting down: 5...
Thread A counting down: 4...
Thread B counting down: 4...
Thread A counting down: 3...
Thread B counting down: 3...
Thread A counting down: 2...
Thread B counting down: 2...
Thread A counting down: 1...
Finished thread A.
Thread B counting down: 1...
Finished thread B.
Finished.
```

An overview of the threading module

There are a lot of choices when it comes to implementing multithreaded programs in Python. One of the most common ways to work with threads in Python is through the `threading` module. Before we dive into the module's usage and its syntax, first, let's explore the `thread` model, which was previously the main thread-based development module in Python.

The thread module in Python 2

Before the `threading` module became popular, the primary thread-based development module was `thread`. If you are using an older version of Python 2, it is possible to use the module as it is. However, according to the module documentation page, the `thread` module was, in fact, renamed `_thread` in Python 3.

For readers that have been working with the `thread` module to build multithreaded applications and are looking to port their code from Python 2 to Python 3, the 2to3 tool might be a solution. The 2to3 tool handles most of the detectable incompatibilities between the different versions of Python, while parsing the source and traversing the source tree to convert Python 2.x code into Python 3.x code. Another trick to achieve the conversion is to change the import code from `import thread` to `import _thread as thread` in your Python programs.

The main feature of the `thread` module is its fast and sufficient method of creating new threads to execute functions: the `thread.start_new_thread()` function. Aside from this, the module only supports a number of low-level ways to work with multithreaded primitives and share their global data space. Additionally, simple lock objects (for example, mutexes and semaphores) are provided for synchronization purposes.

The threading module in Python 3

The old `thread` module has been considered deprecated by Python developers for a long time, mainly because of its rather low-level functions and limited usage. The `threading` module, on the other hand, is built on top of the `thread` module, providing easier ways to work with threads through powerful, higher-level APIs. Python users have actually been encouraged to utilize the new `threading` module over the `thread` module in their programs.

Additionally, the `thread` module considers each thread a function; when the `thread.start_new_thread()` is called, it actually takes in a separate function as its main argument, in order to spawn a new thread. However, the `threading` module is designed to be user-friendly for those that come from the object-oriented software development paradigm, treating each thread that is created as an object.

In addition to all of the functionality for working with threads that the `thread` module provides, the `threading` module supports a number of extra methods, as follows:

- `threading.activeCount()`: This function returns the number of currently active thread objects in the program
- `threading.currentThread()`: This function returns the number of thread objects in the current thread control from the caller
- `threading.enumerate()`: This function returns a list of all of the currently active thread objects in the program

Following the object-oriented software development paradigm, the `threading` module also provides a `Thread` class that supports the object-oriented implementation of threads. The following methods are supported in this class:

- `run()`: This method is executed when a new thread is initialized and started
- `start()`: This method starts the initialized calling thread object by calling the `run()` method
- `join()`: This method waits for the calling thread object to terminate before continuing to execute the rest of the program
- `isAlive()`: This method returns a Boolean value, indicating whether the calling thread object is currently executing
- `getName()`: This method returns the name of the calling thread object
- `setName()`: This method sets the name of the calling thread object

Creating a new thread in Python

Having provided an overview of the `threading` module and its differences from the old `thread` module, in this section, we will explore a number of examples of creating new threads by using these tools in Python. As mentioned previously, the `threading` module is most likely the most common way of working with threads in Python. Specific situations require use of the `thread` module and maybe other tools, as well, and it is important for us to be able to differentiate those situations.

Starting a thread with the thread module

In the `thread` module, new threads are created to execute functions concurrently. As we have mentioned, the way to do this is by using the `thread.start_new_thread()` function:

```
thread.start_new_thread(function, args[, kwargs])
```

When this function is called, a new thread is spawned to execute the function specified by the parameters, and the identifier of the thread is returned when the function finishes its execution. The `function` parameter is the name of the function to be executed, and the `args` parameter list (which has to be a list or a tuple) includes the arguments to be passed to the specified function. The optional `kwargs` argument, on the other hand, includes a separate dictionary of additional keyword arguments. When the `thread.start_new_thread()` function returns, the thread also terminates silently.

Let's look at an example of using the `thread` module in a Python program. If you have already downloaded the code for this book from the GitHub page, go ahead and navigate to the `Chapter03` folder and the `Chapter03/example2.py` file. In this example, we will look at the `is_prime()` function that we have also used in previous chapters:

```python
# Chapter03/example2.py

from math import sqrt

def is_prime(x):
    if x < 2:
        print('%i is not a prime number.' % x)

    elif x == 2:
        print('%i is a prime number.' % x)

    elif x % 2 == 0:
        print('%i is not a prime number.' % x)

    else:
        limit = int(sqrt(x)) + 1
        for i in range(3, limit, 2):
            if x % i == 0:
                print('%i is not a prime number.' % x)

        print('%i is a prime number.' % x)
```

You may have noticed that there is quite a difference in the way this `is_prime(x)` function returns the result of its computation; instead of returning `true` or `false`, to indicate whether the x parameter is a prime number, this `is_prime()` function directly prints out that result. As you saw earlier, the `thread.start_new_thread()` function executes the parameter function through spawning a new thread, but it actually returns the thread's identifier. Printing out the result inside of the `is_prime()` function is a workaround for accessing the result of that function through the `thread` module.

In the main part of our program, we will loop through a list of potential candidates for prime numbers, and we will call the `thread.start_new_thread()` function on the `is_prime()` function and each number in that list, as follows:

```
# Chapter03/example2.py

import _thread as thread

my_input = [2, 193, 323, 1327, 433785907]

for x in my_input:
    thread.start_new_thread(is_prime, (x, ))
```

You will notice that, in the `Chapter03/example2.py` file, there is a line of code to take in the user's input at the end:

```
a = input('Type something to quit: \n')
```

For now, let's comment out this last line. Then, when we execute the whole Python program, it will be observed that the program terminates without printing out any output; in other words, the program terminates before the threads can finish executing. This is due to the fact that, when a new thread is spawned through the `thread.start_new_thread()` function to process a number in our input list, the program continues to loop through the next input number while the newly created thread executes.

So, by the time the Python interpreter reaches the end of the program, if any thread has not finished executing (in our case, it is all of the threads), that thread will be ignored and terminated, and no output will be printed out. However, once in a while, one of the output is `2 is a prime number.` which will be printed out before the program terminates, because the thread processing the number 2 is able to finish executing prior to that point.

The last line of code is another workaround for the `thread` module—this time, to address the preceding problem. This line prevents the program from exiting until the user presses any key on their keyboard, at which time the program will quit. The strategy is to wait for the program to finish executing all of the threads (that is, to finish processing all of the numbers in our input list). Uncomment the last line and execute the file, and your output should be similar to the following:

```
> python example2.py
Type something to quit:
2 is a prime number.
193 is a prime number.
1327 is a prime number.
323 is not a prime number.
433785907 is a prime number.
```

As you can see, the `Type something to quit:` line, which corresponds to the last line of code in our program, was printed out before the output from the `is_prime()` function; this is consistent with the fact that that line is executed before any of the other threads finish executing, most of the time. I say most of the time because, when the thread that is processing the first input (the number 2) finishes executing before the Python interpreter reaches the last line, the output of the program would be something similar to the following:

```
> python example2.py
2 is a prime number.
Type something to quit:
193 is a prime number.
323 is not a prime number.
1327 is a prime number.
433785907 is a prime number.
```

Starting a thread with the threading module

You now know how to start a thread with the `thread` module, and you know about its limited and low-level use of threading and the need for considerably unintuitive workarounds when working with it. In this subsection, we will explore the preferred `threading` module and its advantages over the `thread` module, with regard to the implementation of multithreaded programs in Python.

To create and customize a new thread using the threading module, there are specific steps that need to be followed:

1. Define a subclass of the threading.Thread class in your program
2. Override the default __init__(self [,args]) method inside of the subclass, in order to add custom arguments for the class
3. Override the default run(self [,args]) method inside of the subclass, in order to customize the behavior of the thread class when a new thread is initialized and started

You actually saw an example of this in the first example of this chapter. As a refresher, the following is what we have to use to customize a threading.Thread subclass, in order to perform a five-step countdown, with a customizable delay between each step:

```python
# Chapter03/my_thread.py

import threading
import time


class MyThread(threading.Thread):
    def __init__(self, name, delay):
        threading.Thread.__init__(self)
        self.name = name
        self.delay = delay

    def run(self):
        print('Starting thread %s.' % self.name)
        thread_count_down(self.name, self.delay)
        print('Finished thread %s.' % self.name)

def thread_count_down(name, delay):
    counter = 5

    while counter:
        time.sleep(delay)
        print('Thread %s counting down: %i...' % (name, counter))
        counter -= 1
```

In our next example, we will look at the problem of determining whether a specific number is a prime number. This time, we will be implementing a multithreaded Python program through the `threading` module. Navigate to the `Chapter03` folder and the `example3.py` file. Let's first focus on the `MyThread` class, as follows:

```
# Chapter03/example3.py

import threading

class MyThread(threading.Thread):
    def __init__(self, x):
        threading.Thread.__init__(self)
        self.x = x

    def run(self):
        print('Starting processing %i...' % x)
        is_prime(self.x)
```

Each instance of the `MyThread` class will have a parameter called x, specifying the prime number candidate to be processed. As you can see, when an instance of the class is initialized and started (that is, in the `run(self)` function), the `is_prime()` function, which is the same prime-checking function that we used in the previous example, on the x parameter, before that a message is also printed out by the `run()` function to specify the beginning of the processing.

In our main program, we still have the same list of input for prime-checking. We will be going through each number in that list, spawning and running a new instance of the `MyThread` class with that number, and appending that `MyThread` instance to a separate list. This list of created threads is necessary because, after that, we will have to call the `join()` method on all of those threads, which ensures that all of the threads have finished executing successfully:

```
my_input = [2, 193, 323, 1327, 433785907]

threads = []

for x in my_input:
    temp_thread = MyThread(x)
    temp_thread.start()

    threads.append(temp_thread)

for thread in threads:
    thread.join()

print('Finished.')
```

Notice that, unlike when we used the `thread` module, this time, we do not have to invent a workaround to make sure that all of the threads have finished executing successfully. Again, this is done by the `join()` method provided by the `threading` module. This is only one example of the many advantages of using the more powerful, higher-level API of the `threading` module, rather than using the `thread` module.

Synchronizing threads

As you saw in the previous examples, the `threading` module has many advantages over its predecessor, the `thread` module, in terms of functionality and high-level API calls. Even though some recommend that experienced Python developers know how to implement multithreaded applications using both of these modules, you will most likely be using the `threading` module to work with threads in Python. In this section, we will look at using the `threading` module in thread synchronization.

The concept of thread synchronization

Before we jump into an actual Python example, let's explore the concept of synchronization in computer science. As you saw in previous chapters, sometimes, it is undesirable to have all portions of a program execute in a parallel manner. In fact, in most contemporary concurrent programs, there are sequential portions and concurrent portions of the code; furthermore, even inside of a concurrent portion, some form of coordination between different threads/processes is also required.

Thread/process synchronization is a concept in computer science that specifies various mechanisms to ensure that no more than one concurrent thread/process can process and execute a particular program portion at a time; this portion is known as the **critical section**, and we will discuss it in further detail when we consider common problems in concurrent programming in Chapter 12, *Starvation*, and Chapter 13, *Race Conditions*.

In a given program, when a thread is accessing/executing the critical section of the program, the other threads have to wait until that thread finishes executing. The typical goal of thread synchronization is to avoid any potential data discrepancies when multiple threads access their shared resources; allowing only one thread to execute the critical section of the program at a time guarantees that no data conflicts occur in multithreaded applications.

The threading.Lock class

One of the most common ways to apply thread synchronization is through the implementation of a locking mechanism. In our threading module, the threading.Lock class provides a simple and intuitive approach to creating and working with locks. Its main usage includes the following methods:

- threading.Lock(): This method initializes and returns a new lock object.
- acquire(blocking): When this method is called, all of the threads will run synchronously (that is, only one thread can execute the critical section at a time):
  - The optional argument blocking allows us to specify whether the current thread should wait to acquire the lock
  - When blocking = 0, the current thread does not wait for the lock and simply returns 0 if the lock cannot be acquired by the thread, or 1 otherwise
  - When blocking = 1, the current thread blocks and waits for the lock to be released and acquires it afterwards
- release(): When this method is called, the lock is released.

An example in Python

Let's consider a specific example. In this example, we will be looking at the Chapter03/example4.py file. We will go back to the thread example of counting down from five to one, which we looked at at the beginning of this chapter; take a moment to look back if you do not remember the problem. In this example, we will be tweaking the MyThread class, as follows:

```
# Chapter03/example4.py

import threading
import time

class MyThread(threading.Thread):
    def __init__(self, name, delay):
        threading.Thread.__init__(self)
        self.name = name
        self.delay = delay

    def run(self):
        print('Starting thread %s.' % self.name)
        thread_lock.acquire()
```

```
        thread_count_down(self.name, self.delay)
        thread_lock.release()
        print('Finished thread %s.' % self.name)

def thread_count_down(name, delay):
    counter = 5

    while counter:
        time.sleep(delay)
        print('Thread %s counting down: %i...' % (name, counter))
        counter -= 1
```

As opposed to the first example of this chapter, in this example, the MyThread class utilizes a lock object (whose variable is named thread_lock) inside of its run() function. Specifically, the lock object is acquired right before the thread_count_down() function is called (that is, when the countdown begins), and the lock object is released right after its ends. Theoretically, this specification will alter the behavior of the threads that we saw in the first example; instead of executing the countdown simultaneously, the program will now execute the threads separately, and the countdowns will take place one after the other.

Finally, we will initialize the thread_lock variable as well as run two separate instances of the MyThread class:

```
thread_lock = threading.Lock()

thread1 = MyThread('A', 0.5)
thread2 = MyThread('B', 0.5)

thread1.start()
thread2.start()

thread1.join()
thread2.join()


print('Finished.')
```

The output will be as follows:

```
> python example4.py
Starting thread A.
Starting thread B.
Thread A counting down: 5...
Thread A counting down: 4...
Thread A counting down: 3...
Thread A counting down: 2...
Thread A counting down: 1...
```

```
Finished thread A.
Thread B counting down: 5...
Thread B counting down: 4...
Thread B counting down: 3...
Thread B counting down: 2...
Thread B counting down: 1...
Finished thread B.
Finished.
```

Multithreaded priority queue

A computer science concept that is widely used in both non-concurrent and concurrent programming is queuing. A **queue** is an abstract data structure that is a collection of different elements maintained in a specific order; these elements can be the other objects in a program.

A connection between real-life and programmatic queues

Queues are an intuitive concept that can easily be related to our everyday life, such as when you stand in line to board a plane at the airport. In an actual line of people, you will see the following:

- People typically enter at one end of the line and exit from the other end
- If person A enters the line before person B, person A will also leave the line before person B (unless person B has more priority)
- Once everyone has boarded the plane, there will be no one left in the line. In other words, the line will be empty

In computer science, a queue works in a considerably similar way:

- Elements can be added to the end of the queue; this task is called **enqueue**.
- Elements can also be removed from the beginning of the queue; this task is called **dequeue**.

- In a **First In First Out** (**FIFO**) queue, the elements that are added first will be removed first (hence, the name FIFO). This is contrary to another common data structure in computer science, called **stack**, in which the last element that is added will be removed first. This is known as **Last In First Out** (**LIFO**).
- If all of the elements inside of a queue have been removed, the queue will be empty and there will be no way to remove further elements from the queue. Similarly, if a queue is at the maximum capacity of the number of elements it can hold, there is no way to add any other elements to the queue:

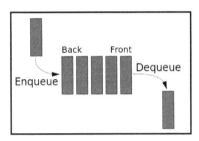

A visualization of the queue data structure

The queue module

The `queue` module in Python provides a simple implementation of the queue data structure. Each queue in the `queue.Queue` class can hold a specific amount of element, and can have the following methods as its high-level API:

- `get()`: This method returns the next element of the calling `queue` object and removes it from the `queue` object
- `put()`: This method adds a new element to the calling `queue` object
- `qsize()`: This method returns the number of current elements in the calling `queue` object (that is, its size)
- `empty()`: This method returns a Boolean, indicating whether the calling `queue` object is empty
- `full()`: This method returns a Boolean, indicating whether the calling `queue` object is full

Queuing in concurrent programming

The concept of a queue is even more prevalent in the sub-field of concurrent programming, especially when we need to implement a fixed number of threads in our program to interact with a varying number of shared resources.

In the previous examples, we have learned to assign a specific task to a new thread. This means that the number of tasks that need to be processed will dictate the number of threads our program should spawn. (For example, in our `Chapter03/example3.py` file, we had five numbers as our input and we therefore created five threads—each took one input number and processed it.)

Sometimes it is undesirable to have as many threads as the tasks we have to process. Say we have a large number of tasks to be processed, then it will be quite inefficient to spawn the same large number of threads and have each thread execute only one task. It could be more beneficial to have a fixed number of threads (commonly known as a thread pool) that would work through the tasks in a cooperative manner.

Here is when the concept of a queue comes in. We can design a structure in which the pool of threads will not hold any information regarding the tasks they should each execute, instead the tasks are stored in a queue (in other words task queue), and the items in the queue will be fed to individual members of the thread pool. As a given task is completed by a member of the thread pool, if the task queue still contains elements to be processed, then the next element in the queue will be sent to the thread that just became available.

This diagram further illustrates this setup:

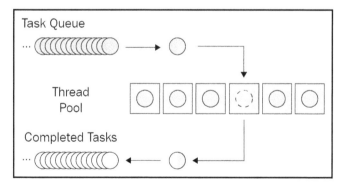

Queuing in threading

Let's consider a quick example in Python, in order to illustrate this point. Navigate to the `Chapter03/example5.py` file. In this example, we will be considering the problem of printing out all of the positive factors of an element in a given list of positive integers. We are still looking at the previous `MyThread` class, but with some adjustments:

```python
# Chapter03/example5.py
import queue
import threading
import time


class MyThread(threading.Thread):
    def __init__(self, name):
        threading.Thread.__init__(self)
        self.name = name

    def run(self):
        print('Starting thread %s.' % self.name)
        process_queue()
        print('Exiting thread %s.' % self.name)

def process_queue():
    while True:
        try:
            x = my_queue.get(block=False)
        except queue.Empty:
            return
        else:
            print_factors(x)

        time.sleep(1)

def print_factors(x):
    result_string = 'Positive factors of %i are: ' % x
    for i in range(1, x + 1):
        if x % i == 0:
            result_string += str(i) + ' '
    result_string += '\n' + '_' * 20

    print(result_string)


# setting up variables
input_ = [1, 10, 4, 3]

# filling the queue
my_queue = queue.Queue()
```

```
for x in input_:
    my_queue.put(x)


# initializing and starting 3 threads
thread1 = MyThread('A')
thread2 = MyThread('B')
thread3 = MyThread('C')

thread1.start()
thread2.start()
thread3.start()

# joining all 3 threads
thread1.join()
thread2.join()
thread3.join()

print('Done.')
```

There is a lot going on, so let's break the program down into smaller pieces. First, let's look at our key function, as follows:

```
# Chapter03/example5.py

def print_factors(x):
    result_string = 'Positive factors of %i are: ' % x
    for i in range(1, x + 1):
        if x % i == 0:
            result_string += str(i) + ' '
    result_string += '\n' + '_' * 20

    print(result_string)
```

This function takes in an argument, x then iterates through all positive numbers between 1 and itself, to check whether a number is a factor of x. It finally prints out a formatted message that contains all of the information that it cumulates through the loop.

In our new `MyThread` class, when a new instance is initialized and started, the `process_queue()` function will be called. This function will first attempt to obtain the next element of the queue object that the `my_queue` variable holds in a non-blocking manner by calling the `get(block=False)` method. If a `queue.Empty` exception occurs (which indicates that the queue currently holds no value), then we will end the execution of the function. Otherwise we simply pass that element we just obtained to the `print_factors()` function.

```
# Chapter03/example5.py

def process_queue():
    while True:
        try:
            x = my_queue.get(block=False)
        except queue.Empty:
            return
        else:
            print_factors(x)

        time.sleep(1)
```

The `my_queue` variable is defined in our main function as a `Queue` object from the `queue` module that contains the elements in the `input_` list:

```
# setting up variables
input_ = [1, 10, 4, 3]

# filling the queue
my_queue = queue.Queue(4)
for x in input_:
    my_queue.put(x)
```

For the rest of the main program, we simply initiate and run three separate threads until all of them finish their respective execution. Here we choose to create only three threads to simulate the design that we discussed earlier—a fixed number of threads processing a queue of input whose number of elements can change independently:

```
# initializing and starting 3 threads
thread1 = MyThread('A')
thread2 = MyThread('B')
thread3 = MyThread('C')

thread1.start()
thread2.start()
thread3.start()
```

```
# joining all 3 threads
thread1.join()
thread2.join()
thread3.join()

print('Done.')
```

Run the program and you will see the following output:

```
> python example5.py
Starting thread A.
Starting thread B.
Starting thread C.
Positive factors of 1 are: 1
_____
Positive factors of 10 are: 1 2 5 10
_____
Positive factors of 4 are: 1 2 4
_____
Positive factors of 3 are: 1 3
_____
Exiting thread C.
Exiting thread A.
Exiting thread B.
Done.
```

In this example, we have implemented the structure that we discussed earlier: a task queue that holds all the tasks to be executed and a thread pool (threads A, B, and C) that interacts with the queue to process its elements individually.

Multithreaded priority queue

The elements in a queue are processed in the order that they were added to the queue; in other words, the first element that is added leaves the queue first (FIFO). Even though this abstract data structure simulates real life in many situations, depending on the application and its purposes, sometimes, we need to redefine/change the order of the elements dynamically. This is where the concept of priority queuing comes in handy.

The **priority queue** abstract data structure is similar to the queue (and even the aforementioned stack) data structure, but each of the elements in a priority queue, as the name suggests, has a priority associated with it; in other words, when an element is added to a priority queue, its priority needs to be specified. Unlike in regular queues, the dequeuing principle of a priority queue relies on the priority of the elements: the elements with higher priorities are processed before those with lower priorities.

The concept of a priority queue is used in a variety of different applications—namely, bandwidth management, Dijkstra's algorithm, best-first search algorithms, and so on. Each of these applications typically uses a definite scoring system/function to determine the priority of its elements. For example, in bandwidth management, prioritized traffic, such as real-time streaming, is processed with the least delay and the least likelihood of being rejected. In best-search algorithms that are used to find the shortest path between two given nodes of a graph, a priority queue is implemented to keep track of unexplored routes; the routes with shorter estimated path lengths are given higher priorities in the queue.

Summary

A thread of execution is the smallest unit of programming commands. In computer science, multithreaded applications allow for multiple threads to exist within the same process simultaneously, in order to implement concurrency and parallelism. Multithreading provides a variety of advantages, in execution time, responsiveness, and the efficiency of resource consumption.

The `threading` module in Python 3, which is commonly considered superior to the old `thread` module, provides an efficient, powerful, and high-level API to work with threads while implementing multithreaded applications in Python, including options to spawn new threads dynamically and synchronize threads through different locking mechanisms.

Queuing and priority queuing are important data structures in the field of computer science, and they are essential concepts in concurrent and parallel programming. They allow for multithreaded applications to efficiently execute and complete their threads in an accurate manner, ensuring that the shared resources are processed in a specific and dynamic order.

In the next chapter, we will discuss a more advanced function of Python, the `with` statement, and how it complements the use of multithreaded programming in Python.

Questions

- What is a thread? What are the core differences between a thread and a process?
- What are the API options provided by the `thread` module in Python?
- What are the API options provided by the `threading` module in Python?
- What are the processes of creating new threads via the `thread` and `threading` modules?
- What is the idea behind thread synchronization using locks?
- What is the process of implementing thread synchronization using locks in Python?
- What is the idea behind the queue data structure?
- What is the main application of queuing in concurrent programming?
- What are the core differences between a regular queue and a priority queue?

Further reading

For more information you can refer to the following links:

- *Python Parallel Programming Cookbook*, Giancarlo Zaccone, Packt Publishing Ltd, 2015
- "Learning Concurrency in Python: Build highly efficient, robust, and concurrent applications", Elliot Forbes (2017)
- *Real-time concepts for embedded systems*, Qing Li and Caroline Yao, CRC Press, 2003

4
Using the with Statement in Threads

The `with` statement in Python sometimes causes confusion for novice and experienced Python programmers alike. This chapter explains in depth the idea behind the `with` statement as a context manager and its usage in concurrent and parallel programming, specifically regarding the use of locks while synchronizing threads. This chapter also provides specific examples of how the `with` statement is most commonly used.

The following topics will be covered in this chapter:

- The concept of context management and the options that the `with` statement provides as a context manager, specifically in concurrent and parallel programming
- The syntax of the `with` statement and how to use it effectively and efficiently
- The different ways of using the `with` statement in concurrent programming

Technical requirements

The following is a list of prerequisites for this chapter:

- Python 3 must be installed on your computer
- Download the GitHub repository at `https://github.com/PacktPublishing/Mastering-Concurrency-in-Python`
- During this chapter, we will be working with the subfolder named `Chapter04`
- Check out the following video to see the Code in Action: `http://bit.ly/2DSGLEZ`

Context management

The new `with` statement was first introduced in Python 2.5 and has been in use for quite some time. However, there still seems to be confusion regarding its usage, even for experienced Python programmers. The `with` statement is most commonly used as a context manager that properly manages resources, which is essential in concurrent and parallel programming, where resources are shared across different entities in the concurrent or parallel application.

Starting from managing files

As an experienced Python user, you have probably seen the `with` statement being used to open and read external files inside Python programs. Looking at this problem at a lower level, the operation of opening an external file in Python will consume a resource—in this case, a file descriptor—and your operating system will set a limit on this resource. This means that there is an upper limit on how many files a single process running on your system can open simultaneously.

Let's consider a quick example to illustrate this point further. Let's take a look at the `Chapter04/example1.py` file, as shown in the following code:

```
# Chapter04/example1.py

n_files = 10
files = []

for i in range(n_files):
    files.append(open('output1/sample%i.txt' % i, 'w'))
```

This quick program simply creates 10 text files inside the `output1` folder: `sample0.txt`, `sample1.txt`, ..., `sample9.txt`. What might be of more interest to us is the fact that the files were opened inside the `for` loop but were not closed—this is a bad practice in programming that we will discuss later. Now, let's say we wanted to reassign the `n_files` variable to a large number—say 10,000—as shown in the following code:

```
# Chapter4/example1.py

n_files = 10000
files = []

# method 1
for i in range(n_files):
    files.append(open('output1/sample%i.txt' % i, 'w'))
```

We would get an error similar to the following:

```
> python example1.py
Traceback (most recent call last):
  File "example1.py", line 7, in <module>
OSError: [Errno 24] Too many open files: 'output1/sample253.txt'
```

Looking closely at the error message, we can see that my laptop can only handle 253 opened files simultaneously (as a side note, if you are working on a UNIX-like system, running `ulimit -n` will give you the number of files that your system can handle). More generally, this situation arose from what is known as **file descriptor leakage**. When Python opens a file inside a program, that opened file is essentially represented by an integer. This integer acts as a reference point that the program can use in order to have access to that file, while not giving the program complete control over the underlying file itself.

By opening too many files at the same time, our program assigned too many file descriptors to manage the open files, hence the error message. File descriptor leakage can lead to a number of difficult problems—especially in concurrent and parallel programming—namely, unauthorized I/O operations on open files. The solution to this is to simply close opened files in a coordinated manner. Let's look at our `Chapter04/example1.py` file in the second method. In the `for` loop, we would do the following:

```python
# Chapter04/example1.py

n_files = 1000
files = []

# method 2
for i in range(n_files):
    f = open('output1/sample%i.txt' % i, 'w')
    files.append(f)
    f.close()
```

The with statement as a context manager

In real-life applications, it is rather easy to mismanage opened files in your programs by forgetting to close them; it can sometimes also be the case that it is impossible to tell whether the program has finished processing a file, and we programmers will therefore be unable to make a decision as to when to put the statement to close the files appropriately. This situation is even more common in concurrent and parallel programming, where the order of execution between different elements changes frequently.

One possible solution to this problem that is also common in other programming languages is to use a `try...except...finally` block every time we want to interact with an external file. This solution still requires the same level of management and significant overhead and does not provide a good improvement in the ease and readability of our programs either. This is when the `with` statement of Python comes into play.

The `with` statement gives us a simple way of ensuring that all opened files are properly managed and cleaned up when the program finishes using them. The most notable advantage of using the `with` statement comes from the fact that, even if the code is successfully executed or it returns an error, the `with` statement always handles and manages the opened files appropriately via context. For example, let's look at our `Chapter04/example1.py` file in more detail:

```
# Chapter04/example1.py

n_files = 254
files = []

# method 3
for i in range(n_files):
    with open('output1/sample%i.txt' % i, 'w') as f:
        files.append(f)
```

While this method accomplishes the same job as the second method we saw earlier, it additionally provides a cleaner and more readable way to manage the opened files that our program interacts with. More specifically, the `with` statement helps us indicate the scope of certain variables—in this case, the variables that point to the opened files—and hence, their context.

For example, in the third method in the preceding code, the `f` variable indicates the current opened file within the `with` block at each iteration of the `for` loop, and as soon as our program exits that `with` block (which is outside the scope of that `f` variable), there is no longer any other way to access it. This architecture guarantees that all cleanup associated with a file descriptor happens appropriately. The `with` statement is hence called a context manager.

The syntax of the with statement

The syntax of the `with` statement can be intuitive and straightforward. With the purpose of wrapping the execution of a block with methods defined by a context manager, it consists of the following simple form:

```
with [expression] (as [target]):
    [code]
```

Note that the `as [target]` part of the `with` statement is actually not required, as we will see later on. Additionally, the `with` statement can also handle more than one item on the same line. Specifically, the context managers created are treated as if multiple `with` statements were nested inside one another. For example, look at the following code:

```
with [expression1] as [target1], [expression2] as [target2]:
    [code]
```

This is interpreted as follows:

```
with [expression1] as [target1]:
    with [expression2] as [target2]:
        [code]
```

The with statement in concurrent programming

Obviously, opening and closing external files does not resemble concurrency very much. However, we mentioned earlier that the `with` statement, as a context manager, is not only used to manage file descriptors, but most resources in general. And if you actually found managing lock objects from the `threading.Lock()` class similar to managing external files while going through Chapter 2, *Amdahl's Law*, then this is where the comparison between the two comes in handy.

As a refresher, locks are mechanisms in concurrent and parallel programming that are typically used to synchronize threads in a multithreaded application (that is, to prevent more than one thread from accessing the critical session simultaneously). However, as we will discuss again in Chapter 12, *Starvation*, locks are also a common source of **deadlock**, during which a thread **acquires** a lock but never **releases** it because of an unhandled occurrence, thereby stopping the entire program.

Example of deadlock handling

Let's look at a quick example in Python. Let's a take look at the `Chapter04/example2.py` file, as shown in the following code:

```
# Chapter04/example2.py

from threading import Lock

my_lock = Lock()

def get_data_from_file_v1(filename):
    my_lock.acquire()

    with open(filename, 'r') as f:
        data.append(f.read())

    my_lock.release()

data = []

try:
    get_data_from_file('output2/sample0.txt')
except FileNotFoundError:
    print('Encountered an exception...')

my_lock.acquire()
print('Lock can still be acquired.')
```

In this example, we have a `get_data_from_file_v1()` function that takes in the path to an external file, reads the data from it, and appends that data to a predeclared list called `data`. Inside this function, a lock object called `my_lock`, which is also predeclared prior to the function being called, is acquired and released as the parameter file is read before and after, respectively.

In the main program, we will try to call `get_data_from_file_v1()` on a nonexistent file, which is one of the most common errors in programming. At the end of the program, we also acquire the lock object again. The point is to see whether our programming could handle the error of reading a nonexistent file appropriately and gracefully with just the `try...except` block that we have.

After running the script, you will notice that our program will print out the error message specified in the `try...except` block, `Encountered an exception...`, which is expected, since the file could not be found. However, the program will also fail to execute the rest of the code; it will never get to the last line of code—`print('Lock acquired.')`—and will hang forever (or until you hit *Ctrl* + *C* to force-quit the program).

This is a deadlock situation, which, again, occurs when `my_lock` is acquired inside the `get_data_from_file_v1()` function, but since our program encountered an error before executing `my_lock.release()`, the lock was never released. This in turn caused the `my_lock.acquire()` line at the end of the program to hang, as the lock could not be acquired in any way. Our program hence could not reach its last line of code, `print('Lock acquired.')`.

This problem, however, could be handled with a `with` statement easily and effortlessly. In the `example2.py` file, simply comment out the line calling `get_data_from_file_v1()` and uncomment the line calling `get_data_from_file_v2()`, and you will have the following:

```
# Chapter04/example2.py

from threading import Lock

my_lock = Lock()

def get_data_from_file_v2(filename):
    with my_lock, open(filename, 'r') as f:
        data.append(f.read())

data = []

try:
    get_data_from_file_v2('output2/sample0.txt')
except:
    print('Encountered an exception...')

my_lock.acquire()
print('Lock acquired.')
```

In the `get_data_from_file_v2()` function, we have the equivalent of a pair of nested `with` statements, as follows:

```
with my_lock:
    with open(filename, 'r') as f:
        data.append(f.read())
```

Since `Lock` objects are context managers, simply using `with my_lock:` would ensure that the lock object is acquired and released appropriately, even if an exception is encountered inside the block. After running the script, you will have the following output:

```
> python example2.py
Encountered an exception...
Lock acquired.
```

We can see that, this time, our program was able to acquire the lock and reach the end of the script gracefully and without errors.

Summary

The `with` statement in Python offers an intuitive and convenient way to manage resources while ensuring that errors and exceptions are handled correctly. This ability to manage resources is even more important in concurrent and parallel programming, where various resources are shared and utilized across different entities—specifically, by using the `with` statement with `threading.Lock` objects that are used to synchronize different threads in a multithreaded application.

Aside from better error handling and guaranteed cleanup tasks, the `with` statement also provides extra readability from your programs, which is one of the strongest features that Python offers its developers.

In the next chapter, we will be discussing one of the most popular uses of Python at the moment: web-scraping applications. We will look at the concept and the basic idea behind web scraping, the tools that Python provides to support web scraping, and how concurrency will significantly help your web-scraping applications.

Questions

- What is a file descriptor and in what ways can it be handled in Python?
- What problem arises when file descriptors are not handled carefully?
- What is a lock and in what ways can it be handled in Python?
- What problem arises when locks are not handled carefully?
- What is the idea behind context managers?
- What options does the `with` statement in Python provide in terms of context management?

Further reading

For more information, you can refer to the following links:

- *Python Parallel Programming Cookbook,* by Zaccone and Giancarlo, published by Packt, 2015
- *Improve Your Python: the with Statement and Context Managers*, Jeff Knupp (`https:/ /jeffknupp.com/blog/2016/03/07/improve-your-python-the-with-statement- and-context-managers/`)
- *Compound statements*, Python Software Foundation (`https://docs.python.org/ 3/reference/compound_stmts.html`)

5
Concurrent Web Requests

This chapter will focus on the application of concurrency in making web requests. Intuitively, making requests to a web page to collect information about it is independent to applying the same task to another web page. Concurrency, specifically threading in this case, therefore can be a powerful tool that provides a significant speedup in this process. In this chapter, we will learn the fundamentals of web requests and how to interact with websites using Python. We will also see how concurrency can help us make multiple requests in an efficient way. Finally, we will look at a number of good practices in web requests.

In this chapter, we will cover the following concepts:

- The basics of web requests
- The requests module
- Concurrent web requests
- The problem of timeout
- Good practices in making web requests

Technical requirements

The following is a list of prerequisites for this chapter:

- Python 3 must be installed on your computer
- Download the GitHub repository at `https://github.com/PacktPublishing/Mastering-Concurrency-in-Python`
- During this chapter, we will be working with the subfolder named `Chapter05`
- Check out the following video to see the Code in Action: `http://bit.ly/2Fy1ZcS`

The basics of web requests

The worldwide capacity to generate data is estimated to double in size every two years. Even though there is an interdisciplinary field known as data science that is entirely dedicated to the study of data, almost every programming task in software development also has something to do with collecting and analyzing data. A significant part of this is, of course, data collection. However, the data that we need for our applications is sometimes not stored nicely and cleanly in a database—sometimes, we need to collect the data we need from web pages.

For example, web scraping is a data extraction method that automatically makes requests to web pages and downloads specific information. Web scraping allows us to comb through numerous websites and collect any data we need in a systematic and consistent manner—the collected data can be analyzed later on by our applications or simply saved on our computers in various formats. An example of this would be Google, which programs and runs numerous web scrapers of its own to find and index web pages for the search engine.

The Python language itself provides a number of good options for applications of this kind. In this chapter, we will mainly work with the `requests` module to make client-side web requests from our Python programs. However, before we look into this module in more detail, we need to understand some web terminology in order to be able to effectively design our applications.

HTML

Hypertext Markup Language (**HTML**) is the standard and most common markup language for developing web pages and web applications. An HTML file is simply a plaintext file with the `.html` file extension. In an HTML document, texts are surrounded and delimited by tags, written in angle brackets: `<p>`, `<img>`, `<i>`, and so on. These tags typically consist of pairs—an opening tag and a closing tag—indicating the styling or the nature of the data included inside.

It is also possible to include other forms of media in HTML code, such as images or videos. There are also numerous other tags that are used in common HTML documents. Some specify a group of elements that share some common characteristics, such as `<id></id>` and `<class></class>`.

The following is an example of HTML code:

```html
<div class="topNavTop">
    <p>Welcome to Chilli restaurant</p>
    <div class="topNavRight">
        <img src="assets/top-nav/icon-phone.png">
        <p>416-455-3221</p>
        <img src="assets/top-nav/icon-email.png">
        <p>info@company.com</p>
        <img src="assets/top-nav/icon-magnifying-glass.png">
    </div>
</div>
<div class="topNavBottom">
    <img src="assets/chilli-logo.png">
    <div class="topNavRightBottom">
        <a href="index.html">HOME</a>
        <a href="menu.html">MENU</a>
        <a href="events.html">EVENTS</a>
        <a href="#contact">CONTACT</a>
    </div>
</div>
```

Sample HTML code

Fortunately, detailed knowledge on what each HTML tag accomplishes is not required for us to be able to make effective web requests. As we will see later on in this chapter, the more essential part of making web requests is the ability to interact with web pages efficiently.

HTTP requests

In a typical communication process on the web, HTML texts are the data that is to be saved and/or further processed. This data needs to be first collected from web pages, but how can we go about doing that? Most of the communication is done via the internet—more specifically, the World Wide Web—and this utilizes the **Hypertext Transfer Protocol (HTTP)**. In HTTP, request methods are used to convey the information of what data is being requested and should be sent back from a server.

For example, when you type `packtpub.com` in your browser, the browser sends a request method via HTTP to the Packt website's main server asking for data from the website. Now, if both your internet connection and Packt's server are working well, then your browser will receive a response back from the server, as shown in the following diagram. This response will be in the form of an HTML document, which will be interpreted by your browser, and your browser will display the corresponding HTML output to the screen.

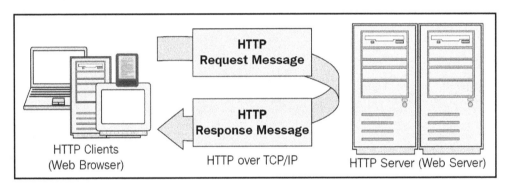

Diagram of HTTP communication

Generally, request methods are defined as verbs that indicate the desired action to be performed while the HTTP client (web browsers) and the server communicate with each other: GET, HEAD, POST, PUT, DELETE, and so on. Of these methods, GET and POST are two of the most common request methods used in web-scraping applications; their function is described in the following list:

- The GET method makes a request for a specific data from the server. This method only retrieves data and has no other effect on the server and its databases.
- The POST method sends data in a specific form that is accepted by the server. This data could be, for example, a message to a bulletin board, mailing list, or a newsgroup; information to be submitted to a web form; or an item to be added to a database.

All general-purpose HTTP servers that we commonly see on the internet are actually required to implement at least the `GET` (and `HEAD`) method, while the `POST` method is considered optional.

HTTP status code

It is not always the case that, when a web request is made and sent to a web server, the server will process the request and return the requested data without fail. Sometimes, the server might be completely down or already busy interacting with other clients and therefore unresponsive to a new request; sometimes, the client itself makes bad requests to a server (for example, incorrectly formatted or malicious requests).

As a way to categorize these problems as well as provide the most information as possible during the communication resulting from a web request, HTTP requires servers to respond to each request from its clients an **HTTP response status code**. A status code is typically a three-digit number that indicates the specific characteristics of the response that the server sends back to a client.

There are in total five large categories of HTTP response status codes, indicated by the first digit of the code. They are as follows:

- **1xx (informational status code)**: The request was received and the server is processing it. For example, 100 means the request header has been received and the server is waiting for the request body; 102 indicates that the request is currently being processed (this is used for large requests and to prevent clients from timing out).
- **2xx (successful status code)**: The request was successfully received, understood, and processed by the server. For example, 200 means the request was successfully fulfilled; 202 indicates that the request has been accepted for processing, but the processing itself is not complete.
- **3xx (redirectional status code)**: Additional actions need to be taken so that the request can be successfully processed. For example, 300 means that there are multiple options regarding how the response from the server should be processed (for example, giving the client multiple video format options when a video file is to be downloaded); 301 indicates that the server has been moved permanently and all requests should be directed to another address (provided in the response from the server).

- **4xx (error status code for the client)**: The request was incorrectly formatted by the client and could not be processed. For example, 400 means that the client sent in a bad request (for example, syntax error or the size of the request is too large); 404 (arguably the most well-known status code) indicates that the request method is not supported by the server.

- **5xx (error status code for the server)**: The request, although valid, could not be processed by the server. For example, 500 means there is an internal server error in which an unexpected condition was encountered; 504 (Gateway Timeout) means that the server, which was acting as a gateway or a proxy, did not receive a response from the final server in time.

A lot more can be said about these status codes, but it is already sufficient for us to keep in mind the big five categories previously mentioned when making web requests from Python. If you would like to find more specific information about the above or other status codes, the **Internet Assigned Numbers Authority** (**IANA**) maintains the official registry of HTTP status codes.

The requests module

The `requests` module allows its users to make and send HTTP request methods. In the applications that we will be considering, it is mainly used to make contact with the server of the web pages we want to extract data from and obtain the response for the server.

 According to the official documentation of the module, the use of Python 3 is **highly recommended** over Python 2 for `requests`.

To install the module on your computer, run the following:

```
pip install requests
```

You should use this code if you are using `pip` as your package manager. If, however, you are using Anaconda instead, simply use the following:

```
conda install requests
```

These commands should install `requests` and any other required dependencies (`idna`, `certifi`, `urllib3`, and so on) for you if your system does not have those already. After this, run `import requests` in a Python interpreter to confirm that the module has been installed successfully.

Making a request in Python

Let's look at an example usage of the module. If you already have the code for this book downloaded from the GitHub page, go ahead and navigate to the `Chapter05` folder. Let's take a look at the `example1.py` file, as shown in the following code:

```
# Chapter05/example1.py

import requests

url = 'http://www.google.com'

res = requests.get(url)

print(res.status_code)
print(res.headers)

with open('google.html', 'w') as f:
    f.write(res.text)

print('Done.')
```

In this example, we are using the `requests` module to download the HTML code of the web page, `www.google.com`. The `requests.get()` method sends a `GET` request method to `url` and we store the response to the `res` variable. After checking the status and headers of the response by printing them out, we create a file called `google.html` and write the HTML code, which is stored in the response text, to the file.

After running the programming (assuming that your internet is working and the Google server is not down), you should get the following output:

```
200
{'Date': 'Sat, 17 Nov 2018 23:08:58 GMT', 'Expires': '-1', 'Cache-Control':
'private, max-age=0', 'Content-Type': 'text/html; charset=ISO-8859-1',
'P3P': 'CP="This is not a P3P policy! See g.co/p3phelp for more info."',
'X-XSS-Protection': '1; mode=block', 'X-Frame-Options': 'SAMEORIGIN',
'Content-Encoding': 'gzip', 'Server': 'gws', 'Content-Length': '4958',
'Set-Cookie': '1P_JAR=2018-11-17-23; expires=Mon, 17-Dec-2018 23:08:58 GMT;
path=/; domain=.google.com, NID=146=NHT7fic3mjBO_vdiFB3-
gqnFPyGN1EGxyMkkNPnFMEVsqjGJ8S0EwrivDBWBgUS7hCPZGHbosLE4uxz31shnr3X4adRpe7u
ICEiK8qh3Asu6LH_bIKSLWStAp8gMK1f9_GnQ0_JKQoMvG-
OLrT_fwV0hwTR5r2UVYsUJ6xHtX2s; expires=Sun, 19-May-2019 23:08:58 GMT;
path=/; domain=.google.com; HttpOnly'}
Done.
```

The response had a `200` status code, which we know means that the request has been successfully completed. The header of the response, stored in `res.headers`, additionally contains further specific information regarding the response. For example, we can see the date and time the request was made or that the content of the response is text and HTML and the total length of the content is `4958`.

The complete data sent from the server was also written to the `google.html` file. When you open the file in a text editor, you will be able to see the HTML code of the web page that we have downloaded using requests. On the other hand, if you use a web browser to open the file, you will see how **most** of the information from the original web page is now being displayed through a downloaded offline file.

For example, the following is how Google Chrome on my system interprets the HTML file:

Downloaded HTML opened offline

There is other information that is stored on the server that web pages of that server make reference to. This means that not all of the information that an online web page provides can be downloaded via a `GET` request, and this is why offline HTML code sometimes fails to contain all of the information available on the online web page that it was downloaded from. (For example, the downloaded HTML code in the preceding screenshot does not display the Google icon correctly.)

Running a ping test

With the basic knowledge of HTTP requests and the `requests` module in Python in mind, we will go through the rest of this chapter with a central problem: running a ping test. A ping test is a process in which you test the communication between your system and specific web servers, simply by making a request to each of the servers in question. By considering the HTTP response status code (potentially) returned by the server, the test is used to evaluate either the internet connection of your own system or the availability of the servers.

Ping tests are quite common among web administrators, who usually have to manage a large number of websites simultaneously. Ping tests are a good tool to quickly identify pages that are unexpectedly unresponsive or down. There are many tools that provide you with powerful options in ping tests and, in this chapter, we will be designing a ping test application that can concurrently send multiple web requests at the same time.

To simulate different HTTP response status codes to be sent back to our program, we will be using `httpstat.us`, a website that can generate various status codes and is commonly used to test how applications that make web requests can handle varying response. Specifically, to use a request that will return a 200 status code in a program, we can simply make a request to `httpstat.us/200` and the same applies for other status codes. In our ping test program, we will have a list of `httpstat.us` URLs with different status codes.

Let's now a take look at the `Chapter05/example2.py` file, as shown in the following code:

```
# Chapter05/example2.py

import requests

def ping(url):
    res = requests.get(url)
    print(f'{url}: {res.text}')

urls = [
    'http://httpstat.us/200',
    'http://httpstat.us/400',
    'http://httpstat.us/404',
    'http://httpstat.us/408',
    'http://httpstat.us/500',
    'http://httpstat.us/524'
]
```

```
for url in urls:
    ping(url)

print('Done.')
```

In this program, the ping() function takes in a URL and attempts to make a GET request to the site. It will then print out the content of the response returned by the server. In our main program, we have a list of different status codes that we mentioned earlier, each of which we will go through and call the ping() function on.

The final output after running the preceding example should be as follows:

```
http://httpstat.us/200: 200 OK
http://httpstat.us/400: 400 Bad Request
http://httpstat.us/404: 404 Not Found
http://httpstat.us/408: 408 Request Timeout
http://httpstat.us/500: 500 Internal Server Error
http://httpstat.us/524: 524 A timeout occurred
Done.
```

We see that our ping test program was able to obtain corresponding responses from the server.

Concurrent web requests

In the context of concurrent programming, we can see that the process of making a request to a web server and obtaining the returned response is independent from the same procedure for a different web server. This is to say that we could apply concurrency and parallelism to our ping test application to speed up our execution.

In the concurrent ping test applications that we are designing, multiple HTTP requests will be made to the server simultaneously and corresponding responses will be sent back to our program, as shown in the following figure. As discussed before, concurrency and parallelism have significant applications in web development, and most servers nowadays have the ability to handle a large amount of requests at the same time:

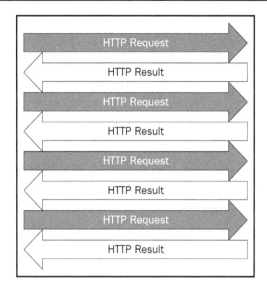

Parallel HTTP requests

Spawning multiple threads

To apply concurrency, we simply use the threading module that we have been discussing to create separate threads to handle different web requests. Let's take a look at the Chapter05/example3.py file, as shown in the following code:

```
# Chapter05/example3.py

import threading
import requests
import time

def ping(url):
    res = requests.get(url)
    print(f'{url}: {res.text}')

urls = [
    'http://httpstat.us/200',
    'http://httpstat.us/400',
    'http://httpstat.us/404',
    'http://httpstat.us/408',
    'http://httpstat.us/500',
    'http://httpstat.us/524'
]
```

```
start = time.time()
for url in urls:
    ping(url)
print(f'Sequential: {time.time() - start : .2f} seconds')

print()

start = time.time()
threads = []
for url in urls:
    thread = threading.Thread(target=ping, args=(url,))
    threads.append(thread)
    thread.start()
for thread in threads:
    thread.join()

print(f'Threading: {time.time() - start : .2f} seconds')
```

In this example, we are including the sequential logic from the previous example to process our URL list, so that we can compare the improvement in speed when we apply threading to our ping test program. We are also creating a thread to ping each of the URLs in our URL list using the `threading` module; these threads will be executing independently from each other. Time taken to process the URLs sequentially and concurrently are also tracked using methods from the `time` module.

Run the program and your output should be similar to the following:

```
http://httpstat.us/200: 200 OK
http://httpstat.us/400: 400 Bad Request
http://httpstat.us/404: 404 Not Found
http://httpstat.us/408: 408 Request Timeout
http://httpstat.us/500: 500 Internal Server Error
http://httpstat.us/524: 524 A timeout occurred
Sequential: 0.82 seconds

http://httpstat.us/404: 404 Not Found
http://httpstat.us/200: 200 OK
http://httpstat.us/400: 400 Bad Request
http://httpstat.us/500: 500 Internal Server Error
http://httpstat.us/524: 524 A timeout occurred
http://httpstat.us/408: 408 Request Timeout
Threading: 0.14 seconds
```

While the specific time that the sequential logic and threading logic take to process all the URLs might be different from system to system, there should still be a clear distinction between the two. Specifically, here we can see that the threading logic was almost six times faster than the sequential logic (which corresponds to the fact that we had six threads processing six URLs in parallel). There is no doubt, then, that concurrency can provide significant speedup for our ping test application specifically and for the process of making web requests in general.

Refactoring request logic

The current version of our ping test application works as intended, but we can improve its readability by refactoring the logic where we make web requests into a thread class. Consider the `Chapter05/example4.py` file, specifically the `MyThread` class:

```
# Chapter05/example4.py

import threading
import requests

class MyThread(threading.Thread):
    def __init__(self, url):
        threading.Thread.__init__(self)
        self.url = url
        self.result = None

    def run(self):
        res = requests.get(self.url)
        self.result = f'{self.url}: {res.text}'
```

In this example, `MyThread` inherits from the `threading.Thread` class and contains two additional attributes: `url` and `result`. The `url` attribute holds the URL that the thread instance should process, and the response returned from the web server to that thread will be written to the `result` attribute (in the `run()` function).

Outside of this class, we now can simply loop through the URL list, and create and manage the threads accordingly while not having to worry about the request logic in the main program:

```
urls = [
    'http://httpstat.us/200',
    'http://httpstat.us/400',
    'http://httpstat.us/404',
    'http://httpstat.us/408',
    'http://httpstat.us/500',
```

```
        'http://httpstat.us/524'
]

start = time.time()

threads = [MyThread(url) for url in urls]
for thread in threads:
    thread.start()
for thread in threads:
    thread.join()
for thread in threads:
    print(thread.result)

print(f'Took {time.time() - start : .2f} seconds')

print('Done.')
```

Note that we are now storing the responses in the `result` attribute of the `MyThread` class, instead of directly printing them out as in the old `ping()` function from the previous examples. This means that, after making sure that all threads have finished, we will need to loop through the threads one more time and print out those responses.

Refactoring the request logic should not greatly affect the performance of our current program; we are keeping track of the execution speed to see if this is actually the case. Execute the program and you will obtain the output similar to the following:

```
http://httpstat.us/200: 200 OK
http://httpstat.us/400: 400 Bad Request
http://httpstat.us/404: 404 Not Found
http://httpstat.us/408: 408 Request Timeout
http://httpstat.us/500: 500 Internal Server Error
http://httpstat.us/524: 524 A timeout occurred
Took 0.14 seconds
Done.
```

Just as we expected, we are still achieving a significant speedup from the sequential version of the program with this refactored request logic. Again, our main program is now more readable, and further adjustments of the request logic (as we will see in the next section) can simply be directed to the `MyThread` class, without affecting the rest of the program.

The problem of timeout

In this section, we will explore a potential improvement to be made to our ping test application: timeout handling. Timeouts typically occur when the server takes an unusually long time to process a specific request, and the connection between the server and its client is terminated.

In the context of a ping test application, we will be implementing a customized threshold for the timeout. Recall that a ping test is used to determine whether specific servers are still responsive, so we can specify in our program that, if a request takes more than our timeout threshold for the server to response, we will categorize that specific server with a timeout.

Support from httpstat.us and simulation in Python

In addition to different options for status codes, the `httpstat.us` website additionally provides a way to simulate a delay in its response when we send in requests. Specifically, we can customize the delay time (in milliseconds) with a query argument in our GET request. For example, `httpstat.us/200?sleep=5000` will return a response after five seconds of delay.

Now, let us see how a delay like this would affect the execution of our program. Consider the `Chapter05/example5.py` file, which contains the current request logic of our ping test application but has a different URL list:

```
# Chapter05/example5.py

import threading
import requests

class MyThread(threading.Thread):
    def __init__(self, url):
        threading.Thread.__init__(self)
        self.url = url
        self.result = None

    def run(self):
        res = requests.get(self.url)
        self.result = f'{self.url}: {res.text}'

urls = [
    'http://httpstat.us/200',
    'http://httpstat.us/200?sleep=20000',
```

```
        'http://httpstat.us/400'
]

threads = [MyThread(url) for url in urls]
for thread in threads:
    thread.start()
for thread in threads:
    thread.join()
for thread in threads:
    print(thread.result)

print('Done.')
```

Here we have a URL that will take around 20 seconds to return a response. Considering that we will block the main program until all threads finish their execution (with the `join()` method), our program will most likely appear to be hanging for 20 seconds before any response is printed out.

Run the program to experience this for yourself. A 20 second delay will occur (which will make the execution take significantly longer to finish) and we will obtain the following output:

```
http://httpstat.us/200: 200 OK
http://httpstat.us/200?sleep=20000: 200 OK
http://httpstat.us/400: 400 Bad Request
Took 22.60 seconds
Done.
```

Timeout specifications

An efficient ping test application should not be waiting for responses from its websites for a long time; it should have a set threshold for timeout that, if a server fails to return a response under that threshold, the application will deem that server non-responsive. We therefore need to implement a way to keep track of how much time has passed since a request is sent to a server. We will do this by counting down from the timeout threshold and, once that threshold is passed, all responses (whether returned or not yet returned) will be printed out.

Additionally, we will also be keeping track of how many requests are still pending and have not had their responses returned. We will be using the `isAlive()` method from the `threading.Thread` class to indirectly determine whether a response has been returned for a specific request: if, at one point, the thread processing a specific request is alive, we can conclude that that specific request is still pending.

Navigate to the `Chapter05/example6.py` file and consider the `process_requests()` function first:

```python
# Chapter05/example6.py

import time

UPDATE_INTERVAL = 0.01

def process_requests(threads, timeout=5):
    def alive_count():
        alive = [1 if thread.isAlive() else 0 for thread in threads]
        return sum(alive)

    while alive_count() > 0 and timeout > 0:
        timeout -= UPDATE_INTERVAL
        time.sleep(UPDATE_INTERVAL)
    for thread in threads:
        print(thread.result)
```

The function takes in a list of threads that we have been using to make web requests in the previous examples, as well as an optional argument specifying the timeout threshold. Inside this function, we have an inner function, `alive_count()`, which returns the count of the threads that are still alive at the time of the function call.

In the `process_requests()` function, as long as there are threads that are currently alive and processing requests, we will allow the threads to continue with their execution (this is done in the `while` loop with the double condition). The `UPDATE_INTERVAL` variable, as you can see, specifies how often we check for this condition. If either condition fails (if there are no alive threads left or if the threshold timeout is passed), then we will proceed with printing out the responses (even if some might have not been returned).

Let's turn our attention to the new `MyThread` class:

```python
# Chapter05/example6.py

import threading
import requests

class MyThread(threading.Thread):
```

```
def __init__(self, url):
    threading.Thread.__init__(self)
    self.url = url
    self.result = f'{self.url}: Custom timeout'

def run(self):
    res = requests.get(self.url)
    self.result = f'{self.url}: {res.text}'
```

This class is almost identical to the one we considered in the previous example, except that the initial value for the `result` attribute is a message indicating a timeout. In the case that we discussed earlier where the timeout threshold specified in the `process_requests()` function is passed, this initial value will be used when the responses are printed out.

Finally, let's consider our main program:

```
# Chapter05/example6.py

urls = [
    'http://httpstat.us/200',
    'http://httpstat.us/200?sleep=4000',
    'http://httpstat.us/200?sleep=20000',
    'http://httpstat.us/400'
]

start = time.time()

threads = [MyThread(url) for url in urls]
for thread in threads:
    thread.setDaemon(True)
    thread.start()
process_requests(threads)

print(f'Took {time.time() - start : .2f} seconds')

print('Done.')
```

Here, in our URL list, we have a request that would take 4 seconds and another that would take 20 seconds, aside from the ones that would respond immediately. As the timeout threshold that we are using is 5 seconds, theoretically we should be able to see that the 4-second-delay request will successfully obtain a response, while the 20-second-delay one will not.

There is another point to be made about this program: daemon threads. In the process_requests() function, if the timeout threshold is passed while there is still at least one thread processing, then the function will proceed to print out the result attribute of each thread:

```
while alive_count() > 0 and timeout > 0:
    timeout -= UPDATE_INTERVAL
    time.sleep(UPDATE_INTERVAL)
for thread in threads:
    print(thread.result)
```

This means that we do not block our program until all of the threads have finished their execution by using the join() function, and the program therefore can simply move forward if the timeout threshold is reached. However, this means that the threads themselves do not terminate at this point. The 20-second-delay request, specifically, will still most likely be running after our program exits out of the process_requests() function.

If the thread processing this request is not a daemon thread (as we know, daemon threads execute in the background and never terminate), it will block the main program from finishing until the thread itself finishes. By making this thread, and any other thread, a daemon thread, we allow the main program to finish as soon as it executes the last line of its instructions, even if there are threads still running.

Let us see this program in action. Execute the code and your output should be similar to the following:

```
http://httpstat.us/200: 200 OK
http://httpstat.us/200?sleep=4000: 200 OK
http://httpstat.us/200?sleep=20000: Custom timeout
http://httpstat.us/400: 400 Bad Request
Took 5.70 seconds
Done.
```

As you can see, it took around 5 seconds for our program to finish this time. This is because it spent 5 seconds waiting for the threads that were still running and, as soon as the 5-second threshold was passed, the program printed out the results. Here we see that the result from the 20-second-delay request was simply the default value of the result attribute of the MyThread class, while the rest of the requests were able to obtain the correct response from the server (including the 4-second-delay request, since it had enough time to obtain the response).

If you would like to see the effect of non-daemon threads that we discussed earlier, simply comment out the corresponding line of code in our main program, as follows:

```
threads = [MyThread(url) for url in urls]
for thread in threads:
    #thread.setDaemon(True)
    thread.start()
process_requests(threads)
```

You will see that the main program will hang for around 20 seconds, as the non-daemon thread processing the 20-second-delay request is still running, before being able to finish its execution (even though the output produced will be identical).

Good practices in making web requests

There are a few aspects of making concurrent web requests that require careful consideration and implementation. In this section, we will be going over those aspects and some of the best practices that you should use when developing your applications.

Consider the terms of service and data-collecting policies

Unauthorized data collection has been the topic of discussion in the technology world for the past few years, and it will continue to be for a long time—and for good reason too. It is therefore extremely important for developers who are making automated web requests in their applications to look for websites' policies on data collecting. You can find these policies in their terms of service or similar documents. When in doubt, it is generally a good rule of thumb to contact the website directly to ask for more details.

Error handling

Error is something that no one can easily avoid in the field of programming, and this is especially true in making web requests. Errors in these programs can include making bad requests (invalid requests or even bad internet connections), mishandling downloaded HTML code, or unsuccessfully parsing HTML code. It is therefore important to make use of `try...except` blocks and other error-handling tools in Python to avoid crashing your application. Avoiding crashes is especially important if your code/applications are used in production and larger applications.

Specifically in concurrent web scraping, it might be possible for some threads to collect data successfully, while others fail. By implementing error-handling functionalities in multithreaded parts of your program, you can make sure that a failed thread will not be able to crash the entirety of your program and ensure that successful threads can still return their results.

However, it is important to note that blind error-catching is still undesirable. This term indicates the practice where we have a large `try...expect` block in our program that will catch any and all errors that occur in the program execution, and no further information regarding the errors can be obtained; this practice might also be known as error swallowing. It's highly recommended to have specific error handling code in a program, so that not only appropriate actions can be taken with regards to that specific error, but other errors that have not been taken into account might also reveal themselves.

Update your program regularly

It is quite common for websites to change their request-handling logic as well as their displayed data regularly. If a program that makes requests to a website has considerably inflexible logic to interact with the server of the website (for example, structuring its requests in a specific format, only handling one kind of response), then if and when the website alters the way it handles its client requests, the program will most likely stop functioning correctly. This situation happens frequently with web scraping programs that look for data in specific HTML tags; when the HTML tags are changed, these programs will fail to find their data.

This practice is implemented to prevent automated data collecting programs from functioning. The only way to keep using a website that recently changed its request-handling logic is to analyze the updated protocols and alter our programs accordingly.

Avoid making a large number of requests

Each time one of the programs that we have been discussing runs, it makes HTTP requests to a server that manages the site that you'd like to extract data from. This process happens significantly more frequently and over a shorter amount of time in a concurrent program, where multiple requests are being submitted to that server.

As mentioned before, servers nowadays have the ability to handle multiple requests simultaneously with ease. However, to avoid having to overwork and overconsume resources, servers are also designed to stop answering requests that come in too frequently. Websites of big tech companies, such as Amazon or Twitter, look for large amounts of automated requests that are made from the same IP address and implement different response protocols; some requests might be delayed, some might be refused a response, or the IP address might even be banned from making further requests for a specific amount of time.

Interestingly, making repeated, heavy-duty requests to servers is actually a form of hacking a website. In **Denial of Service (DoS)** and **Distributed Denial of Service (DDoS)** attacks, a very large number of requests are made at the same time to the server, flooding the bandwidth of the targeted server with traffic, and as a result, normal, nonmalicious requests from other clients are denied because the servers are busy processing the concurrent requests, as illustrated in the following diagram:

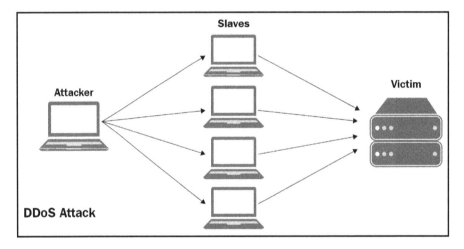

A of a DDoS attack

It is therefore important to space out the concurrent requests that your application makes to a server so that the application would not be considered an attacker and be potentially banned or treated as a malicious client. This could be as simple as limiting the maximum number of threads/requests that can be implemented at a time in your program or pausing the threading for a specific amount of time (for example, using the time.sleep() function) before making a request to the server.

Summary

In this chapter, we have learned about the basics of HTML and web requests. The two most common web requests are GET and POST requests. There are five main categories for HTTP response status code, each indicating a different concept regarding the communication between the server and its client. By considering the status codes received from different websites, we can write a ping test application that effectively checks for the responsiveness of those websites.

Concurrency can be applied to the problem of making multiple web requests simultaneously via threading to provide a significant improvement in application speed. However, it is important to keep in mind a number of considerations when make concurrent web requests.

In the next chapter, we will start discussing another major player in concurrent programming: processes. We will be considering the concept of and the basic idea behind a process, and the options that Python provides for us to work with processes.

Questions

- What is HTML?
- What are HTTP requests?
- What are HTTP response status codes?
- How does the requests module help with making web requests?
- What is a ping test and how is one typically designed?
- Why is concurrency applicable in making web requests?
- What are the considerations that need to be made while developing applications that make concurrent web requests?

Further reading

For more information, you can refer to the following links:

- *Automate the boring stuff with Python: practical programming for total beginners*, Al. Sweigart, No Starch Press, 2015
- *Web Scraping with Python*, Richard Lawson, Packt Publishing Ltd, 2015
- *Instant Web Scraping with Java*, Ryan Mitchell, Packt Publishing Ltd, 2013

6
Working with Processes in Python

This chapter is the first of three chapters on using concurrency through multiprocessing programming in Python. We have seen various examples of processes being used in concurrent and parallel programming. In this chapter, you will be introduced to the formal definition of a process, as well as the `multiprocessing` module in Python. This chapter will go through some of the most common ways of working with processes using the API of the `multiprocessing` module, such as the `Process` class, the `Pool` class, and interprocess communication tools such as the `Queue` class. This chapter will also look at the key differences between multithreading and multiprocessing in concurrent programming.

The following topics will be covered in this chapter:

- The concept of a process in the context of concurrent programming in computer science
- The basic API of the `multiprocessing` module in Python
- How to interact with processes and the advanced functionalities that the `multiprocessing` module provides
- How the `multiprocessing` module supports interprocess communication
- The key differences between multiprocessing and multithreading in concurrent programming

Technical requirements

The following is a list of prerequisites for this chapter:

- Install Python 3 on your computer
- Download the GitHub repository at `https://github.com/PacktPublishing/Mastering-Concurrency-in-Python`
- Ensure that you can access the subfolder named `Chapter06`
- Check out the following video to see the Code in Action: `http://bit.ly/2BtwlJw`

The concept of a process

In the field of computer science, a **process of execution** is an instance of a specific computer program or software that is being executed by the operating system. A process contains both the program code and its current activities and interactions with other entities. Depending on the operating system, the implementation of a process can be made up of multiple threads of execution that can execute instructions concurrently or in parallel.

It is important to note that a process is not equivalent to a computer program. While a program is simply a static collection of instructions (program code), a process is instead the actual execution of those instructions. This also means that the same program could be run concurrently by spawning multiple processes. These processes execute the same code from the parent program.

For example, the internet browser Google Chrome usually manages a process called **Google Chrome Helper** for its main program in order to facilitate web browsing and other processes, to assist with various purposes. An easy way to see what different processes your system is running and managing involves using **Task Manager** for Windows, **Activity Monitor** for iOS, and **System Monitor** for Linux operating systems.

The following is a screenshot of my **Activity Monitor**. Multiple processes with the name **Google Chrome Helper** can be seen in the list. The **PID** column (which stands for **process ID**) reports the unique ID that each process has:

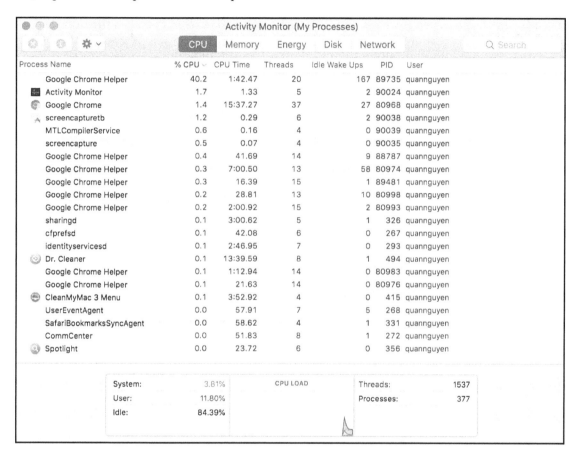

Process Name	% CPU ⌄	CPU Time	Threads	Idle Wake Ups	PID	User
Google Chrome Helper	40.2	1:42.47	20	167	89735	quannguyen
Activity Monitor	1.7	1.33	5	2	90024	quannguyen
Google Chrome	1.4	15:37.27	37	27	80968	quannguyen
screencapturetb	1.2	0.29	6	2	90038	quannguyen
MTLCompilerService	0.6	0.16	4	0	90039	quannguyen
screencapture	0.5	0.07	4	0	90035	quannguyen
Google Chrome Helper	0.4	41.69	14	9	88787	quannguyen
Google Chrome Helper	0.3	7:00.50	13	58	80974	quannguyen
Google Chrome Helper	0.3	16.39	15	1	89481	quannguyen
Google Chrome Helper	0.2	28.81	13	10	80998	quannguyen
Google Chrome Helper	0.2	2:00.92	15	2	80993	quannguyen
sharingd	0.1	3:00.62	5	1	326	quannguyen
cfprefsd	0.1	42.08	6	0	267	quannguyen
identityservicesd	0.1	2:46.95	7	0	293	quannguyen
Dr. Cleaner	0.1	13:39.59	8	1	494	quannguyen
Google Chrome Helper	0.1	1:12.94	14	0	80983	quannguyen
Google Chrome Helper	0.1	21.63	14	0	80976	quannguyen
CleanMyMac 3 Menu	0.1	3:52.92	4	0	415	quannguyen
UserEventAgent	0.0	57.91	7	5	268	quannguyen
SafariBookmarksSyncAgent	0.0	58.62	4	1	331	quannguyen
CommCenter	0.0	51.83	8	1	272	quannguyen
Spotlight	0.0	23.72	6	0	356	quannguyen

System:	3.81%	CPU LOAD	Threads:	1537
User:	11.80%		Processes:	377
Idle:	84.39%			

Sample list of processes

Processes versus threads

One of the most common mistakes that programmers make when developing concurrent and parallel applications is to confuse the structure and functionalities of processes and threads. As we have seen from Chapter 3, *Working with Threads in Python*, a thread is the smallest unit of programming code, and is typically a component of a process. Furthermore, more than one thread can be implemented within the same process to access and share memory or other resources, while different processes do not interact in this way. This relationship is shown in the following diagram:

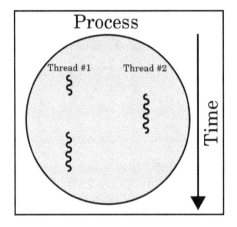

Diagram of two threads executing in one process

Since a process is a larger programming unit than a thread, it is also more complicated and consists of more programming components. A process, therefore, also requires more resources, while a thread does not and is sometimes called a lightweight process. In a typical computer system process, there are a number of main resources, as shown in the following list:

- An image (or copy) of the code being executed from the parent program.
- Memory associated with an instance of a program. This might include executable code, input and output for that specific process, a call stack to manage program-specific events, or a heap that contains generated computation data and is currently being used by the process during runtime.
- Descriptors for the resources allocated to that specific process by the operating system. We have seen an example of these—file descriptors—in Chapter 4, *Using the with Statement in Threads*.

- Security components of a specific process, namely the owner of the process and its permissions and allowed operations.
- The processor state, also known as the process context. The context data of a process is often located in processor registers, the memory used by the process, or in control registers used by the operating system to manage the process.

Because each process has a state dedicated to it, processes hold more state information than threads; multiple threads within a process in turn share process states, memory, and other various resources. For similar reasons, processes only interact with each other through system-facilitated interprocess communication methods, while threads can communicate with one another easily through shared resources.

Additionally, context-switching—the act of saving the state data of a process or a thread to interrupt the execution of a task and resume it at a later time—takes more time between different processes than between different threads within the same process. However, while we have seen that communication between threads requires careful memory synchronization to ensure correct data handling, since there is less communication between separate processes, little or no memory synchronization is needed for processes.

Multiprocessing

A common concept in computer science is multitasking. When multitasking, an operating system simply switches between different processes at high speed to give the appearance that these processes are being executed simultaneously, even though it is usually the case that only one process is executing on one single **central processing unit** (**CPU**) at any given time. In contrast, multiprocessing is the method of using more than one CPU to execute a task.

While there are a number of different uses of the term multiprocessing, in the context of concurrency and parallelism multiprocessing refers to the execution of multiple concurrent processes in an operating system, in which each process is executed on a separate CPU, as opposed to a single process being executed at any given time. By the nature of processes, an operating system needs to have two or more CPUs in order to be able to implement multiprocessing tasks, as it needs to support many processors at the same time and allocate tasks between them appropriately.

This relationship is shown in the following diagram:

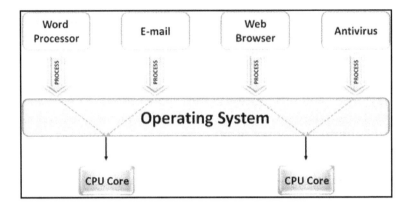

Example diagram of multiprocessing using two CPU cores

We have seen in Chapter 3, *Working with Threads in Python*, that multithreading shares a somewhat similar definition to multiprocessing. Multithreading means that only one processor is utilized, and the system switches between tasks within that processor (also known as **time slicing**), while multiprocessing generally denotes the actual concurrent/parallel execution of multiple processes using multiple processors.

Multiprocessing applications have enjoyed significant popularity in the field of concurrent and parallel programming. Some reasons for this are listed as follows:

- **Faster execution time**: As we know, when done correctly concurrency always provides additional speedups for your programs, provided that some parts of them can be executed independently.
- **Synchronization free**: Given the fact that separate processes do not share resources among themselves in a multiprocessing application, developers rarely need to spend their time coordinating the sharing and synchronization of these resources, unlike multithreaded applications, where efforts need to be made to make sure that data is being manipulated correctly.
- **Safety from crashes**: As processes are independent from each other in terms of both computing procedures and input/output, the failure of one process will not affect the execution of another in a multiprocessing program, if handled correctly. This implies that programmers could afford to spawn a larger number of processes (that their system can still handle) and the chance of crashing the entire application would not increase.

With that being said, there are also noteworthy disadvantages to using multiprocessing that we should consider, as shown in the following list:

- **Multiple processors are needed**: Again, multiprocessing requires the operating system to have more than one CPU. Even though multiple processors are fairly common for computer systems nowadays, if yours does not have more than one, then the implementation of multiprocessing will not be possible.
- **Processing time and space**: As mentioned before, there are many complex components involved in implementing a process and its resources. It therefore takes significant computing time and power to spawn and manage processes in comparison to doing the same with threads.

Introductory example in Python

To illustrate the concept of running multiple processes on one operating system, let's look at a quick example in Python. Let's take a look at the `Chapter06/example1.py` file, as shown in the following code:

```
# Chapter06/example1.py

from multiprocessing import Process
import time


def count_down(name, delay):
    print('Process %s starting...' % name)

    counter = 5

    while counter:
        time.sleep(delay)
        print('Process %s counting down: %i...' % (name, counter))
        counter -= 1

    print('Process %s exiting...' % name)


if __name__ == '__main__':
    process1 = Process(target=count_down, args=('A', 0.5))
    process2 = Process(target=count_down, args=('B', 0.5))

    process1.start()
    process2.start()
```

```
        process1.join()
        process2.join()

        print('Done.')
```

In this file, we are going back to the counting-down example that we saw in Chapter 3, *Working with Threads in Python*, while we look at the concept of a thread. Our count_down() function takes in a string as a process identifier and a delay time range. It will then count down from 5 to 1 while sleeping between iterations for a number of seconds specified by the delay parameter. The function also prints out a message with the process identifier at each iteration.

As we saw in Chapter 3, *Working with Threads in Python*, the point of this counting-down example is to show the concurrent nature of running separate tasks at the same time, this time through different processes by using the Process class from the multiprocessing module. In our main program, we initialize two processes at the same time to implement two separate time-based countdowns simultaneously. Similar to how two separate threads would do this, our two processes will carry out their own countdowns concurrently.

After running the Python script, your output should be similar to the following:

```
> python example1.py
Process A starting...
Process B starting...
Process B counting down: 5...
Process A counting down: 5...
Process B counting down: 4...
Process A counting down: 4...
Process B counting down: 3...
Process A counting down: 3...
Process B counting down: 2...
Process A counting down: 2...
Process A counting down: 1...
Process B counting down: 1...
Process A exiting...
Process B exiting...
Done.
```

Just as we expected, the output tells us that the two countdowns from the separate processes were executed concurrently; instead of finishing the first process' countdown and then starting the second's, the program ran the two countdowns at almost the same time. Even though processes are more expensive and contain more overhead than threads, multiprocessing also allows double the improvement in terms of speed for programs such as the preceding one.

Remember that in multithreading we saw a phenomenon in which the order of the printed output changed between different runs of the program. Specifically, sometimes process B would get ahead of process A during the countdown and finish before process A, even though it was initialized later. This is, again, a direct result of implementing and starting two processes that execute the same function at almost the same time. By executing the script many times, you will see that it is quite likely for you to obtain changing output in terms of the order of the counting and the completion of the countdowns.

An overview of the multiprocessing module

The `multiprocessing` module is one of the most commonly used implementations of multiprocessing programming in Python. It offers methods to spawn and interact with processes using an API similar to the `threading` module (as we saw with the `start()` and `join()` methods in the preceding example). According to its documentation website, the module allows both local and remote concurrency and effectively avoids the **global interpreter lock** (**GIL**) in Python (which we will discuss in more detail later in `Chapter 15`, *The Global Interpreter Lock*) by using subprocesses instead of threads.

The process class

In the `multiprocessing` module, processes are typically spawned and managed through the `Process` class. Each `Process` object represents an activity that executes in a separate process. Conveniently, the `Process` class has equivalent methods and APIs that can be found in the `threading.Thread` class.

Specifically, utilizing an object-oriented programming approach, the `Process` class from `multiprocessing` provides the following resources:

- `run()`: This method is executed when a new process is initialized and started
- `start()`: This method starts the initialized calling `Process` object by calling the `run()` method
- `join()`: This method waits for the calling `Process` object to terminate before continuing with the execution of the rest of the program

- `isAlive()`: This method returns a Boolean value indicating whether the calling `Process` object is currently executing
- `name`: This attribute contains the name of the calling `Process` object
- `pid`: This attribute contains the process ID of the calling `Process` object
- `terminate()`: This method terminates the calling `Process` object

As you can see from our previous example, while initializing a `Process` object, we can pass parameters to a function and execute it in a separate process by specifying the `target` (for the target function) and `args` (for target function arguments) parameters. Note that one could also override the default `Process()` constructor and implement one's own `run()` function.

As it is a major player in the `multiprocessing` module and in concurrency in Python in general, we will look at the `Process` class again in the next section.

The Pool class

In the `multiprocessing` module, the `Pool` class is mainly used to implement a pool of processes, each of which will carry out tasks submitted to a `Pool` object. Generally, the `Pool` class is more convenient than the `Process` class, especially if the results returned from your concurrent application should be ordered.

Specifically, we have seen that the order of completion for different items in a list is considerably likely to change when put through a function concurrently as the program runs over and over again. This leads to difficulty when reordering the outputs of the program with respect to the order of the inputs that produced them. One possible solution to this is to create tuples of processes and their outputs, and to sort them by process ID.

This problem is addressed by the `Pool` class: the `Pool.map()` and `Pool.apply()` methods follow the convention of Python's traditional `map()` and `apply()` methods, ensuring that the returned values are ordered in the same way that the input is. These methods, however, block the main program until a process has finished processing. The `Pool` class, therefore, also has the `map_async()` and `apply_async()` functions to better assist concurrency and parallelism.

Determining the current process, waiting, and terminating processes

The Process class provides a number of ways to easily interact with processes in a concurrent program. In this section, we will explore the options of managing different processes by determining the current process, waiting, and terminating processes.

Determining the current process

Working with processes is at times considerably difficult, and significant debugging is therefore required. One of the methods of debugging a multiprocessing program is to identify the processes that encounter errors. As a refresher, in the previous countdown example we passed a name parameter to the count_down() function to determine where each process is during the countdown.

This is, however, unnecessary as each Process object has a name parameter (with a default value) that can be changed. Naming processes is a better way to keep track of running processes than passing an identifier to the target function itself (as we did earlier), especially in applications with different types of processes running at the same time. One powerful functionality that the multiprocessing module provides is the current_process() method, which will return the Process object that is currently running at any point of a program. This is another way to keep track of running processes effectively and effortlessly.

Let's look at this in more detail using an example. Navigate to the Chapter06/example2.py file, as shown in the following code:

```
# Chapter06/example2.py

from multiprocessing import Process, current_process
import time


def f1():
    pname = current_process().name
    print('Starting process %s...' % pname)
    time.sleep(2)
    print('Exiting process %s...' % pname)

def f2():
    pname = current_process().name
    print('Starting process %s...' % pname)
    time.sleep(4)
```

```
        print('Exiting process %s...' % pname)


if __name__ == '__main__':
    p1 = Process(name='Worker 1', target=f1)
    p2 = Process(name='Worker 2', target=f2)
    p3 = Process(target=f1)

    p1.start()
    p2.start()
    p3.start()

    p1.join()
    p2.join()
    p3.join()
```

In this example, we have two dummy functions, `f1()` and `f2()`, each of which prints out the name of the process that executes the function before and after sleeping for a specified period of time. In our main program, we initialize three separate processes. The first two we name `Worker 1` and `Worker 2` respectively, and the last we purposefully leave blank to give it the default value of its name (that is, `'Process-3'`). After running the script, you should have an output similar to the following:

```
> python example2.py
Starting process Worker 1...
Starting process Worker 2...
Starting process Process-3...
Exiting process Worker 1...
Exiting process Process-3...
Exiting process Worker 2...
```

We can see that the `current_process()` successfully helped us access the correct process that ran each function, and the third process was assigned the name `Process-3` by default. Another way to keep track of the running processes in your program is to look at the individual process IDs using the `os` module. Let's take a look at a modified example in the `Chapter06/example3.py` file, as shown in the following code:

```
# Chapter06/example3.py

from multiprocessing import Process, current_process
import time
import os


def print_info(title):
    print(title)
```

```
    if hasattr(os, 'getppid'):
        print('Parent process ID: %s.' % str(os.getppid()))

    print('Current Process ID: %s.\n' % str(os.getpid()))

def f():
    print_info('Function f')

    pname = current_process().name
    print('Starting process %s...' % pname)
    time.sleep(1)
    print('Exiting process %s...' % pname)


if __name__ == '__main__':
    print_info('Main program')

    p = Process(target=f)
    p.start()
    p.join()

    print('Done.')
```

Our main focus for this example is the `print_info()` function, which uses the `os.getpid()` and `os.getppid()` functions to identify the current process using its process ID. Specifically, `os.getpid()` returns the process ID of the current process, and `os.getppid()` (which is only available on Unix systems) returns the ID of the parent process. The following is my input after running the script:

```
> python example3.py
Main program
Parent process ID: 14806.
Current Process ID: 29010.

Function f
Parent process ID: 29010.
Current Process ID: 29012.

Starting process Process-1...
Exiting process Process-1...
Done.
```

The process IDs might vary from system to system, but their relative relationship should be the same. Specifically for my output, we can see that, while the ID for the main Python program was `29010`, the ID of its parent process was `14806`. Using **Activity Monitor**, I crosschecked this ID and connected it to my Terminal and Bash profile, which makes sense since I ran this Python script from my Terminal. You can see the displayed results from Activity Monitor in the following screenshot:

Process Name	% CPU	CPU Time	Threads	Idle Wake Ups	PID ∧	User
Terminal	0.0	41.16	6	0	14803	quannguyen
MTLCompilerService	0.0	0.13	2	0	14804	quannguyen
bash	0.0	0.39	1	0	14806	quannguyen

Screenshot of Activity Monitor being used to crosscheck PIDs

In addition to the main Python program, we also called `print_info()` inside the `f()` function, whose process ID was `29012`. We can also see that the parent process of the process running the `f()` function is actually our main process, whose ID was `29010`.

Waiting for processes

Oftentimes, we'd like to wait for all of our concurrent processes to finish executing before moving to a new section of the program. As mentioned before, the `Process` class from the `multiprocessing` module provides the `join()` method in order to implement a way to wait until a process has completed its task and exits.

However, sometimes developers want to implement processes that run in the background and do not block the main program from exiting. This specification is commonly used when there is no easy way for the main program to tell whether it is appropriate to interrupt the process at any given time, or when exiting the main program without completing the worker does not affect the end result.

These processes are called **daemon processes**. The `Process` class also provides an easy option to specify whether a process is a daemon through the `daemon` attribute, which takes a Boolean value. The default value for the `daemon` attribute is `False`, so setting it to `True` will turn a given process into a daemon. Let's look at this in more detail using an example in the `Chapter06/example4.py` file, as shown in the following code:

```
# Chapter06/example4.py

from multiprocessing import Process, current_process
import time
```

```
def f1():
    p = current_process()
    print('Starting process %s, ID %s...' % (p.name, p.pid))
    time.sleep(4)
    print('Exiting process %s, ID %s...' % (p.name, p.pid))

def f2():
    p = current_process()
    print('Starting process %s, ID %s...' % (p.name, p.pid))
    time.sleep(2)
    print('Exiting process %s, ID %s...' % (p.name, p.pid))


if __name__ == '__main__':
    p1 = Process(name='Worker 1', target=f1)
    p1.daemon = True
    p2 = Process(name='Worker 2', target=f2)

    p1.start()
    time.sleep(1)
    p2.start()
```

In this example, we have a long-running function (represented by f1(), which has a sleep period of 4 seconds) and a faster function (represented by f2(), which has a sleep period of only 2 seconds). We also have two separate processes, as shown in the following list:

- The p1 process, which is a daemon process assigned to run f1()
- The p2 process, which is a regular process assigned to run f2()

In our main program, we start both processes without calling the join() method on either of them at the end of the program. Since p1 is a long-running process, it will most likely not finish executing before p2 (which is the faster process of the two) finishes. We also know that p1 is a daemon process, so our program should exit before it finishes executing. After running the Python script, your output should be similar to the following code:

```
> python example4.py
Starting process Worker 1, ID 33784...
Starting process Worker 2, ID 33788...
Exiting process Worker 2, ID 33788...
```

Again, even though the process IDs might be different when you yourself run the script, the general format of the output should be the same. As we can see, the output is consistent with what we discussed: both p1 and p2 processes were initialized and started by our main program, and the program terminated after the nondaemon process exited without waiting for the daemon process to finish.

The ability to terminate the main program without having to wait for specific tasks that the daemon is processing is indeed extremely useful. However, sometimes we might want to wait for daemon processes for a specified amount of time before exiting; this way, if the specifications of the program allow some waiting time for the process' execution, we could complete some potential daemon processes instead of terminating all of them prematurely.

The combination of daemon processes and the `join()` method from the `multiprocessing` module can help us implement this architecture, especially given that, while the `join()` method blocks the program execution indefinitely (or at least until the task finishes), it is also possible to pass a timeout argument to specify the number of seconds to wait for the process before exiting. Let's consider a modified version of the previous example in `Chapter06/example5.py`. With the same `f1()` and `f2()` functions, in the following script, we are changing the way we handle the daemon process in the main program:

```
# Chapter06/example5.py

if __name__ == '__main__':
    p1 = Process(name='Worker 1', target=f1)
    p1.daemon = True
    p2 = Process(name='Worker 2', target=f2)

    p1.start()
    time.sleep(1)
    p2.start()

    p1.join(1)
    print('Whether Worker 1 is still alive:', p1.is_alive())
    p2.join()
```

Instead of terminating without waiting for the daemon process, in this example, we are calling the `join()` method on both processes: we allow one second for p1 to finish while we block the main program until p2 finishes. If p1 has not finished executing after that one second, the main program simply continues executing the rest of the program and exits, at which time we will see that p1—or `Worker 1`—is still alive. After running the Python script, your output should be similar to the following:

```
> python example5.py
Starting process Worker 1, ID 36027...
Starting process Worker 2, ID 36030...
Whether Worker 1 is still alive: True
Exiting process Worker 2, ID 36030...
```

We see that p1 was indeed still alive by the time the program moved on after waiting for it for one second.

Terminating processes

The `terminate()` method from the `multiprocessing.Process` class offers a way to quickly terminate a process. When the method is called, exit handlers, finally causes, or similar resources that are specified in the `Process` class or an overridden class will not be executed. However, descendant processes of the terminated process will not be terminated. These processes are known as **orphaned processes**.

Although terminating processes is sometimes frowned upon, it is sometimes necessary because some processes interact with interprocess-communication resources, such as locks, semaphores, pipes, or queues, and forcibly stopping those processes is likely to cause those resources to become corrupted or unavailable to other processes. If, however, the processes in your program never interact with the aforementioned resources, the `terminate()` method is considerably useful, especially if a process appears to be unresponsive or deadlocked.

One thing to note when using the `terminate()` method is that, even though the `Process` object is effectively killed after calling the method, it is important that you call `join()` on the object as well. Since the `alive` status of `Process` objects is sometimes not immediately updated after the `terminate()` method, this practice gives the background system an opportunity to implement the update itself to reflect the termination of the processes.

Interprocess communication

While locks are one of the most common synchronization primitives that are used for communication among threads, pipes and queues are the main way of communicating between different processes. Specifically, they provide message-passing options to facilitate communication between processes—pipes for connections between two processes and queues for multiple producers and consumers.

In this section, we will be exploring the usage of queues, specifically the `Queue` class from the `multiprocessing` module. The implementation of the `Queue` class is, in fact, both thread-and process-safe, and we have already seen the use of queues in `Chapter 3`, *Working with Threads in Python*. All pickleable objects in Python can be passed through a `Queue` object; in this section, we will be using queues to pass messages back and forth between processes.

Using a message queue for interprocess communication is preferred over having shared resources since, if certain processes mishandle and corrupt shared memory and resources while those resources are being shared, then there will be numerous undesirable and unpredictable consequences. If, however, a process failed to handle its message correctly, other items in the queue will remain intact. The following diagram represents the differences in architecture between using a message queue and shared resources (specifically memory) for interprocess communication:

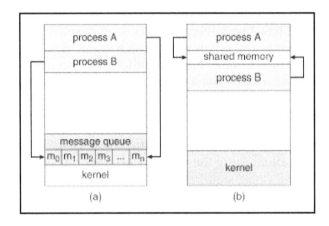

The architecture involved in using a message queue and shared resources for interprocess communication

Message passing for a single worker

Before we dive into the example code in Python, first we need to discuss specifically how we use a `Queue` object in our multiprocessing application. Let's say that we have a `worker` class that performs heavy computations and does not require significant resource sharing and communication. Yet these worker instances still need to be able to receive information from time to time during their execution.

This is where the use of a queue comes in: when we put all the workers in a queue. At the same time, we will also have a number of initialized processes, each of which will go through that queue and process one worker. If a process has finished executing a worker and there are still other workers in the queue, it will move on to another worker and execute it. Looking back at the earlier diagram, we can see that there are two separate processes that keep picking up and executing messages from a queue.

From a `Queue` object, we will be using two main methods, as shown in the following list:

- `get()`: This method returns the next item in the calling `Queue` object
- `put()`: This method adds the parameter passed to it as an additional item to the calling `Queue` object

Let's look at an example script showing the use of a queue in Python. Navigate to and open the `Chapter06/example6.py` file, as shown in the following code:

```
# Chapter06/example6.py

import multiprocessing

class MyWorker():
    def __init__(self, x):
        self.x = x

    def process(self):
        pname = multiprocessing.current_process().name
        print('Starting process %s for number %i...' % (pname, self.x))

def work(q):
    worker = q.get()
    worker.process()

if __name__ == '__main__':
    my_queue = multiprocessing.Queue()

    p = multiprocessing.Process(target=work, args=(my_queue,))
    p.start()

    my_queue.put(MyWorker(10))

    my_queue.close()
    my_queue.join_thread()
    p.join()

    print('Done.')
```

In this script, we have a `MyWorker` class that takes in a number x parameter and performs a computation from it (for now, it will only print out the number). In our main function, we initialize a `Queue` object from the `multiprocessing` module and add a `MyWorker` object with the number `10` in it. We also have the `work()` function, which upon being called will get the first item from the queue and process it. Finally, we have a process whose task is to call the `work()` function.

The structure is designed to pass a message—in this case, a `MyWorker` object—to one single process. The main program then waits for the process to finish executing. After running the script, your output should be similar to the following:

```
> python example6.py
Starting process Process-1 for number 10...
Done.
```

Message passing between several workers

As mentioned earlier, our goal is to have a structure where there are several processes constantly executing workers from a queue, and if a process finishes executing one worker, then it will pick up another. To do this, we will be utilizing a subclass of `Queue` called `JoinableQueue`, which will provide the additional `task_done()` and `join()` methods, as described in the following list:

- `task_done()`: This method tells the program that the calling `JoinableQueue` object is complete
- `join()`: This method blocks until all items in the calling `JoinableQueue` object have been processed

Now the goal here, again, is to have a `JoinableQueue` object holding all the tasks that are to be executed—we will call this the task queue—and a number of processes. As long as there are items (messages) in the task queue, the processes will take their turn to execute those items. We will also have a `Queue` object to store all the results returned from the processes—we will call this the result queue.

Navigate to the `Chapter06/example7.py` file and take a look at the `Consumer` class and the `Task` class, as shown in the following code:

```python
# Chapter06/example7.py

from math import sqrt
import multiprocessing

class Consumer(multiprocessing.Process):

    def __init__(self, task_queue, result_queue):
        multiprocessing.Process.__init__(self)
        self.task_queue = task_queue
        self.result_queue = result_queue

    def run(self):
```

```
        pname = self.name

        while not self.task_queue.empty():

            temp_task = self.task_queue.get()

            print('%s processing task: %s' % (pname, temp_task))

            answer = temp_task.process()
            self.task_queue.task_done()
            self.result_queue.put(answer)

class Task():
    def __init__(self, x):
        self.x = x

    def process(self):
        if self.x < 2:
            return '%i is not a prime number.' % self.x

        if self.x == 2:
            return '%i is a prime number.' % self.x

        if self.x % 2 == 0:
            return '%i is not a prime number.' % self.x

        limit = int(sqrt(self.x)) + 1
        for i in range(3, limit, 2):
            if self.x % i == 0:
                return '%i is not a prime number.' % self.x

        return '%i is a prime number.' % self.x

    def __str__(self):
        return 'Checking if %i is a prime or not.' % self.x
```

The Consumer class, which is an overridden subclass of the multiprocessing.Process class, is our processor logic, which takes in a task queue and a result queue. When started, each Consumer object will get the next item in its task queue, execute it, and finally call task_done() and put the returned result to its result queue. Each item in the task queue is in turn represented by the Task class, whose main functionality is to prime-check its x parameter. As one instance of the Consumer class interacts with one instance of the Task class, it will also print out a help message for us to easily keep track of which consumer is executing which task.

Let's move on and consider our main program, as shown in the following code:

```
# Chapter06/example7.py

if __name__ == '__main__':
    tasks = multiprocessing.JoinableQueue()
    results = multiprocessing.Queue()

    # spawning consumers with respect to the
    # number cores available in the system
    n_consumers = multiprocessing.cpu_count()
    print('Spawning %i consumers...' % n_consumers)
    consumers = [Consumer(tasks, results) for i in range(n_consumers)]
    for consumer in consumers:
        consumer.start()

    # enqueueing jobs
    my_input = [2, 36, 101, 193, 323, 513, 1327, 100000, 9999999,
433785907]
    for item in my_input:
        tasks.put(Task(item))

    tasks.join()

    for i in range(len(my_input)):
        temp_result = results.get()
        print('Result:', temp_result)

    print('Done.')
```

As we said earlier, we create a task queue and a result queue in our main program. We also create a list of `Consumer` objects and start all of them; the number of processes created corresponds to the number of CPUs available in our system. Next, from a list of inputs that requires heavy computation from the `Task` class, we initialize a `Task` object with each input and put them all in the task queue. At this point our processes—our `Consumer` objects—will start executing these tasks.

Finally, at the end of our main program, we call `join()` on our task queue to ensure that all items have been executed and print out the result by looping through our result queue. After running the script, your output should be similar to the following:

```
> python example7.py
Spawning 4 consumers...
Consumer-3 processing task: Checking if 2 is a prime or not.
Consumer-2 processing task: Checking if 36 is a prime or not.
Consumer-3 processing task: Checking if 101 is a prime or not.
Consumer-2 processing task: Checking if 193 is a prime or not.
```

```
Consumer-3 processing task: Checking if 323 is a prime or not.
Consumer-2 processing task: Checking if 1327 is a prime or not.
Consumer-3 processing task: Checking if 100000 is a prime or not.
Consumer-4 processing task: Checking if 513 is a prime or not.
Consumer-3 processing task: Checking if 9999999 is a prime or not.
Consumer-2 processing task: Checking if 433785907 is a prime or not.
Result: 2 is a prime number.
Result: 36 is not a prime number.
Result: 193 is a prime number.
Result: 101 is a prime number.
Result: 323 is not a prime number.
Result: 1327 is a prime number.
Result: 100000 is not a prime number.
Result: 9999999 is not a prime number.
Result: 513 is not a prime number.
Result: 433785907 is a prime number.
Done.
```

Everything seems to be working, but if we look closely at the messages our processes have printed out, we will notice that most of the tasks were executed by either `Consumer-2` or `Consumer-3`, and that `Consumer-4` executed only one task while `Consumer-1` failed to execute any. What happened here?

Essentially, when one of our consumers—let's say `Consumer-3`—finished executing a task, it tried to look for another task to execute immediately after. Most of the time, it would get priority over other consumers, since it was already being run by the main program. So while `Consumer-2` and `Consumer-3` were constantly finishing their tasks' executions and picking up other tasks to execute, `Consumer-4` was only able to "squeeze" itself in once, and `Consumer-1` failed to do this altogether.

When running the script over and over again, you will notice a similar trend: only one or two consumers executed most of the tasks, while others failed to do this. This situation is undesirable for us, since the program is not utilizing all of the available processes that were created at the beginning of the program.

To address this issue, a technique has been developed, to stop consumers from immediately taking the next item from the task queue, called **poison pill**. The idea is that, after setting up the real tasks in the task queue, we also add in dummy tasks that contain "stop" values and that will have the current consumer hold and allow other consumers to get the next item in the task queue first; hence the name "poison pill."

To implement this technique, we need to add in our `tasks` value in the main program's special objects, one per consumer. Additionally, in our `Consumer` class, the implementation of the logic to handle these special objects is also required. Let's take a look at the `example8.py` file (a modified version of the previous example, containing the implementation of the poison pill technique), specifically in the `Consumer` class and the main program, as shown in the following code:

```
# Chapter06/example8.py

class Consumer(multiprocessing.Process):

    def __init__(self, task_queue, result_queue):
        multiprocessing.Process.__init__(self)
        self.task_queue = task_queue
        self.result_queue = result_queue

    def run(self):
        pname = self.name

        while True:
            temp_task = self.task_queue.get()

            if temp_task is None:
                print('Exiting %s...' % pname)
                self.task_queue.task_done()
                break

            print('%s processing task: %s' % (pname, temp_task))

            answer = temp_task.process()
            self.task_queue.task_done()
            self.result_queue.put(answer)

class Task():
    def __init__(self, x):
        self.x = x

    def process(self):
        if self.x < 2:
            return '%i is not a prime number.' % self.x

        if self.x == 2:
            return '%i is a prime number.' % self.x

        if self.x % 2 == 0:
            return '%i is not a prime number.' % self.x
```

```
            limit = int(sqrt(self.x)) + 1
            for i in range(3, limit, 2):
                if self.x % i == 0:
                    return '%i is not a prime number.' % self.x

            return '%i is a prime number.' % self.x

    def __str__(self):
        return 'Checking if %i is a prime or not.' % self.x

if __name__ == '__main__':

    tasks = multiprocessing.JoinableQueue()
    results = multiprocessing.Queue()

    # spawning consumers with respect to the
    # number cores available in the system
    n_consumers = multiprocessing.cpu_count()
    print('Spawning %i consumers...' % n_consumers)
    consumers = [Consumer(tasks, results) for i in range(n_consumers)]
    for consumer in consumers:
        consumer.start()

    # enqueueing jobs
    my_input = [2, 36, 101, 193, 323, 513, 1327, 100000, 9999999,
433785907]
    for item in my_input:
        tasks.put(Task(item))

    for i in range(n_consumers):
        tasks.put(None)

    tasks.join()

    for i in range(len(my_input)):
        temp_result = results.get()
        print('Result:', temp_result)

    print('Done.')
```

The `Task` class remains the same as our previous example. We can see that our poison pill is the `None` value: in the main program, we add in `None` values of a number equal to the number of consumers we have spawned to the task queue; in the `Consumer` class, if the current task to be executed holds the value `None`, then the class object will print out a message indicating the poison pill, call `task_done()`, and exit.

Run the script; your output should be similar to the following:

```
> python example8.py
Spawning 4 consumers...
Consumer-1 processing task: Checking if 2 is a prime or not.
Consumer-2 processing task: Checking if 36 is a prime or not.
Consumer-3 processing task: Checking if 101 is a prime or not.
Consumer-4 processing task: Checking if 193 is a prime or not.
Consumer-1 processing task: Checking if 323 is a prime or not.
Consumer-2 processing task: Checking if 513 is a prime or not.
Consumer-3 processing task: Checking if 1327 is a prime or not.
Consumer-1 processing task: Checking if 100000 is a prime or not.
Consumer-2 processing task: Checking if 9999999 is a prime or not.
Consumer-3 processing task: Checking if 433785907 is a prime or not.
Exiting Consumer-1...
Exiting Consumer-2...
Exiting Consumer-4...
Exiting Consumer-3...
Result: 2 is a prime number.
Result: 36 is not a prime number.
Result: 323 is not a prime number.
Result: 101 is a prime number.
Result: 513 is not a prime number.
Result: 1327 is a prime number.
Result: 100000 is not a prime number.
Result: 9999999 is not a prime number.
Result: 193 is a prime number.
Result: 433785907 is a prime number.
Done.
```

This time, as well as seeing the poison pill messages being printed out, the output also shows a significantly better distribution in terms of which consumer executed which task.

Summary

In the field of computer science, a process is an instance of a specific computer program or software that is being executed by the operating system. A process contains both the program code and its current activities and interactions with other entities. More than one thread can be implemented within the same process to access and share memory or other resources, while different processes do not interact in this way.

In the context of concurrency and parallelism, multiprocessing refers to the execution of multiple concurrent processes from an operating system, in which each process is executed on a separate CPU, as opposed to a single process being executed at any given time. The `multiprocessing` module in Python provides a powerful and flexible API to spawn and manage processes for a multiprocessing application. It also allows complex techniques for interprocess communication via the `Queue` class.

In the next chapter, we will be discussing a more advanced function of Python—reduction operations—and how it is supported in multiprocessing programming.

Questions

- What is a process? What are the core differences between a process and a thread?
- What is multiprocessing? What are the core differences between multiprocessing and multithreading?
- What are the API options provided by the `multiprocessing` module?
- What are the core differences between the `Process` class and the `Pool` class from the `multiprocessing` module?
- What are the options to determine the current process in a Python program?
- What are daemon processes? What are their purposes in terms of waiting for processes in a multiprocessing program?
- How do you terminate a process? Why is it sometimes acceptable to terminate processes?
- What is one of the ways to facilitate interprocess communication in Python?

Further reading

For more information, you can refer to the following links:

- *Python Parallel Programming Cookbook*, by Giancarlo Zaccone, Packt Publishing Ltd (2015).
- "Learning Concurrency in Python: Build highly efficient, robust, and concurrent applications", Elliot Forbes (2017).
- Python Module of The Week. "Communication Between Processes" (pymotw.com/2/multiprocessing/communication.html). This contains functions that you can use to identify the current process.

7
Reduction Operators in Processes

The concept of reduction operators—in which many or all elements of an array are reduced into one single result—is closely associated with concurrent and parallel programming. Specifically, because of the associative and communicative nature of the operators, concurrency and parallelism can be applied to greatly improve their execution time.

This chapter discusses the theoretical concurrent approach to designing and writing a reduction operator from the perspective of programmers and developers. From here, this chapter also makes connections to similar problems that can be solved using concurrency in similar ways.

The following topics will be covered in this chapter:

- The concept of a reduction operator in computer science
- The communicative and associative properties of reduction operators, and therefore the reason why concurrency can be applied
- How to identify problems that are equivalent to a reduction operator and how to apply concurrent programming in such cases

Technical requirements

The following is a list of prerequisites for this chapter:

- You must have Python 3 installed on your computer
- Download the GitHub repository from `https://github.com/PacktPublishing/Mastering-Concurrency-in-Python`
- During this chapter, we will be working with the subfolder titled `Chapter07`
- Check out the following video to see the Code in Action: `http://bit.ly/2TD5odl`

The concept of reduction operators

As experienced programmers, you have undoubtedly encountered situations where you need to calculate the sum or the product of all the numbers in an array, or compute the result of applying the AND operator to all Boolean elements of an array to see whether there is any false value in that array. These are called **reduction operators**, which take a set or an array of elements and perform some form of computation to return only one single result.

Properties of a reduction operator

Not every mathematical or computer science operator is a reduction operator. In fact, even if an operator is capable of reducing an array of elements into one single value, there is no guarantee that it is a reduction operator. An operator is a reduction operator if it satisfies the following conditions:

- The operator can reduce an array of elements into one scalar value
- The end result (the scalar value) must be obtained through creating and computing partial tasks

The first condition is indicative of the phrase "reduction operators", as all elements of the input array have to be combined and reduced into one single value. However, the second condition is, essentially, in terms of concurrency and parallelism. It requires the computation of any reduction operator to be able to be divided into smaller partial computations.

First, let's consider one of the most common reduction operators: addition. For example, consider the input array [1, 4, 8, 3, 2, 5]—the sum of the elements in this array is as follows:

```
1 + 4 + 8 + 3 + 2 + 5
= ((((1 + 4) + 8) + 3) + 2) + 5
= (((5 + 8) + 3) + 2) + 5
= ((13 + 3) + 2) + 5
= (16 + 2) + 5
= 18 + 5
= 23
```

In the preceding computation, we reduced the numbers in our array into their sum, 23, in a sequential order. In other words, we went through each and every element of the array from the beginning to the end and added the current sum. Now, we know that addition is a commutative and associative operator, which means: $a + b = b + a$ and $(a + b) + c = a + (b + c)$.

Therefore, we can perform the preceding computation in a more efficient way by breaking the summation into smaller summations:

```
1 + 4 + 8 + 3 + 2 + 5
= ((1 + 4) + (8 + 3)) + (2 + 5)
= (5 + 11) + 7
= 16 + 7
= 23
```

This technique is at the heart of applying concurrency and parallelism (specifically multiprocessing) to a reduction operator. By breaking the whole task into smaller subtasks, multiple processes can perform those small computations simultaneously, and the system as a whole can arrive at the result much more quickly.

For the same reason, the communicative and associative properties are considered to be equivalent to the requirements for a reduction operator that we discussed earlier. In other words, the operator $\circ$ is a reduction operator that's communicative and associative. Specifically the following:

- Communicative: $a \circ b = b \circ a$
- Associative: $(a \circ b) \circ c = a \circ (b \circ c)$

Here a, b, and c are elements of input arrays.

So, if an operator is a reduction operator, it has to be communicative and associative, and therefore has the ability to break down a big task into smaller, more manageable subtasks, which can be computed in a more efficient way using multiprocessing.

Examples and non-examples

So far, we have seen that addition is one example of a reduction operator. To perform addition as a reduction operator, we first divide the elements from our input array into groups of two, each of which is one of our subtasks. We then perform addition on each group, take the added result from each group, and divide them into groups of two again.

This process continues until we arrive at one single number. This process follows a model called binary tree reduction, which utilizes groups of two to form the subtasks:

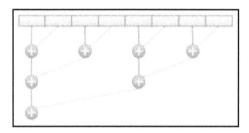

Diagram of binary tree reduction for addition

In the preceding example with the array [1, 4, 8, 3, 2, 5], after dividing the numbers into three different groups of two numbers (1 and 4, 8 and 3, 2 and 5), we used three separate processes to add the pairs of numbers together. We then obtained the array [5, 11, 7], which we used for one process to obtain [16, 7], and again another process to finally obtain 23. So, with three CPUs or more, an addition operator of six elements can be done in $\log_2 6 = 3$ steps instead of five steps in sequential addition.

Other common examples of reduction operators are multiplication and logical AND. For example, reducing the same array of numbers [1, 4, 8, 3, 2, 5] using multiplication as a reduction operator would be done as follows:

```
1 x 4 x 8 x 3 x 2 x 5
= ((1 x 4) x (8 x 3)) x (2 x 5)
= (4 x 24) x 10
= 96 x 10
= 960
```

To reduce an array of Boolean values, for example (`True`, `False`, `False`, `True`), using the logical `AND` operator, we could do the following:

```
True AND False AND False AND True
= (True AND False) AND (False AND True)
= False AND False
= False
```

A non-example of reduction operators is the power function, as changing the order of computation would change the final result (that is, the function is not communicative). For example, reducing the array [2, 1, 2] sequentially would give us the following:

```
2 ^ 1 ^ 2 = 2 ^ (1 ^ 2) = 2 ^ 1 = 2
```

And if we were to change the order of operation as follows:

```
(2 ^ 1) ^ 2 = 2 ^ 2 = 4
```

We would obtain a different value. Therefore, the power function is not a reduction operation.

Example implementation in Python

As we mentioned previously, due to their communicative and associative properties, reduction operators can have their partial tasks created and processed independently, and this is where concurrency can be applied. To truly understand how a reduction operator utilizes concurrency, let's try implementing a concurrent, multiprocessing reduction operator from scratch—specifically the add operator.

Similar to what we saw in the previous chapter, in this example, we will be using a task queue and a result queue to facilitate our interprocess communication. Specifically, the program will store all of the numbers in the input array in the task queue as individual tasks. As each of our consumers (individual processes) executes, it will call get() on the task queue **twice** to obtain two task numbers (except for some edge cases where there is no or only one number left in the task queue), add them together, and put the result in the result queue.

Similar to adding pairs of numbers together, like we did in the previous section, after our processes iterate through the tasks queue one time and put the added pairs of task numbers in the result queue, the number of elements in the input array will have been reduced by half. For example, an input array of [1, 4, 8, 3, 2, 5] will become [5, 11, 7].

Now, our program will assign the new task queue to be the result queue (so, in this example, [5, 11, 7] is now the new task queue), and our processes will continue going through it and adding pairs of numbers together to generate a new result queue, which will become the next task queue. This process repeats itself until the result queue only contains one element, since we know that that single number is the sum of the numbers in the original input array.

The following diagram shows the changes in the task queue and the result queue in each iteration of processing the input array [1, 4, 8, 3, 2, 5]; the process stops when the result queue contains only one number (23):

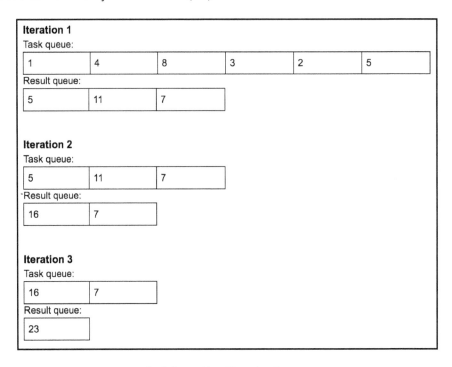

Sample diagram of the multiprocessing add operator

Let's take a look at the ReductionConsumer class in the Chapter07/example1.py file:

```
# Chapter07/example1.py

class ReductionConsumer(multiprocessing.Process):

    def __init__(self, task_queue, result_queue):
        multiprocessing.Process.__init__(self)
        self.task_queue = task_queue
        self.result_queue = result_queue

    def run(self):
        pname = self.name
        print('Using process %s...' % pname)

        while True:
            num1 = self.task_queue.get()
```

```
if num1 is None:
    print('Exiting process %s.' % pname)
    self.task_queue.task_done()
    break

self.task_queue.task_done()
num2 = self.task_queue.get()
if num2 is None:
    print('Reaching the end with process %s and number
        %i.' % (pname, num1))
    self.task_queue.task_done()
    self.result_queue.put(num1)
    break

print('Running process %s on numbers %i and %i.' % (
    pname, num1, num2))
self.task_queue.task_done()
self.result_queue.put(num1 + num2)
```

We implement the ReductionConsumer class by overriding the
multiprocessing.Process class. This consumer class takes in a task queue and a result
queue when initialized, and handles the consumer process logic of the program, which calls
get() twice on the task queue to obtain two numbers from the queue, and adds their sum
to the result queue.

While doing this, the ReductionConsumer class also handles cases where there is no or
only one number left in the task queue (that is, when either the num1 or num2 variable is
None, which, as we know from the previous chapter, is what we use to indicate a poison
pill).

Additionally, recall that the JoinableQueue class of the multiprocessing module is
used to implement our task queues, and that it requires the task_done() function to be
called after each time the get() function is called, otherwise the subsequent join()
function that we will call on the task queue later will block indefinitely. So, in the case
where the consumer process calls get() two times, it is important to call task_done() on
the current task queue twice, and when we only call get() once (when the first number is a
poison pill), then we should call task_done() only once. This is one of the more complex
considerations while working with multiprocessing programs that facilitate interprocess
communication.

To process and coordinate different consumer processes as well as manipulate the task queue and the result queue after each iteration, we have a separate function called `reduce_sum()`:

```
def reduce_sum(array):
    tasks = multiprocessing.JoinableQueue()
    results = multiprocessing.JoinableQueue()
    result_size = len(array)

    n_consumers = multiprocessing.cpu_count()

    for item in array:
        results.put(item)

    while result_size > 1:
        tasks = results
        results = multiprocessing.JoinableQueue()

        consumers = [ReductionConsumer(tasks, results)
                     for i in range(n_consumers)]
        for consumer in consumers:
            consumer.start()

        for i in range(n_consumers):
            tasks.put(None)

        tasks.join()
        result_size = result_size // 2 + (result_size % 2)
        #print('-' * 40)

    return results.get()
```

This function takes in a Python list of numbers to compute the sum of its elements. Aside from a task queue and a result queue, the function also keeps track of another variable called `result_size`, which indicates the number of elements in the current result queue.

After initializing its base variables, the function spawns its consumer processes to reduce the current task queue inside a while loop. As we discussed previously, in each iteration of the while loop, the elements in the task queue are added together pairwise, and the added results are stored in the result queue. After that, the task queue will take over the elements of that result queue, and add additional `None` values to the queue to implement the poison pill technique.

In each iteration, a new empty result queue is also initialized as a `JoinableQueue` object—this is different from the `multiprocessing.Queue` class that we used for our result queue in the previous chapter, since we will be assigning `tasks = results` at the beginning of the next iteration, and the task queue needs to be a `JoinableQueue` object.

We also update the value of `result_size` at the end of each iteration through `result_size = result_size // 2 + (result_size % 2)`. It is important to note here that while the `qsize()` method from the `JoinableQueue` class is a potential method to keep track of the length of its object (that is, the number of elements in a `JoinableQueue` object), this method is usually considered to be unreliable for various reasons—it is not even implemented in Unix operating systems.

Since we can easily predict how the number of remaining numbers from our input array will change after each iteration (it is halved if it is an even number, otherwise it is halved by integer division, and then `1` is added to that result), we can keep track of that number using a separate variable called `result_size`.

As for our main program for this example, we simply pass a Python list to the `reduce_sum()` function. Here, we are adding numbers from 0 to 19:

```
my_array = [i for i in range(20)]

result = reduce_sum(my_array)
print('Final result: %i.' % result)
```

After running the script, your output should be similar to the following:

```
> python example1.py
Using process ReductionConsumer-1...
Running process ReductionConsumer-1 on numbers 0 and 1.
Using process ReductionConsumer-2...
Running process ReductionConsumer-2 on numbers 2 and 3.
Using process ReductionConsumer-3...

[...Truncated for readability..]

Exiting process ReductionConsumer-17.
Exiting process ReductionConsumer-18.
Exiting process ReductionConsumer-19.
Using process ReductionConsumer-20...
Exiting process ReductionConsumer-20.
Final result: 190.
```

Real-life applications of concurrent reduction operators

The communicative and associative nature of the way reduction operators process their data enables the subtasks of an operator to be processed independently, and is thus highly connected to concurrency and parallelism. Consequently, various topics in concurrent programming could be related to reduction operators, and by applying the same principles of reduction operators, problems regarding those topics could be made more intuitive and efficient.

As we have seen, add and multiply operators are reduction operators. More generally, number-crunching problems that usually involve communicative and associative operators are prime candidates for applying concurrency and parallelism. This is actually a true case for the famous, and arguably one of the most used modules in Python—NumPy, whose code is implemented to be as parallelizable as possible.

Furthermore, applying the logic operators AND, OR, or XOR to an array of Boolean values works the same way as reduction operators. Some real-world applications for concurrent bitwise reduction operators include the following:

- Finite state machines, which commonly take advantage of logic operators while processing logic gates. Finite state machines can be found in both hardware structures and software designs.
- Communication across sockets/ports, which typically involves parity and stop bits to check for data errors, or flow control algorithms. These techniques utilize logic values of individual bytes to process information through the use of logic operators.
- Compression and encryption techniques, which heavily depend on bitwise algorithms.

Summary

Careful considerations need to be made while implementing multiprocessing reduction operators in Python, especially if the program utilizes task queues and result queues to facilitate communication across the consumer processes.

The operations of various real-world problems resemble reduction operators, and the use of concurrency and parallelism for these problems could greatly improve efficiency and thus productivity of the programs processing them. It is therefore important to be able to identify these problems, and relate back to the concept of reduction operators to implement their solutions.

In the next chapter, we will be discussing a specific real-world application for multiprocessing programs in Python: image processing. We will be going over the basic ideas behind image processing and how concurrency—specifically multiprocessing—could be applied to image-processing applications.

Questions

- What is a reduction operator? What conditions must be satisfied so that an operator can be a reduction one?
- What properties do reduction operators have that are equivalent to the required conditions?
- What is the connection between reduction operators and concurrent programming?
- What are some of the considerations that must be made while working with multiprocessing programs that facilitate interprocess communication in Python?
- What are some real-life applications of concurrent reduction operators?

Further reading

For more information, you can refer to the following links:

- *Python Parallel Programming Cookbook*, Giancarlo Zaccone, Packt Publishing Ltd, 2015
- *Learning Concurrency in Python: Build highly efficient, robust, and concurrent applications.*, Elliot Forbes (2017)
- *Parallel Programming in OpenMP*, Morgan Kaufmann, Chandra, Rohit (2001)
- *Fundamentals of Parallel Multicore Architecture*, Yan Solihin (2016), CRC Press

Concurrent Image Processing

8

This chapter analyzes the process of processing and manipulating images through concurrent programming, especially multiprocessing. Since images are processed independently of one another, concurrent programming can provide image processing with a significant speedup. This chapter discusses the basics behind image processing techniques, illustrates the improvements that concurrent programming provides, and finally, goes over some of the best practices used in image processing applications.

The following topics will be covered in this chapter:

- The idea behind image processing and a number of basic techniques in image processing
- How to apply concurrency to image processing, and how to analyze the improvements it provides
- Best practices in concurrent image processing

Technical requirements

Following is a list of prerequisites for this chapter:

- You must have Python 3 installed on your computer
- You must have OpenCV and NumPy installed for your Python 3 distribution
- Download the GitHub repository from `https://github.com/PacktPublishing/Mastering-Concurrency-in-Python`
- During this chapter, we will be working with the subfolder named `Chapter08`
- Check out the following video to see the Code in Action: `http://bit.ly/2R8ydN8`

Image processing fundamentals

Digital/computational image processing (which we will refer to simply as image processing from this point forward) has become so popular in the modern era that it exists in numerous aspects in our everyday life. Image processing and manipulation is involved when you take a picture with your camera or phone using different filters, or when advanced image editing software such as Adobe Photoshop is used, or even when you simply edit images using Microsoft Paint.

Many of the techniques and algorithms used in image processing were developed in the early 1960s for various purposes such as medical imaging, satellite image analysis, character recognition, and so on. However, these image processing techniques required significant computing power, and the fact that the available computer equipment at the time was unable to accommodate the need for fast number-crunching slowed down the use of image processing.

Fast-forwarding to the future, where powerful computers with fast, multicore processors were developed, image processing techniques consequently became much more accessible, and research on image processing increased significantly. Nowadays, numerous image processing applications are being actively developed and studied, including pattern recognition, classification, feature extraction, and so on. Specific image processing techniques, which take advantage of concurrent and parallel programming and would otherwise be extremely computationally time-consuming, include Hidden Markov models, independent component analysis, and even up-and-coming neural network models:

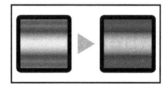

One sample use of image processing: grayscaling

Python as an image processing tool

As we have stated multiple times throughout this book, the Python programming language is on its way to becoming the most popular programming language. This is especially true in the field of computational image processing, which, most of the time, requires fast prototyping and designing, and significant automation capabilities.

As we will find out in the following section, digital images are represented in two-dimensional and three-dimensional matrices so that computers can process them easily. Consequently, most of the time, digital image processing involves matrix calculation. Multiple Python libraries and modules not only provide efficient matrix calculation options, but also interact seamlessly with other libraries that handle image reading/writing.

As we already know, automating tasks and making them concurrent are both Python's strong suit. This makes Python the prime candidate to implement your image processing applications. For this chapter, we will be working with two main Python libraries: **OpenCV** (which stands for **Open Source Computer Vision**), which is a library that provides image processing and computer vision options in C++, Java, and Python, and NumPy, which, as we know, is one of the most popular Python modules and performs efficient and parallelizable number-crunching calculations.

Installing OpenCV and NumPy

To install NumPy for your Python distribution using the `pip` package manager, run the following command:

```
pip install numpy
```

If, however, you are using Anaconda/Miniconda to manage your packages, run the following command:

```
conda install numpy
```

Installing OpenCV might be more complicated, depending on your operating system. The easiest option is to have Anaconda handle the installation process by following this guide (`https://anaconda.org/conda-forge/opencv`) after installing Anaconda (`https://www.anaconda.com/download/`) as your main Python package manager. If, however, you are not using Anaconda, the main option for installing OpenCV is to follow its official documentation guide, which can be found at `https://docs.opencv.org/master/df/d65/tutorial_table_of_content_introduction.html`. After successfully installing OpenCV, open a Python interpreter and try importing the library, as follows:

```
>>> import cv2
>>> print(cv2.__version__)
3.1.0
```

We import OpenCV using the name `cv2`, which is the library alias of OpenCV in Python. The success message indicates the version of my OpenCV library that has been downloaded (3.1.0).

Computer image basics

Before we jump into processing and manipulating digital image files, we first need to discuss the fundamentals of those files, and how computers interpret data from them. Specifically, we need to understand how data regarding the colors and coordinates of individual pixels in an image file is represented, and how to extract it using Python.

RGB values

RGB values are the basics of how colors are represented digitally. Standing for **Red**, **Green**, and **Blue**, **RGB** values are constructed from the fact that all colors can be generated from a specific combination of red, green, and blue. An RGB value therefore is a tuple of three integer numbers, each of which ranges from 0 (which indicates no color at all) to 255 (which indicates the deepest shade of that specific color).

For example, the color red corresponds to the tuple (255, 0, 0); in the tuple, there is only the highest value for red and no value for the other colors, so the whole tuple represents the pure color red. Similarly, blue is represented by (0, 0, 255), and green is represented by (0, 255, 0). The color yellow is the result of mixing equal amounts of red and green, and is therefore represented by (255, 255, 0) (the maximum amount of red and green, with no blue). White, which is the combination of all three colors, is (255, 255, 255), while black, which is the opposite of white and therefore lacks all colors, is represented by (0, 0, 0).

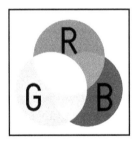

RGB values basics

Pixels and image files

So, an RGB value indicates a specific color, but how do we connect this to a computer image? If we were to view an image on our computer and try to zoom in as much as we can, we would observe that as we zoom in deeper and deeper, the image will start breaking apart into increasingly discernible colored squares—these squares are called pixels, which are the smallest units of color on a computer display or in a digital image:

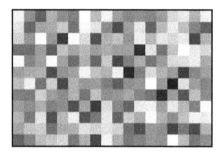

Examples of pixels in digital images

A set of different pixels arranged in a tabular format (rows and columns of pixels) makes up a computer image. Each pixel, in turn, is an RGB value; in other words, a pixel is a tuple of three integers. This means that a computer image is simply a two-dimensional array of tuples, whose sides correspond to the size of the image. For example, a 128 x 128 image has 128 rows and 128 columns of RGB tuples for its data.

Coordinates inside an image

Similar to indexing for two-dimensional arrays, the coordinate for a digital image pixel is a pair of two integers, representing the x- and y-coordinates of that pixel; the x-coordinate indicates the pixel's location along the horizontal axis starting from the left, and the y-coordinate indicates the pixel's location along the vertical axis starting from the top.

Here, we can see how heavy computational number-crunching processes are typically involved when it comes to image processing, as each image is a matrix of integer tuples. This also suggests that, with the help of the NumPy library and concurrent programming, we can implement significant improvements in execution time for Python image processing applications.

Following the convention of indexing two-dimensional arrays in NumPy, the location of a pixel is still a pair of integers, but the first number indicates the index of the row containing the pixel, which corresponds to the *y*-coordinate, and similarly, the second number indicates the *x*-coordinate of the pixel.

OpenCV API

There are a surprising number of methods to read in, perform image processing, and display a digital image file in Python. However, OpenCV provides some of the easiest and most intuitive APIs to do this. One important thing to note regarding OpenCV is that it actually inverts RGB values to BGR values when interpreting its images, so instead of red, green, and blue in order, the tuples in an image matrix will represent blue, green, and red, in that order.

Let's look at an example of interacting with OpenCV in Python. Let's a take look at the `Chapter08/example1.py` file:

```
# Chapter08/example1.py

import cv2

im = cv2.imread('input/ship.jpg')
cv2.imshow('Test', im)
cv2.waitKey(0) # press any key to move forward here

print(im)
print('Type:', type(im))
print('Shape:', im.shape)
print('Top-left pixel:', im[0, 0])

print('Done.')
```

There are a few methods from OpenCV that have been used in this script that we need to discuss:

- `cv2.imread()`: This method takes in a path to an image file (common file extensions include `.jpeg`, `.jpg`, `.png`, and so on) and returns an image object, which, as we will see later, is represented by a NumPy array.
- `cv2.imshow()`: This method takes in a string and an image object and displays it in a separate window. The title of the window is specified by the passed-in string. The method should always be followed by the `cv2.waitKey()` method.

- `cv2.waitKey()`: This method takes in a number and blocks the program for a corresponding number of milliseconds, unless the number 0 is passed in, in which case it will block indefinitely until the user presses a key on their keyboard. This method should always follow the `cv2.imshow()` method.

After calling `cv2.imshow()` on the `ship.jpg` file inside the input subfolder so that it's displayed from the Python interpreter, the program will stop until a key is pressed, at which point it will execute the rest of the program. If run successfully, the script will display the following image:

You should also obtain the following output for the rest of the main program after pressing any key to close the displayed picture:

```
> python example1.py
[[[199 136 86]
  [199 136 86]
  [199 136 86]
  ...,
```

```
  [198 140 81]
  [197 139 80]
  [201 143 84]]

[...Truncated for readability...]

 [[ 56 23 4]
  [ 59 26 7]
  [ 60 27 7]
  ...,
  [ 79 43 7]
  [ 80 44 8]
  [ 75 39 3]]]
Type: <class 'numpy.ndarray'>
Shape: (1118, 1577, 3)
Top-left pixel: [199 136 86]
Done.
```

The output confirms a few of the things that we discussed earlier:

- First, when printing out the image object returned from the `cv2.imread()` function, we obtained a matrix of numbers.
- Using the `type()` method from Python, we found out that the class of this matrix is indeed a NumPy array: `numpy.ndarray`.
- Calling the `shape` attribute of the array, we can see that the image is a three-dimensional matrix of the shape (`1118`, `1577`, `3`), which corresponds to a table with `1118` rows and `1577` columns, each element of which is a pixel (three-number tuple). The numbers for the rows and columns also correspond to the size of the image.
- Focusing on the top-left pixel in the matrix (the first pixel in the first row, that is, `im[0, 0]`), we obtained the BGR value of (`199`, `136`, `86`)—`199` blue, `136` green, and `86` red. By looking up this BGR value through any online converter, we can see that this is a light blue that corresponds to the sky, which is the upper part of the image.

Image processing techniques

We have already seen some Python APIs that are provided by OpenCV to read in data from image files. Before we can use OpenCV to perform various image processing tasks, let's discuss the theoretical foundation for a number of techniques that are commonly used in image processing.

Grayscaling

We saw an example of grayscaling earlier in this chapter. Arguably one of the most used image processing techniques, grayscaling is the process of reducing the dimensionality of the image pixel matrix by only considering the intensity information of each pixel, which is represented by the amount of light available.

As a result, pixels of grayscale images no longer hold three-dimensional information (red, green, and blue), and only one-dimensional black-and-white data. These images are exclusively composed of shades of gray, with black indicating the weakest light intensity and white indicating the strongest.

Grayscaling serves a number of important purposes in image processing. Firstly, as mentioned, it reduces the dimensionality of the image pixel matrix by mapping traditional three-dimensional color data to one-dimensional gray data. So, instead of having to analyze and process three layers of color data, image processing programs only have to do one third of the job with grayscale images. Additionally, by only representing colors using one spectrum, important patterns in the image are more likely to be recognized with just black and white data.

There are multiple algorithms for converting color to grayscale: colorimetric conversion, luma coding, single channel, and so on. Luckily, we do not have to implement one ourselves, as the OpenCV library provides a one-line method to convert normal images to grayscale ones. Still using the image of a ship from the last example, let's look at the `Chapter08/example2.py` file:

```
# Chapter08/example2.py

import cv2

im = cv2.imread('input/ship.jpg')
gray_im = cv2.cvtColor(im, cv2.COLOR_BGR2GRAY)

cv2.imshow('Grayscale', gray_im)
cv2.waitKey(0) # press any key to move forward here

print(gray_im)
print('Type:', type(gray_im))
print('Shape:', gray_im.shape)
cv2.imwrite('output/gray_ship.jpg', gray_im)

print('Done.')
```

In this example, we are using the `cvtColor()` method from OpenCV to convert our original image to a grayscale one. After running this script, the following image should be displayed on your computer:

Output from Grayscaling

Pressing any key to unblock your program, you should obtain the following output:

```
> python example2.py
[[128 128 128 ..., 129 128 132]
 [125 125 125 ..., 129 128 130]
 [124 125 125 ..., 129 129 130]
 ...,
 [ 20 21 20 ..., 38 39 37]
 [ 19 22 21 ..., 41 42 37]
 [ 21 24 25 ..., 36 37 32]]
Type: <class 'numpy.ndarray'>
Shape: (1118, 1577)
Done.
```

We can see that the structure of our grayscale image object is different from what we saw with our original image object. Even though it is still represented by a NumPy array, it is now a two-dimensional array of integers, each of which ranges from 0 (for black) to 255 (for white). The table of pixels, however, still consists of `1118` rows and `1577` columns.

In this example, we also used the `cv2.imwrite()` method, which saves the image object to your local computer. The grayscale image can therefore be found in the output subfolder of this chapter's folder, as specified in our code.

Thresholding

Another important technique in image processing is thresholding. With the goal of categorizing each pixel in a digital image into different groups (also known as image segmentation), thresholding provides a quick and intuitive way to create binary images (with just black and white pixels).

The idea behind thresholding is to replace each pixel in an image with a white pixel if the pixel's intensity is greater than a previously specified threshold, and with a black pixel if the pixel's intensity is less than that threshold. Similar to the goal of grayscaling, thresholding amplifies the differences between high- and low-intensity pixels, and from that important features and patterns in an image can be recognized and extracted.

Recall that grayscaling converts a fully colored image to a version that only has different shades of gray; in this case, each pixel has a value of an integer ranging from 0 to 255. From a grayscale image, thresholding can convert it to a fully black-and-white one, each pixel of which is now only either 0 (black) or 255 (white). So, after performing thresholding on an image, each pixel of that image can only hold two possible values, also significantly reducing the complexity of our image data.

The key to an effective thresholding process is therefore finding an appropriate threshold so that the pixels in an image are segmented in a way that allows separate regions in the image to become more obvious. The most simple form of thresholding is to use a constant threshold to process all pixels throughout a whole image. Let's consider an example of this method in the `Chapter08/example3.py` file:

```
# Chapter08/example3.py

import cv2

im = cv2.imread('input/ship.jpg')
gray_im = cv2.cvtColor(im, cv2.COLOR_BGR2GRAY)

ret, custom_thresh_im = cv2.threshold(gray_im, 127, 255, cv2.THRESH_BINARY)
```

```
cv2.imwrite('output/custom_thresh_ship.jpg', custom_thresh_im)

print('Done.')
```

In this example, after converting the image of a ship that we have been using to grayscale, we call the `threshold(src, thresh, maxval, type)` function from OpenCV, which takes in the following arguments:

- `src`: This argument takes in the input/source image.
- `thresh`: The constant threshold to be used throughout the image. Here, we are using `127`, as it is simply the middle point between 0 and 255.
- `maxval`: Pixels whose original values are greater than the constant threshold will take this value after the thresholding process. We pass in 255 to specify that those pixels should be completely white.
- `type`: This value indicates the thresholding type used by OpenCV. We are performing a simple binary thresholding, so we pass in `cv2.THRESH_BINARY`.

After running the script, you should be able to find the following image in the output with the name `custom_thresh_ship.jpg`:

Output from simple thresholding

We can see that with a simple threshold (`127`), we have obtained an image that highlights separate regions of the image: the sky, the ship, and the sea. However, there are a number of problems that this method of simple thresholding poses, the most common of which is finding the appropriate constant threshold. Since different images have different color tones, lighting conditions, and so on, it is undesirable to use a static value across different images as their threshold.

This issue is addressed by adaptive thresholding methods, which calculate the dynamic thresholds for small regions of an image. This process allows the threshold to adjust according to the input image, and not depend solely on a static value. Let's consider two examples of these adaptive thresholding methods, namely Adaptive Mean Thresholding and Adaptive Gaussian Thresholding. Navigate to the `Chapter08/example4.py` file:

```
# Chapter08/example4.py

import cv2

im = cv2.imread('input/ship.jpg')
im = cv2.cvtColor(im, cv2.COLOR_BGR2GRAY)

mean_thresh_im = cv2.adaptiveThreshold(im, 255, cv2.ADAPTIVE_THRESH_MEAN_C,
cv2.THRESH_BINARY, 11, 2)
cv2.imwrite('output/mean_thresh_ship.jpg', mean_thresh_im)

gauss_thresh_im = cv2.adaptiveThreshold(im, 255,
cv2.ADAPTIVE_THRESH_GAUSSIAN_C, cv2.THRESH_BINARY, 11, 2)
cv2.imwrite('output/gauss_thresh_ship.jpg', gauss_thresh_im)

print('Done.')
```

Similar to what we did with the `cv2.threshold()` method earlier, here, we again convert the original image to its grayscale version, and then we pass it to the `adaptiveThreshold()` method from OpenCV. This method takes in similar arguments to the `cv2.threshold()` method, except that, instead of taking in a constant to be the threshold, it takes in an argument for the adaptive method. We used `cv2.ADAPTIVE_THRESH_MEAN_C` and `cv2.ADAPTIVE_THRESH_GAUSSIAN_C`, respectively.

The second to last argument specifies the size of the window to perform thresholding; this number has to be an odd positive integer. Specifically, we used 11 in our example, so for each pixel in the image, the algorithm will consider the neighboring pixels (in an 11 x 11 square surrounding the original pixel). The last argument specifies the adjustment to make for each pixel in the final output. These two arguments, again, help localize the threshold for different regions of the image, thus making the thresholding process more dynamic and, as the name suggests, adaptive.

After running the script, you should be able to find the following images as output with the names mean_thresh_ship.jpg and gauss_thresh_ship.jpg. The output for mean_thresh_ship.jpg is as follows:

Output from mean thresholding

The output for `gauss_thresh_ship.jpg` is as follows:

Output from Gaussian thresholding

We can see that with adaptive thresholding, details in specific regions will be thresholded and highlighted in the final output image. These techniques are useful when we need to recognize small details in an image, while simple thresholding is useful when we only want to extract big regions of an image.

Applying concurrency to image processing

We have talked a lot about the basics of image processing and some common image processing techniques. We also know why image processing is a heavy number-crunching task, and that concurrent and parallel programming can be applied to speed up independent processing tasks. In this section, we will be looking at a specific example on how to implement a concurrent image processing application that can handle a large number of input images.

First, head to the current folder for this chapter's code. Inside the input folder, there is a subfolder called large_input, which contains 400 images that we will be using for this example. These pictures are different regions in our original ship image, which have been cropped from it using the array-indexing and -slicing options that NumPy provides to slice OpenCV image objects. If you are curious as to how these images were generated, check out the Chapter08/generate_input.py file.

Our goal in this section is to implement a program that can concurrently process these images using thresholding. To do this, let's look at the example5.py file:

```
from multiprocessing import Pool
import cv2

import sys
from timeit import default_timer as timer


THRESH_METHOD = cv2.ADAPTIVE_THRESH_GAUSSIAN_C
INPUT_PATH = 'input/large_input/'
OUTPUT_PATH = 'output/large_output/'

n = 20
names = ['ship_%i_%i.jpg' % (i, j) for i in range(n) for j in range(n)]


def process_threshold(im, output_name, thresh_method):
    gray_im = cv2.cvtColor(im, cv2.COLOR_BGR2GRAY)
    thresh_im = cv2.adaptiveThreshold(gray_im, 255, thresh_method,
            cv2.THRESH_BINARY, 11, 2)

    cv2.imwrite(OUTPUT_PATH + output_name, thresh_im)


if __name__ == '__main__':

    for n_processes in range(1, 7):
```

```
        start = timer()

        with Pool(n_processes) as p:
            p.starmap(process_threshold, [(
                cv2.imread(INPUT_PATH + name),
                name,
                THRESH_METHOD
            ) for name in names])

        print('Took %.4f seconds with %i process(es).
            ' % (timer() - start, n_processes))

    print('Done.')
```

In this example, we are using the `Pool` class from the `multiprocessing` module to manage our processes. As a refresher, a `Pool` object supplies convenient options to map a sequence of inputs to separate processes using the `Pool.map()` method. We are using the `Pool.starmap()` method in our example, however, to pass multiple arguments to the target function.

At the beginning of our program, we make a number of house-keeping assignments: the thresholding method to perform adaptive thresholding when processing the images, paths for the input and output folders, and the names of the images to process. The `process_threshold()` function is what we use to actually process the images; which takes in an image object, the name for the processed version of the image, and which thresholding method to use. Again, this is why we need to use the `Pool.starmap()` method instead of the traditional `Pool.map()` method.

In the main program, to demonstrate the differences between sequential and multiprocessing image processing, we want to run our program with different numbers of processes, specifically from one single process to six different processes. In each iteration of the `for` loop, we initialize a `Pool` object and map the necessary arguments of each image to the `process_threshold()` function, while keeping track of how much time it takes to process and save all of the images.

After running the script, the processed images can be found in the `output/large_output/` subfolder in our current chapter's folder. You should obtain an output similar to the following:

```
> python example5.py
Took 0.6590 seconds with 1 process(es).
Took 0.3190 seconds with 2 process(es).
Took 0.3227 seconds with 3 process(es).
Took 0.3360 seconds with 4 process(es).
Took 0.3338 seconds with 5 process(es).
```

```
Took 0.3319 seconds with 6 process(es).
Done.
```

We can see a big difference in execution time when we go from one single process to two separate processes. However, there is negligible or even negative speedup after going from two to higher numbers of processes. Generally, this is because of the heavy overhead, which is the product of implementing a large number of separate processes, in comparison to a relatively low number of inputs. Even though we are not implementing this comparison in the interest of simplicity, with an increased number of inputs we would see better improvements from a high number of working processes.

So far, we have seen that concurrent programming could provide a significant speedup for image processing applications. However, if we take a look at our preceding program, we can see that there are additional adjustments that we can make to improve the execution time even further. Specifically, in our preceding program, we are reading in images in a sequential way by using list comprehension in the following line:

```
with Pool(n_processes) as p:
    p.starmap(process_threshold, [(
        cv2.imread(INPUT_PATH + name),
        name,
        THRESH_METHOD
    ) for name in names])
```

Theoretically, if we were to make the process of reading in different image files concurrent, we could also gain additional speedup with our program. This is especially true in an image processing application that deals with large input files, where significant time is spent on waiting for input to be read. With that in mind, let's consider the following example, in which we will implement concurrent input/output processing. Navigate to the example6.py file:

```
from multiprocessing import Pool
import cv2

import sys
from functools import partial
from timeit import default_timer as timer


THRESH_METHOD = cv2.ADAPTIVE_THRESH_GAUSSIAN_C
INPUT_PATH = 'input/large_input/'
OUTPUT_PATH = 'output/large_output/'

n = 20
names = ['ship_%i_%i.jpg' % (i, j) for i in range(n) for j in range(n)]
```

```
def process_threshold(name, thresh_method):
    im = cv2.imread(INPUT_PATH + name)
    gray_im = cv2.cvtColor(im, cv2.COLOR_BGR2GRAY)
    thresh_im = cv2.adaptiveThreshold(gray_im, 255, thresh_method,
cv2.THRESH_BINARY, 11, 2)

    cv2.imwrite(OUTPUT_PATH + name, thresh_im)


if __name__ == '__main__':

    for n_processes in range(1, 7):
        start = timer()

        with Pool(n_processes) as p:
            p.map(partial(process_threshold, thresh_method=THRESH_METHOD),
names)

        print('Took %.4f seconds with %i process(es).' % (timer() - start,
n_processes))
    print('Done.')
```

The structure of this program is similar to that of the previous one. However, instead of preparing the necessary images to be processed and other relevant input information, we implement them inside the `process_threshold()` function, which now only takes the name of the input image and handles reading the image itself.

As a side note, we are using Python's built-in `functools.partial()` method in our main program to pass in a partial argument (hence the name), specifically `thresh_method`, to the `process_threshold()` function, as this argument is fixed across all images and processes. More information about this tool can be found at `https://docs.python.org/3/library/functools.html`.

After running the script, you should obtain an output similar to the following:

```
> python example6.py
Took 0.5300 seconds with 1 process(es).
Took 0.4133 seconds with 2 process(es).
Took 0.2154 seconds with 3 process(es).
Took 0.2147 seconds with 4 process(es).
Took 0.2213 seconds with 5 process(es).
Took 0.2329 seconds with 6 process(es).
Done.
```

Compared to our last output, this implementation of the application indeed gives us a significantly better execution time.

Good concurrent image processing practices

Up until this point, you have most likely realized that image processing is quite an involved process, and implementing concurrent and parallel programming in an image processing application can add more complexity to our work. There are, however, good practices that will guide us in the right direction while developing our image processing applications. The following section discusses some of the most common practices that we should keep in mind.

Choosing the correct way (out of many)

We have hinted at this practice briefly when we learned about thresholding. How an image processing application handles and processes its image data heavily depends on the problems it is supposed to solve, and what kind of data will be fed to it. Therefore, there is significant variability when it comes to choosing specific parameters when processing your image.

For example, as we have seen earlier, there are various ways to threshold an image, and each will result in very different output: if you want to focus on only the large, distinct regions of an image, simple constant thresholding will prove to be more beneficial than adaptive thresholding; if, however, you want to highlight small changes in the details of an image, adaptive thresholding will be significantly better.

Let's consider another example, in which we will see how tuning a specific parameter for an image processing function results in better output. In this example, we are using a simple Haar Cascade model to detect faces in images. We will not go too deeply into how the model handles and processes its data, since it is already built into OpenCV; again, we are only using this model on a high level, changing its parameters to obtain different results.

Navigate to the `example7.py` file in this chapter's folder. The script is designed to detect faces in the `obama1.jpeg` and `obama2.jpg` images in our input folder:

```
import cv2

face_cascade =
cv2.CascadeClassifier('input/haarcascade_frontalface_default.xml')

for filename in ['obama1.jpeg', 'obama2.jpg']:
    im = cv2.imread('input/' + filename)
    gray_im = cv2.cvtColor(im, cv2.COLOR_BGR2GRAY)
```

```
faces = face_cascade.detectMultiScale(im)

for (x, y, w, h) in faces:
    cv2.rectangle(im, (x, y), (x + w, y + h), (0, 255, 0), 2)

cv2.imshow('%i face(s) found' % len(faces), im)
cv2.waitKey(0)

print('Done.')
```

First, the program loads the pretrained Haar Cascade model from the input folder using the cv2.CascadeClassifier class. For each input image, the script converts it to grayscale and feeds it to the pretrained model. The script then draws a green rectangle around each face found in the image, and finally displays it in a separate window.

Run the program, and you will see the following image with the title 5 face(s) found:

Correct face detection

It looks like our program is working well so far. Press any key to continue, and you should see the following image with the title 7 face(s) found:

Incorrect face detection

Now, our program is mistaking some other objects as actual faces, resulting in two false-positives. The reason behind this involves how the pretrained model was created. Specifically, the Haar Cascade model used a training dataset with images of specific (pixel) sizes, and when an input image contains faces of different sizes—which is common when it is a group picture with some people being close to the camera, while others are far away—is fed into this model, it will cause false-positives in the output.

The scaleFactor parameter in the detectMultiScale method of the cv2.CascadeClassifier class addresses this issue. This parameter will scale down different areas of the input image before trying to predict whether those areas contain a face or not—doing this negates the potential difference in face sizes. To implement this, change the line where we pass the input images to the model to the following to specify the scaleFactor parameter as 1.2:

```
faces = face_cascade.detectMultiScale(im, scaleFactor=1.2)
```

Run the program, and you will see that this time our application is able to correctly detect all of the faces in our input images without making any false-positives.

From this example, we can see that it is important to know about the potential challenges that the input images will pose to your image processing application in execution, and to try different methods or parameters within one method of processing to achieve the best results.

Spawning an appropriate number of processes

One point we noticed in our example for concurrent image processing is that the task of spawning processes takes a considerable amount of time. Due to this, if the number of processes available to analyze the data is too high in comparison to the amount of input, the improvement in execution time received from increasing the number of working processes will diminish and sometimes even become negative.

However, there is no concrete way to tell whether a specific number of separate processes is appropriate for a program unless we also take into account its input images. For example, if the input images are relatively large files, and it takes a significant amount of time for the program to load them from storage, having a larger number of processes might be beneficial; when some processes are waiting for their images to load, others can proceed to perform processing on theirs. In other words, having a larger number of processes will allow for some overlapping between loading and processing time, which will result in better speedup.

In short, it is important to test out different processes that are available for your image processing application to see what the optimal number for scalability is.

Processing input/output concurrently

We saw that loading input images in a sequential way might have a negative effect on the execution time of an image processing application, as opposed to allowing separate processes to load their own inputs. This is specifically true if the image files are significantly large, as the loading time in separate processes might overlap with the loading/processing time in other processes. The same is applicable for writing output images to files.

Summary

Image processing is the task of analyzing and manipulating digital image files to create new versions of the images or to extract important data from them. These digital images are represented by tables of pixels, which are RGB values, or in essence, tuples of numbers. Therefore, digital images are simply multidimensional matrices of numbers, which results in the fact that image processing tasks typically come down to heavy number-crunching.

Since images can be analyzed and processed independently from each other in an image processing application, concurrent and parallel programming – specifically multiprocessing – provides a way to achieve significant improvements in execution time for the application. Additionally, there are a number of good practices to follow while implementing your own concurrent image processing program.

So far in this book, we have covered the main two forms of concurrent programming: multithreading and multiprocessing. In the next chapter, we will be moving on to the topic of asynchronous I/O, which is also one of the key elements of concurrency and parallelism.

Questions

- What is an image processing task?
- What is the smallest unit of digital imaging? How is it represented in computers?
- What is grayscaling? What purpose does this technique serve?
- What is thresholding? What purpose does this technique serve?
- Why should image processing be made concurrent?
- What are some good practices for concurrent image processing?

Further reading

For more information, you can refer to the following links:

- Automate the Boring Stuff with Python: Practical Programming for Total Beginners, Al Sweigart, No Starch Press, 2015
- *Learning Image Processing with OpenCV*, Garcia, Gloria Bueno, et al, Packt Publishing Ltd, 2015
- A Computational Introduction to Digital Image Processing, Alasdair McAndrew, Chapman and Hall/CRC, 2015
- Howse, J., P. Joshi, and M. Beyeler. OpenCV: *Computer Vision Projects with Python.* Packt Publishing Ltd, 2016

Introduction to Asynchronous Programming

9

In this chapter, we will introduce readers to the formal definition of asynchronous programming. We will be discussing the basic idea behind asynchronous processing, the differences between asynchronous programming and other programming models that we have seen, and the reason why asynchronous programming is such a major factor in concurrency.

The following topics will be covered in this chapter:

- The concept of asynchronous programming
- The key differences between asynchronous programming and other programming models

Technical requirements

The following is a list of prerequisites for this chapter:

- You must have Python 3 installed on your computer
- Download the GitHub repository from `https://github.com/PacktPublishing/Mastering-Concurrency-in-Python`
- During this chapter, we will be working with the subfolder titled `Chapter09`, so make sure that you have it at the ready
- Check out the following video to see the Code in Action: `http://bit.ly/2DF700L`

A quick analogy

Asynchronous programming is a model of programming that focuses on coordinating different tasks in an application. Its goal is to ensure that the application finishes executing those tasks in the smallest amount of time possible. From this perspective, asynchronous programming is about switching from one task to another when it is appropriate to create overlapping between waiting and processing time, and from there, shorten the total time taken to finish the whole program.

To understand the underlying idea of asynchronous programming, let's consider a quick, real-life analogy. Imagine a scenario in which you are cooking a three-course meal that contains the following:

- An appetizer that will take 2 minutes of preparation and 3 minutes of cooking/waiting
- A main course that will take 5 minutes of preparation and 10 minutes of cooking/waiting
- A dessert that will take 3 minutes of preparation and 5 minutes of cooking/waiting

Now, considering the order in which the courses finish cooking, your goal is to determine a way to produce the three courses that will take the least amount of time. For example, if we are cooking the courses in a sequential way, we will finish the appetizer first, which will take 5 minutes, then we will move on to the main course, which will take 15 minutes, and then finally the dessert, which will take 8 minutes, respectively. In total, the whole meal will take 28 minutes to finish.

The key to finding a quicker way to go about this is to **overlap** the cooking/waiting time of one course with the preparation time of another. Since you will not be occupied while waiting for the food that has already been prepared for cooking, this time could be saved by preparing the food for another dish. For example, improvements could be achieved through the following steps:

- Preparing the appetizer: 2 minutes.
- Preparing the main course while waiting for the appetizer to cook: 5 minutes. The appetizer will have finished during this step.
- Preparing and cooking the dessert while waiting for the main course to cook: 8 minutes. The dessert will have finished during this step, and the main course will have 2 minutes of cooking remaining.
- Waiting for the main course to finish cooking: 2 minutes. The main course will have cooking finished during this step.

By overlapping the time, we have saved a significant amount of time cooking the three meals, which now takes only 17 minutes in total, compared to 28 minutes if we had done this in the sequential way. However, there is obviously more than one way to decide which dish we should start first, and which dish should be cooked second and last. Another variation of the cooking order could be as follows:

- Preparing the main course: 5 minutes.
- Preparing the appetizer while waiting for the main course to cook: 2 minutes. The main course will have 8 minutes of cooking left.
- Preparing the dessert while waiting for the appetizer and the main course to cook: 3 minutes. The appetizer will have finished during this step, and the main course will have 5 minutes of cooking left.
- Waiting for the main course and the dessert to finish cooking: 5 minutes. Both the main course and the dessert will have finished during this step.

This time, it only takes 15 minutes in total to produce the whole meal. As we can see, different variations of the cooking order might result in a different total cooking time. Finding the best order to execute and switch between tasks in a program is the main idea behind asynchronous programming: instead of executing all of the instructions of that program in a sequential way, we coordinate those instructions so that we can create overlapped waiting and processing times and finally achieve a better execution time.

Asynchronous versus other programming models

Asynchronous programming is one of the major concepts in concurrency specifically, and in programming in general. However, it is quite a complex concept that can be considerably challenging for us to sometimes differentiate it from other programming models. In this section, we will be comparing asynchronous programming with synchronous programming and other concurrent programming models that we have seen (that is, threading and multiprocessing).

Asynchronous versus synchronous programming

Again, asynchronous programming is fundamentally different from synchronous programming because of its task-switching nature. In synchronous programming, the instructions of a program are executed sequentially: a task has to have finished executing before the next task in the program starts processing. With asynchronous programming, if the current task takes significant time to finish, you have the option to specify a time during the task at which the execution is switched to another task. As we have observed, doing this would result in potential improvements in the execution time of the whole program.

One common example of asynchronous programming is the interaction between a server and a client during an HTTP request. If HTTP requests were synchronous, clients would have to wait after making a request until receiving the response from the server. Imagine a scenario in which your browser would hang every time you go to a new link or start playing a video until the actual data returns from the server. This would be extremely inconvenient and inefficient for HTTP communication.

A better approach is asynchronous communication, where the client is free to continue working, and when data from the requests made returns from the server is when the client will be notified and proceed to process that data. Asynchronous programming is so common in web development that a whole programming model called **AJAX** (short for **Asynchronous JavaScript and XML**) is now used in almost every website. Additionally, if you have used common libraries in JavaScript such as jQuery or Node.js, chances are you have worked with, or at least heard the term **callback**, which simply means a function that can be passed to another function to execute later in the future. Switching back and forth between the execution of functions is the main idea of asynchronous programming, and we will actually analyze an advanced example of callback usage in `Chapter 18`, *Building a Server from Scratch*.

The following diagram further illustrates the difference between synchronous and asynchronous client-server communication:

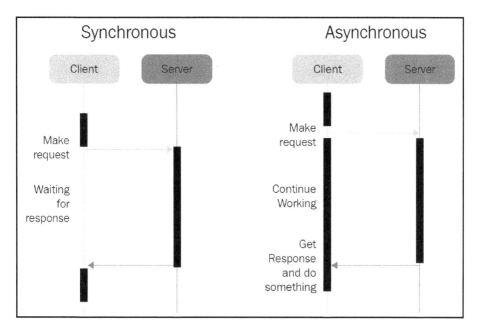

Differences between synchronous and asynchronous HTTP requests

Asynchronous programming is, of course, not limited to HTTP requests. Tasks that involve general network communication, software data processing, interaction with databases, and so on all take advantage of asynchronous programming. Contrary to synchronous programming, asynchronous programming provides responsiveness for users by preventing the program from hanging while waiting for data. Therefore, it is a great tool to implement in programs that deal with a large amount of data.

Asynchronous versus threading and multiprocessing

While providing somewhat similar benefits to those that threading and multiprocessing provide, asynchronous programming is fundamentally different from these two programming models, especially in the Python programming language.

As we know, in multiprocessing, multiple copies of our main program—together with its instructions and variables—are created and executed independently across different cores. Threads, which are also known as lightweight processes, operate on the same basis: although the code is not executed in separate cores, independent portions of the code that are executed in separate threads do not interact with one another either.

Asynchronous programming, on the other hand, keeps all of the instructions of a program in the same thread and process. The main idea behind asynchronous programming is to have a single executor to switch from one task to another if it is more efficient (in terms of execution time) to simply wait for the first task while processing the second. This means that asynchronous programming will not take advantage of the multiple cores that a system might have.

An example in Python

While we will go into more depth regarding how asynchronous programming can be implemented in Python and the main tools we will be using, including the `asyncio` module, let's consider how asynchronous programming can improve the execution time of our Python programs.

Let's take a look at the `Chapter09/example1.py` file:

```python
# Chapter09/example1.py

from math import sqrt

def is_prime(x):
    print('Processing %i...' % x)

    if x < 2:
        print('%i is not a prime number.' % x)

    elif x == 2:
        print('%i is a prime number.' % x)

    elif x % 2 == 0:
        print('%i is not a prime number.' % x)

    else:
        limit = int(sqrt(x)) + 1
        for i in range(3, limit, 2):
            if x % i == 0:
                print('%i is not a prime number.' % x)
                return
```

```
        print('%i is a prime number.' % x)

if __name__ == '__main__':

    is_prime(9637529763296797)
    is_prime(427920331)
    is_prime(157)
```

Here, we have our familiar prime-checking `is_prime()` function, which takes in an integer and prints out a message indicating whether that input is a prime number or not. In our main program, we call `is_prime()` on three different numbers. We are also keeping track of how much time it takes for our program to process all three numbers.

Once you execute the script, your output should be similar to the following:

```
> python example1.py
Processing 9637529763296797...
9637529763296797 is a prime number.
Processing 427920331...
427920331 is a prime number.
Processing 157...
157 is a prime number.
```

You have probably noticed that the program took quite some time to process the first input. Because of the way the `is_prime()` function is implemented, if the input of the prime number is large, then it takes `is_prime()` longer to process it. So, since we have a large prime number as the first input, our Python program will hang for a significant amount of time before printing out the output. This typically creates a non-responsive feel for our program, which is not desirable in both software engineering and web development.

To improve the responsiveness of the program, we will take advantage of the `asyncio` module, which has been implemented in the `Chapter09/example2.py` file:

```
# Chapter09/example2.py

from math import sqrt

import asyncio

async def is_prime(x):
    print('Processing %i...' % x)

    if x < 2:
        print('%i is not a prime number.' % x)

    elif x == 2:
```

```
            print('%i is a prime number.' % x)

        elif x % 2 == 0:
            print('%i is not a prime number.' % x)

        else:
            limit = int(sqrt(x)) + 1
            for i in range(3, limit, 2):
                if x % i == 0:
                    print('%i is not a prime number.' % x)
                    return
                elif i % 100000 == 1:
                    #print('Here!')
                    await asyncio.sleep(0)

            print('%i is a prime number.' % x)

async def main():

    task1 = loop.create_task(is_prime(9637529763296797))
    task2 = loop.create_task(is_prime(427920331))
    task3 = loop.create_task(is_prime(157))

    await asyncio.wait([task1, task2, task3])

if __name__ == '__main__':
    try:
        loop = asyncio.get_event_loop()
        loop.run_until_complete(main())
    except Exception as e:
        print('There was a problem:')
        print(str(e))
    finally:
        loop.close()
```

We will go into the details of this code in the next chapter. For now, simply run the script, and you will see an improvement in responsiveness in the printed output:

```
> python example2.py
Processing 9637529763296797...
Processing 427920331...
427920331 is a prime number.
Processing 157...
157 is a prime number.
9637529763296797 is a prime number.
```

Specifically, while `9637529763296797` (our largest input) was being processed, the program decided to switch to the next inputs. Therefore, the results for `427920331` and `157` were returned before it, hence improving the responsiveness of the program.

Summary

Asynchronous programming is a programming model that is based on task coordination through task switching. It is different from traditional sequential (or synchronous) programming since it creates an overlap between processing and waiting time, which provides potential improvements in speed. Asynchronous programming is also different from threading and multiprocessing, as it only takes place within one single thread in one single process.

Asynchronous programming is mostly used to improve the responsiveness of a program. When a large input takes a significant amount of time to process, the sequential version of a program will appear to be hanging, while the asynchronous program will move to other less heavy tasks. This allows small inputs to finish executing first and help the program to be more responsive.

In the next chapter, we will learn about the main structure of an asynchronous program and look into the `asyncio` module and its functionalities in more detail.

Questions

- What is the idea behind asynchronous programming?
- How is asynchronous programming different from synchronous programming?
- How is asynchronous programming different from threading and multiprocessing?

Further reading

For more information, you can refer to the following links:

- *Parallel Programming with Python*, by Jan Palach, Packt Publishing Ltd, 2014
- *Python Parallel Programming Cookbook*, by Giancarlo Zaccone, Packt Publishing Ltd, 2015
- *RabbitMQ Cookbook*, by Sigismondo Boschi and Gabriele Santomaggio, Packt Publishing Ltd, 2013

10
Implementing Asynchronous Programming in Python

This chapter will introduce you to the `asyncio` module in Python. It will cover the idea behind this new concurrency module, which utilizes event loops and coroutines and provides an API that is as readable as synchronous code. In this chapter, we will also discuss the implementation of asynchronous programming, in addition to threading and multiprocessing through the `concurrent.futures` module. During this process, we will cover the application of asynchronous programming via the most common uses of `asyncio`, including asynchronous input/output and avoiding blocking tasks.

The following topics will be covered in this chapter:

- The fundamental elements of implementing asynchronous programming using `asyncio`
- The framework for asynchronous programming provided by `asyncio`
- The `concurrent.futures` module and its usage, in respect to `asyncio`

Technical requirements

The following is the list a prerequisites for this chapter:

- Ensure that you have Python 3 installed on your computer
- Download the GitHub repository at `https://github.com/PacktPublishing/Mastering-Concurrency-in-Python`
- During this chapter, we will be working with the subfolder titled `Chapter10`
- Check out the following video to see the Code in Action: `http://bit.ly/2TAtTrA`

The asyncio module

As you saw in the previous chapter, the `asyncio` module provides an easy way to convert a sequential program to an asynchronous one. In this section, we will be discussing the general structure of an asynchronous program, and subsequently, how to implement the conversion from a sequential to an asynchronous program in Python.

Coroutines, event loops, and futures

There are a few common elements that most asynchronous programs have, and coroutines, event loops, and futures are three of those elements. They are defined as follows:

- **Event loops** are the main coordinators of tasks in an asynchronous program. An event loop keeps track of all of the tasks that are to be run asynchronously, and decides which of those tasks should be executed at a given moment. In other words, event loops handle the task switching aspect (or the execution flow) of asynchronous programming.
- **Coroutines** are a special type of function that wrap around specific tasks, so that they can be executed asynchronously. A coroutine is required in order to specify where in the function the task switching should take place; in other words, they specify when the function should give back the flow of execution to the event loop. The tasks for coroutines are typically either stored in a task queue or created inside the event loop.
- **Futures** are placeholders for the results returned from coroutines. These future objects are created as soon as coroutines are initiated in the event loop, so futures can represent actual results, pending results (if the coroutines have not finished executing), or even an exception (if that is what the coroutine will return).

An event loop, coroutines, and their corresponding futures, are the core elements of an asynchronous programming process. First, the event loop is started and interacts with its task queue, in order to obtain the first task. The coroutine for this task and its corresponding future are then created. When a task switching has to take place inside of that coroutine, the coroutine suspends, and the next coroutine is called; all data and the context from the first coroutine are also saved.

Now, if that coroutine is blocking (for example, input/output processing or sleeping), the flow of execution is released back to the event loop, which will move on to the next item in the task queue. The event loop will initiate the last item in the task queue before it switches back to the first coroutine, and will proceed the execution from where it was last suspended.

As each task finishes executing, it will be dequeued from the task queue, its coroutine will be terminated, and the corresponding future will register the returned result from the coroutine. This process will go on until all tasks in the task queue are completely executed. The following diagram further illustrates the general structure of the asynchronous process described earlier:

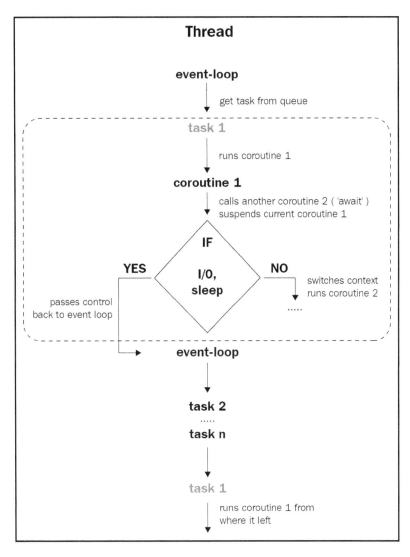

Asynchronous programming process

Asyncio API

With the general structure of an asynchronous program in mind, let's consider the specific APIs that the `asyncio` module and Python provide for the implementation of asynchronous programs. The first foundation for this API is the `async` and `await` keywords that were added to Python 3.5. These keywords are used to specify the main elements of an asynchronous program to Python.

Specifically, `async` is typically put in front of the `def` keyword when a function is declared. A function with the `async` keyword in front of it will be interpreted by Python as a coroutine. As we discussed, inside of each coroutine, there has to be a specification regarding when the task switching events will take place. The `await` keyword is then used to specify where and when, exactly, to give back the flow of execution to the event loop; this is typically done through waiting for another coroutine to produce a result (`await coroutine`) or through helper functions from the `asyncio` module, such as the `asyncio.sleep()` and `asyncio.wait()` functions.

It is important to note that the `async` and `await` keywords are actually provided by Python and are not managed by the `asyncio` module. This means that asynchronous programming can actually be implemented without `asyncio`, but, as you will see, `asyncio` provides a framework and infrastructure to streamline this process, and is therefore the primary tool in Python for the implementation of asynchronous programming.

Specifically, the most commonly used API from the `asyncio` module is event-loop-managing functionalities. With `asyncio`, you can start to manipulate your tasks and event loop with intuitive and easy function calls, without extensive boilerplate code. These include the following:

- `asyncio.get_event_loop()`: This method returns the event loop for the current context, which is an `AbstractEventLoop` object. Most of the time, we do not need to worry about this class, as the `asyncio` module already provides a high-level API to manage our event loops.
- `AbstractEventLoop.create_task()`: This method is to be called by an event loop. It adds its input to the current task queue of the calling event loop; the input is typically a coroutine (that is, a function with the `async` keyword).

- `AbstractEventLoop.run_until_complete()`: This method is also to be called by an event loop. It takes in the main coroutine of an asynchronous program and executes it until the corresponding future of the coroutine is returned. While the method initiates the event loop execution, it also blocks all subsequent code following it, until all futures are complete.
- `AbstractEventLoop.run_forever()`: This method is somewhat similar to `AbstractEventLoop.run_until_complete()`, except for the fact that, as suggested by the method name, the calling event loop will run forever, unless the `AbstractEventLoop.stop()` method is called. So, instead of exiting, the loop will continue to run, even upon obtaining the returned futures.
- `AbstractEventLoop.stop()`: This method causes the calling event loop to stop executing and exit at the nearest appropriate opportunity, without causing the whole program to crash.

Aside from these methods, we use a number of non-blocking functions to facilitate the task switching event. These include the following:

- `asyncio.sleep()`: While in itself a coroutine, this function creates an additional coroutine that completes after a given time (specified by the input, in seconds). It is typically used as `asyncio.sleep(0)`, to cause an immediate task switching event.
- `asyncio.wait()`: This function is also a coroutine, and hence, it can be used to switch tasks. It takes in a sequence (usually a list) of futures and waits for them to complete their execution.

The asyncio framework in action

As you have seen, `asyncio` provides a simple and intuitive way to implement the framework of an asynchronous program with Python's asynchronous programming keywords. With that, let's consider the process of applying the framework provided to a synchronous application in Python, and convert it to an asynchronous one.

Asynchronously counting down

Let's take a look at the `Chapter10/example1.py` file, as follows:

```
# Chapter10/example1.py

import time

def count_down(name, delay):
    indents = (ord(name) - ord('A')) * '\t'

    n = 3
    while n:
        time.sleep(delay)

        duration = time.perf_counter() - start
        print('-' * 40)
        print('%.4f \t%s%s = %i' % (duration, indents, name, n))

        n -= 1

start = time.perf_counter()

count_down('A', 1)
count_down('B', 0.8)
count_down('C', 0.5)

print('-' * 40)
print('Done.')
```

The goal of this example is to illustrate the asynchronous nature of overlapping the processing and waiting time of independent tasks. To do this, we will be analyzing a countdown function (`count_down()`) that takes in a string and a delay time. It will then count down from three to one, in seconds, while printing out the time elapsed from the beginning of the function's execution and the input string (with the current countdown number).

In our main program, we will call the `count_down()` function on the letters A, B, and C, with different delay times. After running the script, your output should be similar to the following:

```
> python example1.py
----------------------------------------
1.0006 A = 3
----------------------------------------
2.0041 A = 2
----------------------------------------
```

```
3.0055 A = 1
-----------------------------------------
3.8065          B = 3
-----------------------------------------
4.6070          B = 2
-----------------------------------------
5.4075          B = 1
-----------------------------------------
5.9081                    C = 3
-----------------------------------------
6.4105                    C = 2
-----------------------------------------
6.9107                    C = 1
-----------------------------------------
Done.
```

The numbers at the beginning of the lines indicate the total numbers of seconds elapsed from the beginning of the program. You can see that the program counted down for letter A first, with one-second intervals, and it moved on to letter B, with 0.8-second intervals, and finally, to letter C, with 0.5-second intervals. This is a purely sequential, synchronous program, since there is no overlapping between processing and waiting time. Additionally, it took approximately 6.9 seconds to run the program, which is the sum of the counting down time of all three letters:

```
1 second x 3 (for A) + 0.8 seconds x 3 (for B) + 0.5 seconds x 3 (for C) =
6.9 seconds
```

Keeping the idea behind asynchronous programming in mind, we can see that it is actually possible for us to convert this program to an asynchronous one. Specifically, let's suppose that during the first second of the program, while we are waiting to count down the letter A, we can switch tasks to move to other letters. In fact, we will implement this setup for all of the letters inside the count_down() function (in other words, we will turn count_down() into a coroutine).

Theoretically, now that all counting down tasks are coroutines in an asynchronous program, we should achieve better execution time and responsiveness for our program. Since all three tasks are processed independently, the countdown messages should be printed out of order (jumping between different letters), and the asynchronous program should only take about the same time as the largest task takes (that is, three seconds for letter A).

But first, let's make our program asynchronous. To do this, we first need to make `count_down()` into a coroutine and specify a point inside the function to be a task switching event. In other words, we will add the keyword `async` in front of the function, and, instead of the `time.sleep()` function, we will be using the `asyncio.sleep()` function along with the `await` keyword; the rest of the function should remain the same. Our `count_down()` coroutine should now be as follows:

```python
# Chapter10/example2.py

async def count_down(name, delay):
    indents = (ord(name) - ord('A')) * '\t'

    n = 3
    while n:
        await asyncio.sleep(delay)

        duration = time.perf_counter() - start
        print('-' * 40)
        print('%.4f \t%s%s = %i' % (duration, indents, name, n))

        n -= 1
```

As for our main program, we will need to initialize and manage an event loop. Specifically, we will create an empty event loop with the `asyncio.get_event_loop()` method, add all of the three counting down tasks into the task queue with `AbstractEventLoop.create_task()`, and, finally, start running the event loop with `AbstractEventLoop.run_until_complete()`. Our main program should look like the following:

```python
# Chapter10/example2.py

loop = asyncio.get_event_loop()
tasks = [
    loop.create_task(count_down('A', 1)),
    loop.create_task(count_down('B', 0.8)),
    loop.create_task(count_down('C', 0.5))
]

start = time.perf_counter()
loop.run_until_complete(asyncio.wait(tasks))

print('-' * 40)
print('Done.')
```

The complete script can also be found in the code repository of the book, inside the `Chapter10` subfolder, named `example2.py`. After running the script, your output should look similar to the following:

```
> python example2.py
-------------------------------------------
0.5029                    C = 3
-------------------------------------------
0.8008          B = 3
-------------------------------------------
1.0049 A = 3
-------------------------------------------
1.0050                    C = 2
-------------------------------------------
1.5070                    C = 1
-------------------------------------------
1.6011          B = 2
-------------------------------------------
2.0090 A = 2
-------------------------------------------
2.4068          B = 1
-------------------------------------------
3.0147 A = 1
-------------------------------------------
Done.
```

Now, you can see how having an asynchronous program can improve the execution time and responsiveness of our programs. Instead of executing individual tasks sequentially, our program now switches between different countdowns and overlaps their processing/waiting times. This, as we discussed, results in different letters being printed out in between each other, or simultaneously.

At the beginning of the program, instead of waiting for the whole first second to print out the first message A = 3, the program switches to the next task in the task queue (in this case, it is waiting for 0.8 seconds for the letter B). This process continues until 0.5 seconds have passed and C = 3 is printed out, and 0.3 seconds later (at the time 0.8 seconds), B = 3 is printed out. This all happens before A = 3 is printed out.

This task-switching property of our asynchronous program makes it significantly more responsive. Instead of hanging for one second before the first message is printed, the program now only takes 0.5 seconds (the shortest waiting period) to print out its first message. As for the execution time, you can see that this time, it only takes three seconds, in total, to execute the whole program (instead of 6.9 seconds). This corresponds to what we speculated: that the execution time would be right around the time it takes to execute the largest task.

A note about blocking functions

As you have seen, we have to replace our original `time.sleep()` function with its equivalent from the `asyncio` module. This is because `time.sleep()` is, by nature, a blocking function, which means that it cannot be used to implement a task switching event. To test this, in our `Chapter10/example2.py` file (our asynchronous program), we will replace the following line of code:

```
await asyncio.sleep(delay)
```

The preceding code will be replaced with the following code:

```
time.sleep(delay)
```

After running this new script, your output will simply be the same as that of our original sequential, synchronous program. So, replacing `await asyncio.sleep()` with `time.sleep()` actually converts our program back to synchronous, ignoring the event loop that we implemented. What happened was, when our program proceeded to that line inside of the `count_down()` function, `time.sleep()` actually blocked and prevented the release of the execution flow, essentially rendering the whole program synchronous once again. Revert `time.sleep()` back to `await asyncio.sleep()` to fix this problem.

The following diagram illustrates an example of the difference in execution time between blocking and non-blocking file handling:

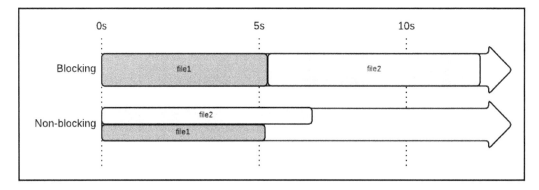

Blocking versus non-blocking

This phenomenon raises an interesting issue: if a heavy, long-running task is blocking, then it is literally impossible to implement asynchronous programming with that task as a coroutine. So, if we really wanted to achieve what a blocking function returns in an asynchronous application, we would need to implement another version of that blocking function, which could be made into a coroutine and allow for task switching events to take place at at least one point inside the function.

Luckily, after implementing `asyncio` as one of the official features of Python, Python core developers have been on working to produce the coroutine version of the most commonly used Python blocking functions. This means that if you ever find blocking functions that prevent your program from being truly asynchronous, you will most likely be able to find the coroutine versions of those functions to implement in your program.

However, the fact that there are asynchronous versions of traditionally blocking functions in Python with potentially different APIs means that you will need to familiarize yourself with those APIs from separate functions. Another way to handle blocking functions without having to implement their coroutine versions is to use an executor to run the functions in separate threads or separate processes, to avoid blocking the thread of the main event loop.

Asynchronous prime-checking

Moving on from our starting counting-down example, let's reconsider the example from the previous chapter. As a refresher, the following is the code for the synchronous version of the program:

```python
# Chapter09/example1.py

from math import sqrt

def is_prime(x):
    print('Processing %i...' % x)

    if x < 2:
        print('%i is not a prime number.' % x)

    elif x == 2:
        print('%i is a prime number.' % x)

    elif x % 2 == 0:
        print('%i is not a prime number.' % x)

    else:
        limit = int(sqrt(x)) + 1
```

```
        for i in range(3, limit, 2):
            if x % i == 0:
                print('%i is not a prime number.' % x)
                return

        print('%i is a prime number.' % x)

if __name__ == '__main__':

    is_prime(9637529763296797)
    is_prime(427920331)
    is_prime(157)
```

As we discussed in the last chapter, here, we have a simple prime-checking function, `is_prime(x)`, that prints out messages indicating whether the input integer that it takes in, x, is a prime number. In our main program, we call `is_prime()` on three prime numbers, in an order of decreasing magnitude sequentially. This setup again creates a significant period of time during which the program appears to be hanging while processing the large input, resulting in a low responsiveness for the program.

The output produced by the program will look similar to the following:

```
Processing 9637529763296797...
9637529763296797 is a prime number.
Processing 427920331...
427920331 is a prime number.
Processing 157...
157 is a prime number.
```

To implement asynchronous programming for this script, first, we will have to create our first main component: the event loop. To do this, instead of using the '__main__' scope, we will convert it to a separate function. This function and our `is_prime()` prime-checking function will be the coroutines in our final asynchronous program.

Now, we need to convert both the `is_prime()` and `main()` functions into coroutines; again, this means putting the `async` keyword in front of the `def` keyword, and the `await` keyword inside each function, to specify the task-switching event. For `main()`, we simply implement that event while waiting for the task queue by using `aysncio.wait()`, as follows:

```
# Chapter09/example2.py

async def main():

    task1 = loop.create_task(is_prime(9637529763296797))
    task2 = loop.create_task(is_prime(427920331))
```

```
        task3 = loop.create_task(is_prime(157))

        await asyncio.wait([task1, task2, task3])
```

Things are more complicated in the `is_prime()` function, as there is no clear point during which the execution flow should be released back to the event loop, like in our previous counting-down example. Recall that the goal of asynchronous programming is to achieve a better execution time and responsiveness, and to implement this, the task-switching event should take place during a heavy, long-running task. This requirement, however, is dependent on the specifics of your program—particularly, the coroutine, the task queue of the program, and the individual tasks in the queue.

For example, the task queue of our program consists of three numbers: `9637529763296797`, `427920331`, and `157`; in order, we can consider them as a large task, a medium task, and a small task. To improve responsiveness, we would like to switch tasks during the large task, and not during the small task. This setup will allow the medium and small tasks to be started, processed, and maybe finished during the execution of the large task, even if the large task is in front in the task queue of the program.

Then, we will consider our `is_prime()` coroutine. After checking for some specific edge cases, it iterates in a `for` loop through every odd number under the square root of the input integer and tests for the divisibility of the input with regards to the current odd number in question. Inside this long-running `for` loop, then, is the perfect place to switch tasks—that is, to release the execution flow back to the event loop.

However, we still need to decide at which specific points in the `for` loop to implement the task-switching event. Again, taking into account the individual tasks in the task queue, we are looking for a point that is fairly common in the large task, not so common in the medium task, and non-existent in the small task. I have decided that this point is every 1,00,000-number period, which does satisfy our requirements, and I have used the `await asyncio.sleep(0)` command to facilitate the task-switching event, as follows:

```python
# Chapter09/example2.py

from math import sqrt
import asyncio

async def is_prime(x):
    print('Processing %i...' % x)

    if x < 2:
        print('%i is not a prime number.' % x)

    elif x == 2:
```

```
        print('%i is a prime number.' % x)

    elif x % 2 == 0:
        print('%i is not a prime number.' % x)

    else:
        limit = int(sqrt(x)) + 1
        for i in range(3, limit, 2):
            if x % i == 0:
                print('%i is not a prime number.' % x)
                return
            elif i % 100000 == 1:
                await asyncio.sleep(0)

        print('%i is a prime number.' % x)
```

Finally, in our main program (not to be confused with the `main()` coroutine), we create our event loop and use it to run our `main()` coroutine, until it completes its execution:

```
try:
    loop = asyncio.get_event_loop()
    loop.run_until_complete(main())
except Exception as e:
    print('There was a problem:')
    print(str(e))
finally:
    loop.close()
```

As you saw in the previous chapter, better responsiveness was achieved through this asynchronous version of the script. Specifically, instead of appearing like it is hanging while processing the first large task, our program now prints out output messages for the other, smaller tasks, before it finishes executing the large task. Our end result will look similar to the following:

```
Processing 9637529763296797...
Processing 427920331...
427920331 is a prime number.
Processing 157...
157 is a prime number.
9637529763296797 is a prime number.
```

Improvements from Python 3.7

As of 2018, Python 3.7 has just come out, with several major new features, such as data classes, guaranteed ordered dictionaries, better timing precision, and so on. Asynchronous programming and the `asyncio` module received a number of important improvements.

First of all, `async` and `await` are now officially reserved keywords in Python. While we have been calling them keywords, Python did not, in fact, treat these words as reserved keywords, up until now. This means that neither `async` nor `await` can be used to name variables or functions in a Python program. If you are using Python 3.7, fire up a Python interpreter and try to use these keywords for variable or function names, and you should receive the following error message:

```
>>> def async():
  File "<stdin>", line 1
    def async():
             ^
SyntaxError: invalid syntax
>>> await = 0
  File "<stdin>", line 1
    await = 0
          ^
SyntaxError: invalid syntax
```

A major improvement in Python 3.7 comes with the `asyncio` module. Specifically, you might have noticed from our previous examples that the main program typically contains a fair amount of boilerplate code to initiate and run the event loop, which most likely remains the same in all asynchronous programs:

```
loop = asyncio.get_event_loop()
asyncio.run_until_complete(main())
```

With `main()` being a coroutine in our program, `asyncio` allows us to simply run it in an event loop by using the `asyncio.run()` method. This eliminates significant boilerplate code in Python asynchronous programming.

So, we can convert the preceding code to a more simplified version in Python 3.7, as follows:

```
asyncio.run(main())
```

There are other improvements regarding asynchronous programming, in both performance and ease in usage, that were implemented in Python 3.7; however, we will not be discussing them in this book.

Inherently blocking tasks

In the first example in this chapter, you saw that asynchronous programming can provide our Python programs with better execution time, but that is not always the case. Asynchronous programming alone can only provide improvements in speed if all processing tasks are non-blocking. However, similar to the comparison between concurrency and inherent sequentiality in programming tasks, some computing tasks in Python are inherently blocking, and therefore, they cannot be taken advantage of by asynchronous programming.

This means that if your asynchronous programming has inherently blocking tasks in some coroutines, the program will not gain any additional improvement in speed from the asynchronous architecture. While task-switching events still take place in those programs, which will improve the responsiveness of the programs, no instructions will be overlapping each other, and no additional speed will thus be gained. In fact, since there is considerable overhead regarding the implementation of asynchronous programming in Python, our programs might even take longer to finish their execution than the original, synchronous programs.

For example, let's look at a comparison in speed between the two versions of our prime-checking program. Since the primary processing portion of the program is the is_prime() coroutine, which solely consists of number crunching, we know that this coroutine contains blocking tasks. So, the asynchronous version is, in fact, expected to run more slowly than the synchronous version.

Navigate to the Chapter10 subfolder of the code repository and take a look at the files example3.py and example4.py. These files contain the same code for the synchronous and asynchronous prime-checking programs that we have been seeing, but with the addition that we are also tracking how much time it takes to run the respective programs. The following is my output after running example3.py, the synchronous version of the program:

```
> python example3.py
Processing 9637529763296797...
9637529763296797 is a prime number.
Processing 427920331...
427920331 is a prime number.
Processing 157...
157 is a prime number.
Took 5.60 seconds.
```

The following code shows my output when running `example4.py`, the asynchronous program:

```
> python example4.py
Processing 9637529763296797...
Processing 427920331...
427920331 is a prime number.
Processing 157...
157 is a prime number.
9637529763296797 is a prime number.
Took 7.89 seconds.
```

While the output that you receive might be different in the specific times it took to run either program, it should be the case that, as we discussed, the asynchronous program actually took longer to run than the synchronous (sequential) one. Again, this is because the number crunching tasks inside our `is_prime()` coroutine are blocking, and, instead of overlapping these tasks in order to gain additional speed, our asynchronous program simply switched between these tasks in its execution. In this case, only responsiveness is achieved through asynchronous programming.

However, this does not mean that if your program contains blocking functions, asynchronous programming is out of the question. As mentioned previously, all execution in an asynchronous program, if not specified otherwise, occurs entirely in the same thread and process, and blocking CPU-bound tasks can thus prevent program instructions from overlapping each other. However, this is not the case if the tasks are distributed to separate threads/processes. In other words, threading and multiprocessing can help asynchronous programs with blocking instructions to achieve better execution time.

concurrent.futures as a solution for blocking tasks

In this section, we will be considering another way to implement threading/multiprocessing: the `concurrent.futures` module, which is designed to be a high-level interface for implementing asynchronous tasks. Specifically, the `concurrent.futures` module works seamlessly with the `asyncio` module, and, in addition, it provides an abstract class called `Executor`, which contains the skeleton of the two main classes that implement asynchronous threading and multiprocessing, respectively (as suggested by their names): `ThreadPoolExecutor` and `ProcessPoolExecutor`.

Changes in the framework

Before we jump into the API from `concurrent.futures`, let's discuss the theoretical basics of asynchronous threading/multiprocessing, and how it plays into the framework of the asynchronous programming that `asyncio` provides.

As a reminder, we have three major elements in our ecosystem of asynchronous programming: the event loop, the coroutines, and their corresponding futures. We still need the event loop while utilizing threading/multiprocessing, to coordinate the tasks and handle their returned results (futures), so these elements typically remain consistent with single-threaded asynchronous programming.

As for the coroutines, since the idea of combining asynchronous programming with threading and multiprocessing involves avoiding blocking tasks in the coroutines by executing them in separate threads and processes, the coroutines do not necessarily have to be interpreted as actual coroutines by Python anymore. Instead, they can simply be traditional Python functions.

One new element that we will need to implement is the executor that facilitates threading or multiprocessing; this can be an instance of the `ThreadPoolExecutor` class or the `ProcessPoolExecutor` class. Now, every time we add a task to our task queue in the event loop, we will also need to reference this executor, so that separate tasks will be executed in separated threads/processes. This is done through the `AbstractEventLoop.run_in_executor()` method, which takes in an executor, a coroutine (though, again, it does not have to be an actual coroutine), and arguments for the coroutines to be executed in separate threads/processes. We will see an example of this API in the next section.

Examples in Python

Let's look at a specific implementation of the `concurrent.futures` module. Recall that in this chapter's first example (the counting down example), the blocking `time.sleep()` function prevented our asynchronous program from becoming truly asynchronous, and had to be replaced with its non-blocking version, `asyncio.sleep()`. Now, we are executing the individual countdowns in separate threads or processes, which means that the blocking `time.sleep()` function will not pose any problems in terms of executing our program asynchronously.

Navigate to the `Chapter10/example5.py` file, as follows:

```python
# Chapter10/example5.py

from concurrent.futures import ThreadPoolExecutor
import asyncio
import time

def count_down(name, delay):
    indents = (ord(name) - ord('A')) * '\t'

    n = 3
    while n:
        time.sleep(delay)

        duration = time.perf_counter() - start
        print('-' * 40)
        print('%.4f \t%s%s = %i' % (duration, indents, name, n))

        n -= 1

async def main():
    futures = [loop.run_in_executor(
        executor,
        count_down,
        *args
    ) for args in [('A', 1), ('B', 0.8), ('C', 0.5)]]

    await asyncio.gather(*futures)

    print('-' * 40)
    print('Done.')

start = time.perf_counter()
executor = ThreadPoolExecutor(max_workers=3)
loop = asyncio.get_event_loop()
loop.run_until_complete(main())
```

Notice that `count_down()` is declared as a typical, non-coroutine Python function. In `main()`, which remains a coroutine, we declare our task queue for the event loop. Again, we are using the `run_in_executor()` method during this process, instead of the `create_task()` method that is used in single-threaded asynchronous programming. In our main program, we also need to initiate an executor, which, in this case, is an instance of the `ThreadPoolExecutor` class from the `concurrent.futures` module.

The decision between using threading and multiprocessing is, as we discussed in previous chapters, dependent on the nature of the program. Here, we need to share the `start` variable (holding the time at which the program starts to execute) among separate coroutines, so that they can perform the act of counting down; so, threading is chosen over multiprocessing.

After running the script, your output should be similar to the following:

```
> python example5.py
----------------------------------------
0.5033                  C = 3
----------------------------------------
0.8052          B = 3
----------------------------------------
1.0052 A = 3
----------------------------------------
1.0079                  C = 2
----------------------------------------
1.5103                  C = 1
----------------------------------------
1.6064          B = 2
----------------------------------------
2.0093 A = 2
----------------------------------------
2.4072          B = 1
----------------------------------------
3.0143 A = 1
----------------------------------------
Done.
```

This output is identical to the one that we obtained from the asynchronous program with pure `asyncio` support. So, even with a blocking processing function, we were able to make the execution of our program asynchronous, with threading implemented by the `concurrent.futures` module.

Let's now apply the same concept to our prime-checking problem. We are first converting our `is_prime()` coroutine to its original, non-coroutine form, and executing it in separate processes again (which are more desirable than threads, as the `is_prime()` function is an intensive number-crunching task). An additional benefit of using the original version of `is_prime()` is that we will not have to perform a check of the task-switching condition that we have in our single-threaded asynchronous program:

```
elif i % 100000 == 1:
    await asyncio.sleep(0)
```

This will provide us with a significant speedup, as well. Let's take a look at the
`Chapter10/example6.py` file, as follows:

```
# Chapter10/example6.py

from math import sqrt
import asyncio
from concurrent.futures import ProcessPoolExecutor
from timeit import default_timer as timer

#async def is_prime(x):
def is_prime(x):
    print('Processing %i...' % x)

    if x < 2:
        print('%i is not a prime number.' % x)

    elif x == 2:
        print('%i is a prime number.' % x)

    elif x % 2 == 0:
        print('%i is not a prime number.' % x)

    else:
        limit = int(sqrt(x)) + 1
        for i in range(3, limit, 2):
            if x % i == 0:
                print('%i is not a prime number.' % x)
                return

        print('%i is a prime number.' % x)

async def main():

    task1 = loop.run_in_executor(executor, is_prime, 9637529763296797)
    task2 = loop.run_in_executor(executor, is_prime, 427920331)
    task3 = loop.run_in_executor(executor, is_prime, 157)

    await asyncio.gather(*[task1, task2, task3])

if __name__ == '__main__':
    try:
        start = timer()

        executor = ProcessPoolExecutor(max_workers=3)
        loop = asyncio.get_event_loop()
        loop.run_until_complete(main())
```

```
            print('Took %.2f seconds.' % (timer() - start))

    except Exception as e:
        print('There was a problem:')
        print(str(e))

    finally:
        loop.close()
```

After running the script, I obtained the following output:

```
> python example6.py
Processing 9637529763296797...
Processing 427920331...
Processing 157...
157 is a prime number.
427920331 is a prime number.
9637529763296797 is a prime number.
Took 5.26 seconds.
```

Again, your execution time will most likely be different from mine, although the comparison between this and the other two versions of our prime-checking program should always be consistent: the original, synchronous version takes less time than the single-threaded asynchronous version, but more than the multiprocessing asynchronous version. In other words, by combining multiprocessing with asynchronous programming, we get the best of both worlds: the consistent responsiveness from asynchronous programming, and the improvement in speed from multiprocessing.

Summary

In this chapter, you learned about asynchronous programming, which is a model of programming that takes advantage of coordinating computing tasks to overlap the waiting and processing times. There are three main components to an asynchronous program: the event loop, the coroutines, and the futures. The event loop is in charge of scheduling and managing coroutines using its task queue. Coroutines are computing tasks that are to be executed asynchronously; each coroutine has to specify inside of its function exactly where it will give the execution flow back to the event loop (that is, the task-switching event). Futures are placeholder objects that contain the results obtained from the coroutines.

The `asyncio` module, together with the Python keywords `async` and `await`, provides an easy-to-use API and an intuitive framework to implement asynchronous programs; additionally, this framework makes the asynchronous code just as readable as synchronous code, which is generally quite rare in asynchronous programming. However, we cannot apply single-threaded asynchronous programming on blocking computing tasks with the `asyncio` module alone. The solution to this is the `concurrent.futures` module, which provides a high-level API to implement asynchronous threading and multiprocessing, and can be used in addition to the `asyncio` module.

In the next chapter, we will be discussing one of the most common applications of asynchronous programming, **Transmission Control Protocol** (**TCP**), as a means of server-client communication. You will learn about the basics of the concept, how it takes advantage of asynchronous programming, and how to implement it in Python.

Questions

- What is asynchronous programming? What advantages does it provide?
- What are the main elements in an asynchronous program? How do they interact with each other?
- What are the `async` and `await` keywords? What purposes do they serve?
- What options does the `asyncio` module provide, in terms of the implementation of asynchronous programming?
- What are the improvements in regards to asynchronous programming provided in Python 3.7?
- What are blocking functions? Why do they pose a problem for traditional asynchronous programming?
- How does `concurrent.futures` provide a solution to blocking functions for asynchronous programming? What options does it provide?

Further reading

For more information, you can refer to the following links:

- Zaccone, Giancarlo. *Python Parallel Programming Cookbook*. Packt Publishing Ltd, 2015
- *A guide to asynchronous programming in Python with asyncio* (`medium.freecodecamp.org/a-guide-to-asynchronous-programming-in-python-with-asyncio`), Mariia Yakimova
- *AsyncIO for the Working Python Developer* (`hackernoon.com/asyncio-for-the-working-python-developer`), Yeray Diaz
- Python Documentation. Tasks and coroutines. `docs.python.org/3/library/asyncio`
- *Modern Concurrency*, (`speakerdeck.com/pybay/2017-luciano-ramalho-modern-concurrency`), PyBay 2017

11
Building Communication Channels with asyncio

Communication channels are a big part of applied concurrency in the field of computer science. In this chapter, we will cover the fundamental theories of transports, which are classes provided by the `asyncio` module in order to abstract various forms of communication channels. We will also cover an implementation of a simple echoing server-client logic in Python, in order to further illustrate the use of `asyncio` and concurrency in communication systems. The code for this example will serve as the foundation for an advanced example that will appear later in this book.

The following topics will be covered in this chapter:

- The fundamentals of communication channels and applying asynchronous programming to them
- How to build an asynchronous server in Python by using `asyncio` and `aiohttp`
- How to make requests to multiple servers asynchronously and handle asynchronous file reading and writing

Technical requirements

The following is a list of prerequisites for this chapter:

- Ensure that you have Python 3 installed on your computer
- Ensure that you have Telnet installed on your computer
- Ensure that you have the Python module `aiohttp` installed with your Python 3 distribution
- Download the GitHub repository at `https://github.com/PacktPublishing/Mastering-Concurrency-in-Python`
- In this chapter, we will be working with the subfolder named `Chapter11`
- Check out the following video to see the Code in Action: `http://bit.ly/2FMwKL8`

The ecosystem of communication channels

Communication channels are used to denote both the physical wiring connection between different systems and the logical communication of data that facilitates computer networks. In this chapter, we will only be concerned with the latter, as it is a problem that is related to computing and is more germane to the idea of asynchronous programming. In this section, we will be discussing the general structure of a communication channel, and two specific elements in that structure that are particularly relevant to asynchronous programming.

Communication protocol layers

Most data transmission processes that are done through communication channels are facilitated in the form of the **Open Systems Interconnection** (**OSI**) model protocol layers. The OSI model lays out the major layers and topics in an intersystem communication process.

The following diagram shows the general structure of an OSI model:

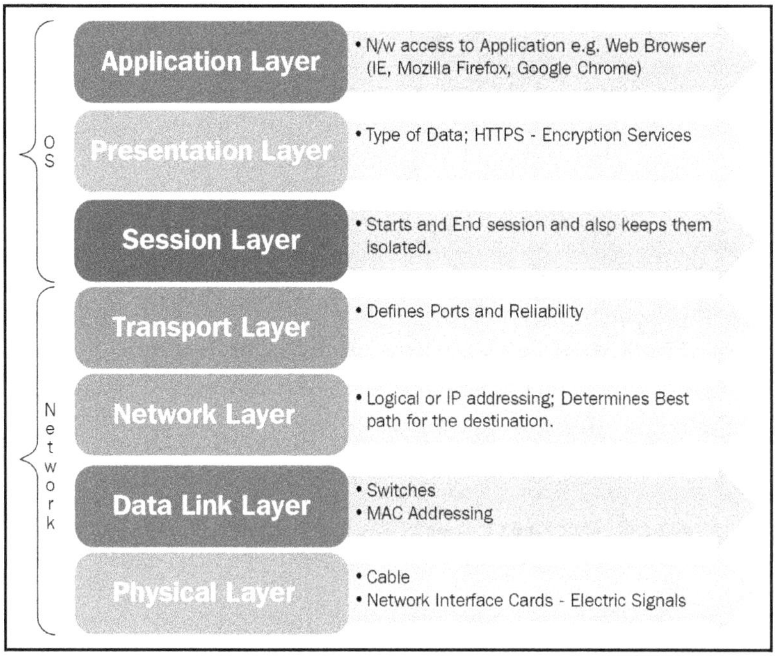

OSI model structure

As indicated in the preceding diagram, there are seven main layers of communication in a data transmission process, with varying degrees of computing level. We will not be going into the details of the purposes and specific functions of each layer, but it is still important that you understand the general ideas behind the media and host layers.

The three bottom layers contain fairly low-level operations that interact with the underlying process of the communication channel. The operations in the physical and data link layers include coding schemes, access schemes, low-level error detection and correction, bit synchronization, and so on. These operations are used to implement and specify the logic of processing and preparing data before transferring it. The network layer, on the other hand, handles forwarding packets of data from one system (for example, the server) to another (for example, the client) in a computer network, via determining the address of the recipient and which path of data transfer to take.

On the other hand, the top layers deal with high-level data communication and manipulation. Among these layers, we will be focusing on the transport layer, as it is directly utilized by the `asyncio` module in implementing communication channels. This layer is often viewed as the conceptual transition between the media layers and the host layers (for example, the client and the server), responsible for sending data along end-to-end connections between different systems. Additionally, because packets of data (prepared by the network layer) might be lost or corrupted during transmission processes due to network errors, the transport layer is also in charge of detecting these errors via methods in error detection code.

The other host layers implement mechanisms for handling, interpreting, and providing the data sent from another system. After receiving data from the transport layer, the session layer handles the authentication, authorization, and session restoration processes. The presentation layer then translates the same data and reorganizes it into an interpretable representation. Finally, the application layer displays that data in user-friendly formats.

Asynchronous programming for communication channels

Given the nature of asynchronous programming, it is no surprise that the programming model can provide functionalities that complement the process of facilitating communication channels efficiently. Using the topic of HTTP communication as an example, the server can asynchronously handle multiple clients at the same time; while it is waiting for a specific client to make an HTTP request, it can switch to another client and process that client's request. Similarly, if a client needs to make HTTP requests to multiple servers, and has to wait for large responses from some servers, it can process the more lightweight responses, which have already been processed and were sent back to the client first. The following diagram shows an example of how servers and clients interact with each other asynchronously in HTTP requests:

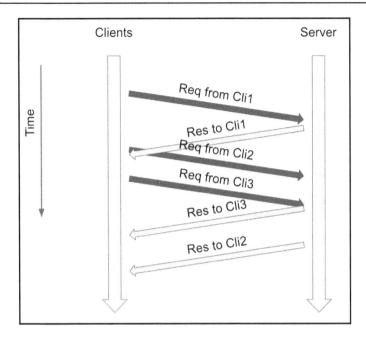

Asynchronous, interleaved HTTP requests

Transports and protocols in asyncio

The `asyncio` module provides a number of different transport classes. In essence, these classes are the implementations of the functionalities of the transport layer that were discussed in the preceding section. You already know that the transport layer plays an integral role in communication channels; the transport classes, therefore, give `asyncio` (and consequently, the developers) more control over the process of implementing our own communication channels.

The `asyncio` module combines the abstract of transports with the implementation of an asynchronous program. Specifically, even though transports are the central elements of communication channels, in order to utilize the transport classes and other relevant communication channel tools, we need to initiate and call an event loop, which is an instance of the `asyncio.AbstractEventLoop` class. The event loop itself will then create the transports and manage the low-level communication procedures.

It is important to note that a `transport` object in an established communication channel in `asyncio` is always associated with an instance of the `asyncio.Protocol` class. As the name suggests, the `Protocol` class specifies the underlying protocols that the communication channels use; for each connection made with another system, a new protocol object from this class will be created. While working closely with a `transport` object, a protocol object can call various methods from the `transport` object; this is the point where we can implement the specific inner workings of a communication channel.

For this reason, generally we need to focus on the implementation of an `asyncio.Protocol` subclass and its methods while building a connection channel. In other words, we use `asyncio.Protocol` as a parent class to derive a subclass that meets the needs of our communication channel. To do this, we overwrite the following methods from the `asyncio.Protocol` base class in our own custom protocol subclass:

- `Protocol.connection_made(transport)`: This method is automatically called whenever a connection from another system is made. The `transport` argument holds the `transport` object that is associated with the connection. Again, each `transport` needs to be paired with a protocol; we generally store this `transport` object as an attribute of this specific protocol object in the `connection_made()` method.
- `Protocol.data_received(data)`: This method is automatically called whenever the one system that we are connected to sends its data. Note that the `data` argument, which holds the sent information, is usually represented in bytes, so the `encode()` function of Python should be used before `data` is processed further.

Next, let us consider the important methods from the transport classes from `asyncio`. All transport classes inherit from a parent transport class, called `asyncio.BaseTransport`, for which we have the following common methods:

- `BaseTransport.get_extra_info()`: This method returns, as the name suggests, additional channel-specific information for the calling `transport` object. The result can include information regarding the socket, the pipe, and the subprocess associated with that transport. Later in this chapter, we will be calling `BaseTransport.get_extra_info('peername')`, in order to obtain the remote address from which the transport traveled.

- `BaseTransport.close()`: This method is used to close the calling `transport` object, after which the connections between different systems will be stopped. The corresponding protocol of the transport will automatically call its `connection_lost()` method.

Out of the many implementations of transport classes, we will focus on the `asyncio.WriteTransport` class, which again inherits the methods from the `BaseTransport` class, and additionally implements other methods that are used to facilitate write-only transport functionalities. Here, we will be using the `WriteTransport.write()` method, which will write the data that we would like to send to the other system that we communicate with via the `transport` object. As a part of the `asyncio` module, this method is not a blocking function; instead, it buffers and sends out the written data in an asynchronous way.

The big picture of asyncio's server client

You have learned that asynchronous programming, and `asyncio` specifically, can drastically improve the execution of your communication channels. You have also seen the specific methods that you will need to use when implementing an asynchronous communication channel. Before we dive into a working example in Python, let us briefly discuss the big picture of what we are trying to accomplish – or, in other words, the general structure of our program.

As mentioned earlier, we need to implement a subclass of `asyncio.Protocol` to specify the underlying organization of our communication channel. Again, there is an event loop at the heart of each asynchronous program, so we also need to create a server outside of the context of the protocol class, and initiate that server inside of the event loop of our program. This process will set up the asynchronous architecture of our entire server, and can be done via the `asyncio.create_server()` method, which we will look at in our upcoming example.

Finally, we will run the event loop of our asynchronous program forever by using the `AbstractEventLoop.run_forever()` method. Similar to an actual, real-life server, we would like to keep our sever running until it encounters a problem, in which case we will close the server gracefully. The following diagram illustrates this whole process:

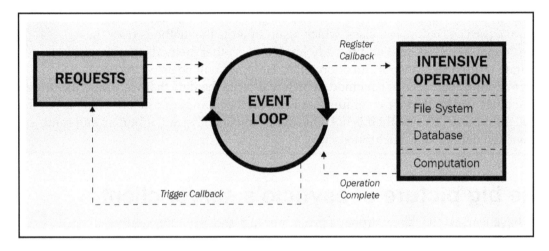

Asynchronous program structure in communication channels

Python example

Now, let us look at a specific Python example that implements a server that facilitates asynchronous communication. Download the code for this book from the GitHub page (`https://github.com/PacktPublishing/Mastering-Concurrency-in-Python`), and navigate to the `Chapter11` folder.

Starting a server

In the `Chapter11/example1.py` file, let's look at the `EchoServerClientProtocol` class, as follows:

```
# Chapter11/example1.py

import asyncio

class EchoServerClientProtocol(asyncio.Protocol):
    def connection_made(self, transport):
        peername = transport.get_extra_info('peername')
```

```
        print('Connection from {}'.format(peername))
        self.transport = transport

    def data_received(self, data):
        message = data.decode()
        print('Data received: {!r}'.format(message))
```

Here, our `EchoServerClientProtocol` class is a subclass of `asyncio.Protocol`. As we discussed earlier, inside of this class, we need to implement the `connection_made(transport)` and `data_received(data)` methods. In the `connection_made()` method, we simply obtain the address of the connected system via the `get_extra_info()` method (with the `'peername'` argument), print a message out with that information, and finally store the `transport` object in an attribute of the class. In order to print out a similar message in the `data_received()` method, again we use the `decode()` method to obtain a string object from byte data.

Let us move on to the main program of our script, as follows:

```
# Chapter11/example1.py

loop = asyncio.get_event_loop()
coro = loop.create_server(EchoServerClientProtocol, '127.0.0.1', 8888)
server = loop.run_until_complete(coro)

# Serve requests until Ctrl+C is pressed
print('Serving on {}'.format(server.sockets[0].getsockname()))
try:
    loop.run_forever()
except KeyboardInterrupt:
    pass

# Close the server
server.close()
loop.run_until_complete(server.wait_closed())
loop.close()
```

We are using the familiar `asyncio.get_event_loop()` function to create an event loop for our asynchronous program. Then, we create a server for our communication by having that event loop call the `create_server()` method; this method takes in a subclass from the `asyncio.Protocol` class, an address for our server (in this case, it is our local host: `127.0.0.1`), and finally, a port for that address (typically, `8888`).

Note that this method does not create the server itself; it only initiates the process of creating the server asynchronously, and returns a coroutine that will finish the process. For this reason, we need to store the returned coroutine from the method in a variable (`coro`, in our case) and have our event loop run that coroutine. After printing out a message using the `sockets` attribute of our server object, we will run the event loop forever, in order to keep the server running, except for the case of a `KeyboardInterrupt` exception being invoked.

Finally, at the end of our program, we will handle the house cleaning portion of the script, which is closing the server gracefully. This is typically done by having the server object call the `close()` method (to initiate the closing process of the server) and using the event loop to run the `wait_closed()` method on the server object, to make sure that the server is properly closed. Finally, we close the event loop.

Installing Telnet

Before we can run our sample Python program, we have to install the Telnet program, in order to correctly simulate a connection channel between a client and a server. Telnet is a program that provides Terminal commands that facilitate protocols for bidirectional, interactive, text-oriented communication. If you already have Telnet working on your computer, simply skip to the next section; otherwise, find the information appropriate to your system in this section.

In Windows systems, Telnet is already installed, but might not be enabled. To enable it, you can either utilize the **Turn Windows features on or off** window and make sure that the **Telnet Client** box is checked, or run the following command:

```
dism /online /Enable-Feature /FeatureName:TelnetClient
```

Linux systems typically come with Telnet preinstalled, so if you own a Linux system, simply move on to the next section.

In macOS systems, it is possible that Telnet has already been installed on your computer. If not, you will need to do it via the package management software Homebrew, as follows:

```
brew install telnet
```

Note that macOS systems do have a preinstalled alternative to Telnet, called Netcat. If you do not want Telnet installed on your macOS computer, simply use the `nc` command instead of `telnet` in the following examples, and you will achieve the same effect.

Simulating a connection channel

There are multiple steps to running the following server example. First, we need to run the script to start the server, from which you will obtain the following output:

```
> python example1.py
Serving on ('127.0.0.1', 8888)
```

Notice that the program will run until you invoke the *Ctrl + C* key combination. With the program still running in one Terminal (this is our server Terminal), open another Terminal and connect to the server (127.0.0.1) at the specified port (8888); this will server as our client Terminal:

```
telnet 127.0.0.1 8888
```

Now, you will see some changes in both the server and the client Terminals. Most likely, your client Terminal will have the following output:

```
> telnet 127.0.0.1 8888
Trying 127.0.0.1...
Connected to localhost.
```

This is from the interface of the Telnet program, which indicates that we have successfully connected to our local server. The more interesting output is on our server Terminal, and it will be similar to the following:

```
> python example1.py
Serving on ('127.0.0.1', 8888)
Connection from ('127.0.0.1', 60332)
```

Recall that this is an information message that we implemented in our `EchoServerClientProtocol` class—specifically in the `connection_made()` method. Again, as a connection between the server and a new client is made, this method will be called automatically, in order to initiate the communication. From the output message, we know that the client is making their requests from port `60332` of server `127.0.0.1` (which is the same as the running server, since they are both local).

Another feature that we implemented in the `EchoServerClientProtocol` class was in the `data_received()` method. Specifically, we print the decoded data that is sent from the client. To simulate this type of communication, simply type a message in your client Terminal and press the *Return* (*Enter*, for Windows) key. You will not see any changes in the client Terminal output, but the server Terminal should print out a message, as specified in the `data_received()` method of our protocol class.

For example, the following is my server Terminal output when I send the message `Hello, World!` from my client Terminal:

```
> python example1.py
Serving on ('127.0.0.1', 8888)
Connection from ('127.0.0.1', 60332)
Data received: 'Hello, World!\r\n'
```

The \r and \n characters are simply the return characters included in the message string. With our current protocol, you can send multiple messages to the server, and can even have multiple clients send messages to the server. To implement this, simply open another Terminal and connect to the local server again. You will see from your server Terminal that a different client (from a different port) has made a connection to the server, while the original communication of our server with the old client is still being maintained. This is another result achieved from asynchronous programming, allowing multiple clients to communicate with the same server seamlessly, without using threading or multiprocessing.

Sending messages back to clients

So, in our current example, we are able to have our asynchronous server receive, read, and process messages from clients. However, in order for our communication channel to be useful, we would also like to send messages from the server to the clients. In this section, we will update our server to an echo server, which, by definition, will send any and all data that it receives from a specific client back to the client.

To do this, we will be using the `write()` method from the `asyncio.WriteTransport` class. Examine the `Chapter11/example2.py` file, in the `data_received()` method of the `EchoServerClientProtocol` class, as follows:

```
# Chapter11/example2.py

import asyncio

class EchoServerClientProtocol(asyncio.Protocol):
    def connection_made(self, transport):
        peername = transport.get_extra_info('peername')
        print('Connection from {}'.format(peername))
        self.transport = transport

    def data_received(self, data):
        message = data.decode()
        print('Data received: {!r}'.format(message))

        self.transport.write(('Echoed back: {}'.format(message)).encode())
```

```
loop = asyncio.get_event_loop()
coro = loop.create_server(EchoServerClientProtocol, '127.0.0.1', 8888)
server = loop.run_until_complete(coro)

# Serve requests until Ctrl+C is pressed
print('Serving on {}'.format(server.sockets[0].getsockname()))
try:
    loop.run_forever()
except KeyboardInterrupt:
    pass

# Close the server
server.close()
loop.run_until_complete(server.wait_closed())
loop.close()
```

After receiving the data from the `transport` object and printing it out, we write a corresponding message to the `transport` object, which will go back to the original client. By running the `Chapter11/example2.py` script and simulating the same communication that we implemented in the last example with Telnet or Netcat, you will see that after typing a message in the client Terminal, the client receives an echoed message from the server. The following is my output after initiating the communication channel and typing in the `Hello, World!` message:

```
> telnet 127.0.0.1 8888
Trying 127.0.0.1...
Connected to localhost.
Hello, World!
Echoed back: Hello, World!
```

In essence, this example illustrates the capability of a bidirectional communication channel that we can implement through a custom `asyncio.Protocol` class. While running a server, we can obtain data sent from various clients connected to the server, process the data, and finally send the desired result back to the appropriate clients.

Closing the transports

Occasionally, we will want to forcefully close a transport in a communication channel. For example, even with asynchronous programming and other forms of concurrency, it is possible for your server to be overwhelmed with constant communications from multiple clients. On the other hand, it is undesirable to have the server completely handle some of the sent requests and plainly reject the rest of the requests as soon as the server is at its maximum capacity.

So, instead of keeping the communication open for each and every client connected to the server, we can specify in our protocol that each connection should be closed after a successful communication. We will do this by using the `BaseTransport.close()` method to forcefully close the calling `transport` object, which will stop the connection between the server and that specific client. Again, we are modifying the `data_received()` method of the `EchoServerClientProtocol` class in `Chapter11/example3.py`, as follows:

```
# Chapter11/example3.py

import asyncio

class EchoServerClientProtocol(asyncio.Protocol):
    def connection_made(self, transport):
        peername = transport.get_extra_info('peername')
        print('Connection from {}'.format(peername))
        self.transport = transport

    def data_received(self, data):
        message = data.decode()
        print('Data received: {!r}'.format(message))

        self.transport.write(('Echoed back: {}'.format(message)).encode())

        print('Close the client socket')
        self.transport.close()

loop = asyncio.get_event_loop()
coro = loop.create_server(EchoServerClientProtocol, '127.0.0.1', 8888)
server = loop.run_until_complete(coro)

# Serve requests until Ctrl+C is pressed
print('Serving on {}'.format(server.sockets[0].getsockname()))
try:
    loop.run_forever()
except KeyboardInterrupt:
    pass

# Close the server
server.close()
loop.run_until_complete(server.wait_closed())
loop.close()
```

Run the script, try to connect to the specified server, and type in some messages, in order to see the changes that we implemented. With our current setup, after a client connects and sends a message to the server, it will receive an echoed message back, and its connection with the server will be closed. The following is the output (again, from the interface of the Telnet program) that I obtained after simulating this process with our current implementation of the protocol:

```
> telnet 127.0.0.1 8888
Trying 127.0.0.1...
Connected to localhost.
Hello, World!
Echoed back: Hello, World!
Connection closed by foreign host.
```

Client-side communication with aiohttp

In previous sections, we covered examples of implementing asynchronous communication channels with the `asyncio` module, mostly from the perspective of the server side of the communication process. In other words, we have been considering handling and processing requests sent from external systems. This, however, is only one side of the equation, and we also have the client side of communication to explore. In this section, we will discuss applying asynchronous programming to make requests to servers.

As you have most likely guessed, the end goal of this process is to efficiently collect data from external systems by asynchronously making requests to those systems. We will be revisiting the concept of web scraping, which is the process of automating HTTP requests to various websites and extracting specific information from their HTML source code. If you have not read Chapter 5, *Concurrent Web Requests*, I highly recommend going through it before proceeding with this section, as that chapter covers the foundational ideas of web scraping, and other relevant, important concepts.

In this section, you will also be introduced to another module that supports asynchronous programming options: `aiohttp` (which stands for **Asynchronous I/O HTTP**). This module provides high-level functionalities that streamline HTTP communication procedures, and it also works seamlessly with the `asyncio` module, in order to facilitate asynchronous programming.

Installing aiohttp and aiofiles

The `aiohttp` module does not come preinstalled with your Python distribution; however, similarly to other packages, you can easily install the module by using the `pip` or `conda` commands. We will also be installing another module, `aiofiles`, which facilitates asynchronous file-writing. If you use `pip` as your package manager, simply run the following commands:

```
pip install aiohttp
pip install aiofiles
```

If you'd like to use Anaconda, run the following commands:

```
conda install aiohttp
conda install aiofiles
```

As always, to confirm that you have successfully installed a package, open your Python interpreter and try to import the module. In this case, run the following code:

```
>>> import aiohttp
>>> import aiofiles
```

There will be no error messages if the package has been successfully installed.

Fetching a website's HTML code

First, let's look at how to make a request and obtain the HTML source code from a single website with `aiohttp`. Note that even with only one task (a website), our application remains asynchronous, and the structure of an asynchronous program still needs to be implemented. Now, navigate to the `Chapter11/example4.py` file, as follows:

```
# Chapter11/example4.py

import aiohttp
import asyncio

async def get_html(session, url):
    async with session.get(url, ssl=False) as res:
        return await res.text()

async def main():
    async with aiohttp.ClientSession() as session:
        html = await get_html(session, 'http://packtpub.com')
        print(html)
```

```
loop = asyncio.get_event_loop()
loop.run_until_complete(main())
```

Let's consider the `main()` coroutine first. We are initiating an instance from the `aiohttp.ClientSession` class within a context manager; note that we are also placing the `async` keyword in front of this declaration, since the whole context block itself will also be treated as a coroutine. Inside of this block, we are calling and waiting for the `get_html()` coroutine to process and return.

Turning our attention to the `get_html()` coroutine, we can see that it takes in a session object and a URL for the website that we want to extract the HTML source code from. Inside of this function, we make another context manager asynchronous, which is used to make a `GET` request and store the response from the server to the `res` variable. Finally, we return the HTML source code stored in the response; since the response is an object returned from the `aiohttp.ClientSession` class, its methods are asynchronous functions, and therefore we need to specify the `await` keyword when we call the `text()` function.

As you run the program, the entire HTML source code of Packt's website will be printed out. For example, the following is a portion of my output:

HTML source code from aiohttp

Writing files asynchronously

Most of the time, we would like to collect data by making requests to multiple websites, and simply printing out the response HTML code is inappropriate (for many reasons); instead, we'd like to write the returned HTML code to output files. In essence, this process is asynchronous downloading, which is also implemented in the underlying architecture of popular download managers. To do this, we will use the `aiofiles` module, in combination with `aiohttp` and `asyncio`.

Navigate to the `Chapter11/example5.py` file. First, we will look at the `download_html()` coroutine, as follows:

```
# Chapter11/example5.py

async def download_html(session, url):
    async with session.get(url, ssl=False) as res:
        filename = f'output/{os.path.basename(url)}.html'

        async with aiofiles.open(filename, 'wb') as f:
            while True:
                chunk = await res.content.read(1024)
                if not chunk:
                    break
                await f.write(chunk)

        return await res.release()
```

This is an updated version of the `get_html()` coroutine from the last example. Instead of using an `aiohttp.ClientSession` instance to make a `GET` request and print out the returned HTML code, now we write the HTML code to the file using the `aiofiles` module. For example, to facilitate asynchronous file writing, we use the asynchronous `open()` function from `aiofiles` to read in a file in a context manager. Furthermore, we read the returned HTML in chunks, asynchronously, using the `read()` function for the `content` attribute of the response object; this means that after reading `1024` bytes of the current response, the execution flow will be released back to the event loop, and the task-switching event will take place.

The `main()` coroutine and the main program of this example remain relatively the same as those in our last example:

```
async def main(url):
    async with aiohttp.ClientSession() as session:
        await download_html(session, url)

urls = [
    'http://packtpub.com',
    'http://python.org',
    'http://docs.python.org/3/library/asyncio',
    'http://aiohttp.readthedocs.io',
    'http://google.com'
]

loop = asyncio.get_event_loop()
loop.run_until_complete(
    asyncio.gather(*(main(url) for url in urls))
)
```

The `main()` coroutine takes in a URL and passes it to the `download_html()` coroutine, along with an `aiohttp.ClientSession` instance. Finally, in our main program, we create an event loop and pass each item in a specified list of URLs to the `main()` coroutine. After running the program, your output should look similar to the following, although the time it takes to run the program might vary:

```
> python3 example5.py
Took 0.72 seconds.
```

Additionally, a subfolder named `output` (inside of the `Chapter11` folder) will be filled with the downloaded HTML code from each website in our list of URLs. Again, these files were created and written asynchronously, via the functionalities of the `aiofiles` module, which we discussed earlier. As you can see, to compare the speed of this program and its corresponding synchronous version, we are also keeping track of the time it takes to run the entire program.

Now, head to the `Chapter11/example6.py` file. This script contains the code of the synchronous version of our current program. Specifically, it makes HTTP `GET` requests to individual websites in order, and the process of file writing is also implemented sequentially. This script produced the following output:

```
> python3 example6.py
Took 1.47 seconds.
```

While it achieved the same results (downloading the HTML code and writing it to files), our sequential program took significantly more time than its asynchronous counterpart.

Summary

There are seven main layers of communication in a data transmission process, with varying degrees of computing level. The media layers contain fairly low-level operations that interact with the underlying process of the communication channel, while the host layers deals with high-level data communication and manipulation. Of the seven, the transport layer is often viewed as the conceptual transition between the media layers and the host layers, responsible for sending data along end-to-end connections between different systems. Asynchronous programming can provide functionalities that complement the process of efficiently facilitating communication channels.

Server-wise, the `asyncio` module combines the abstract of transports with the implementation of an asynchronous program. Specifically, via its `BaseTransport` and `BaseProtocol` classes, `asyncio` provides different ways to customize the underlying architecture of a communication channel. Together with the `aiohttp` module, `asyncio` offers efficiency and flexibility regarding client-side communication processes. The `aiofiles` module, which can work in conjunction with the other two asynchronous programming modules, can also help to facilitate asynchronous file reading and writing.

We have now explored three of the biggest, most important topics in concurrent programming: threading, multiprocessing, and asynchronous programming. We have shown how each of them can be applied to various programming problems and provide significant improvements in speed. In the next chapter of this book, we will start to discuss problems that concurrent programming commonly poses to developers and programmers, starting with deadlocks.

Questions

- What is a communication channel? What is its connection to asynchronous programming?
- What are the two main parts of the OSI model protocol layers? What purposes do each of them serve?
- What is the transport layer? Why is it crucial to communication channels?
- How does `asyncio` facilitate the implementation of server-side communication channels?
- How does `asyncio` facilitate the implementation of client-side communication channels?
- What is `aiofiles`?

Further reading

For more information, you can refer to the following links:

- *IoT Systems and Communication Channels* (`bridgera.com/iot-communication-channels/`), by Bridgera
- *Automate the boring stuff with Python: practical programming for total beginners*, No Starch Press, Al. Sweigart
- *Transports and protocols* (`docs.python.org/3/library/asyncio-protocol`), Python documentation

12
Deadlocks

Deadlocks, one of the most common concurrency problems, will be the first problem that we analyze in this book. In this chapter, we will discuss the theoretical causes of deadlocks in concurrent programming. We will cover a classical synchronization problem in concurrency, called the Dining Philosophers problem, as a real-life example of deadlock. We will also illustrate an actual implementation of deadlock in Python. We will discuss several methods to address the problem. This chapter will also cover the concept of livelock, which is relevant to deadlock and is a relatively common problem in concurrent programming.

The following topics will be covered in this chapter:

- The idea behind deadlock, and how to simulate it in Python
- Common solutions to deadlock, and how to implement them in Python
- The concept of livelock, and its connection to deadlock

Technical requirements

The following is a list of prerequisites for this chapter:

- Ensure that you have Python 3 installed on your computer
- Download the GitHub repository at `https://github.com/PacktPublishing/Mastering-Concurrency-in-Python`
- In this chapter, we will be working with the subfolder titled `Chapter12`
- Check out the following video to see the Code in Action: `http://bit.ly/2r2WKaU`

The concept of deadlock

In the field of computer science, deadlock refers to a specific situation in concurrent programming, in which no progress can be made and the program becomes locked in its current state. In most cases, this phenomenon is caused by a lack of, or mishandled, coordination between different lock objects (for thread synchronization purposes). In this section, we will discuss a thought experiment commonly known as the Dining Philosophers problem, in order to illustrate the concept of deadlock and its causes; from there, you will learn how to simulate the problem in a Python concurrent program.

The Dining Philosophers problem

The Dining Philosophers problem was first introduced by Edgar Dijkstra (who, as you learned in `Chapter 1`, *Advanced Introduction to Concurrent and Parallel Programming* was a leading pioneer in concurrent programming) in 1965. The problem was first demonstrated using different technical terms (resource contention in computer systems), and was later rephrased by Tony Hoare, a British computer scientist and the inventor of the quicksort sorting algorithm. The problem statement is as follows.

Five philosophers sit around a table, and each has a bowl of food in front of them. Placed between these five bowls of food are five forks, so each philosopher has a fork on their left side, and one on their right side. This setup is demonstrated by the following diagram:

An illustration of the Dining Philosophers problem

Each silent philosopher is to alternate between thinking and eating. Each philosopher is required to have both of the forks around them to be able to pick up the food from their individual bowl, and no fork can be shared between two or more different philosophers. When a philosopher finishes eating a specific amount of food, they are to place both of the forks back in their respective, original locations. At this point, the philosophers around that philosopher will be able to use those forks.

Since the philosophers are silent and cannot communicate with each other, they have no method to let each other know they need the forks to eat. In other words, the only way for a philosopher to eat is to have both of the forks already available to them. The question of this problem is to design a set of instructions for the philosophers to efficiently switch between eating and thinking, so that each philosopher is provided with enough food.

Now, a potential approach to this problem would be the following set of instructions:

1. A philosopher must think until the fork on their left side becomes available. When that happens, the philosopher is to pick it up.
2. A philosopher must think until the fork on their right side becomes available. When that happens, the philosopher is to pick it up.
3. If a philosopher is holding two forks, they will eat a specific amount of food from the bowl in front of them, and then the following will apply:
   - Afterwards, the philosopher has to put the right fork down in its original place
   - Afterwards, the philosopher has to put the left fork down in its original place
4. The process repeats from the first bullet point.

It is quite clear how this set of instructions can lead to a situation where no progress can be made; namely, if at the beginning, all of the philosophers start to execute their instructions at the same time. Since all of the forks are on the table at the beginning, and are therefore available to be picked up by nearby philosophers, each philosopher will be able to execute the first instruction (picking up the fork on their left side).

Now, after this step, each philosopher will be holding a fork with their left hand, and no forks will be left on the table. Since no philosopher has both forks in their hands, they cannot proceed to eat their food. Furthermore, the set of instructions that they were given specifies that only after a philosopher has eaten a specific amount of food can they put their forks down on the table. This means that as long as a philosopher has not eaten, they will not release any fork that they are holding.

So, as each philosopher is holding only one fork with their left hand, they cannot proceed to eat or put down the fork they are holding. The only time a philosopher gets to eat their food is when their neighboring philosopher puts their fork down, which is only possible if they can eat their own food; this creates a never-ending circle of conditions that can never be satisfied. This situation is, in essence, the nature of a deadlock, in which all of the elements of a system are stuck in place, and no progress can be made.

Deadlock in a concurrent system

With the example of the Dining Philosophers problem in mind, let us consider the formal concept of deadlock, and the relevant theories around it. Given a concurrent program with multiple threads or processes, the execution flow enters a situation of deadlock if a process (or thread) is waiting on a resource that is being held and utilized by another process, which is, in turn, waiting for another resource that is held by a different process. In other words, processes cannot proceed with their execution instructions while waiting for resources that can only be released after the execution is completed; therefore, these processes are unable to change their execution states.

Deadlock is also defined by the conditions that a concurrent program needs to have at the same time in order for deadlock to occur. These conditions were first proposed by the computer scientist Edward G. Coffman, Jr., and are therefore known as the Coffman conditions. These conditions are as follows:

- At least one resource has to be in a non-shareable state. This means that that resource is being held by an individual process (or thread), and cannot be accessed by others; the resource can only be accessed and held by a single process (or thread) at any given time. This condition is also known as mutual exclusion.
- There exists one process (or thread) that is simultaneously accessing a resource and waiting for another held by other processes (or threads). In other words, this process (or thread) needs access to two resources in order to execute its instructions, one of which it is already holding, the other of which it is waiting for from other processes (or threads). This condition is called hold and wait.
- Resources can only be released by a process (or a thread) holding them if there are specific instructions for the process (or thread) to do so. This is to say that unless the process (or thread) voluntarily and actively releases the resource, that resource remains in a non-shareable state. This is the no preemption condition.
- The final condition is called circular wait. As suggested by the name, this condition specifies that there exists a set of processes (or threads) such that the first process (or thread) in the set is in a waiting state for a resource to be released by the second process (or thread), which, in turn, needs to be waiting for the third process (or thread); finally, the last process (or thread) in the set is waiting for the first one.

Let us quickly take a look at a basic example of deadlock. Consider a concurrent program in which there are two different processes (process **A** and process **B**), and two different resources (resource **R1** and resource **R2**), as follows:

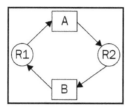

Sample deadlock diagram

Neither of the resources can be shared across separate processes, and each process needs to access both resources to execute its instructions. Take process **A**, for example. It is already holding resource **R1**, but its also needs **R2** to proceed with its execution. However, **R2** cannot be acquired by process **A**, as it is being held by process **B**. So, process **A** cannot proceed. The same goes for process **B**, which is holding **R2** and needs **R1** to proceed. **R1** is, in turn, held by process **A**.

Python simulation

In this section, we will implement the preceding situation in an actual Python program. Specifically, we will have two locks (we will call them lock A and lock B), and two separate threads interacting with the locks (thread A and thread B). In our program, we will set up a situation in which thread A has acquired lock A and is waiting to acquire lock B, which has already been acquired by thread B, which is, in turn, waiting for lock A to be released.

If you have already downloaded the code for this book from the GitHub page, go ahead and navigate to the `Chapter12` folder. Let us consider the `Chapter12/example1.py` file, as follows:

```
# Chapter12/example1.py

import threading
import time

def thread_a():
    print('Thread A is starting...')

    print('Thread A waiting to acquire lock A.')
    lock_a.acquire()
    print('Thread A has acquired lock A, performing some calculation...')
```

```
    time.sleep(2)

    print('Thread A waiting to acquire lock B.')
    lock_b.acquire()
    print('Thread A has acquired lock B, performing some calculation...')
    time.sleep(2)

    print('Thread A releasing both locks.')
    lock_a.release()
    lock_b.release()

def thread_b():
    print('Thread B is starting...')

    print('Thread B waiting to acquire lock B.')
    lock_b.acquire()
    print('Thread B has acquired lock B, performing some calculation...')
    time.sleep(5)

    print('Thread B waiting to acquire lock A.')
    lock_a.acquire()
    print('Thread B has acquired lock A, performing some calculation...')
    time.sleep(5)

    print('Thread B releasing both locks.')
    lock_b.release()
    lock_a.release()

lock_a = threading.Lock()
lock_b = threading.Lock()

thread1 = threading.Thread(target=thread_a)
thread2 = threading.Thread(target=thread_b)

thread1.start()
thread2.start()

thread1.join()
thread2.join()

print('Finished.')
```

In this script, the `thread_a()` and `thread_b()` functions specify our thread A and thread B, respectively. In our main program, we also have two `threading.Lock` objects: lock A and lock B. The general structure of the thread instructions is as follows:

1. Start the thread
2. Try to acquire the lock with the same name as the thread (thread A will try to acquire lock A, and thread B will try to acquire lock B)
3. Perform some calculations
4. Try to acquire the other lock (thread A will try to acquire lock B, and thread B will try to acquire lock A)
5. Perform some other calculations
6. Release both locks
7. End the thread

Note that we are using the `time.sleep()` function to simulate the action of some calculations being processed.

First of all, we are starting both thread A and thread B almost simultaneously, within the main program. With the structure of the thread instruction set in mind, we can see that at this point, both threads will be initiated; thread A will try to acquire lock A, and will succeed in doing so, since lock A is still available at this point. The same goes for thread B and lock B. The two threads will then go on to perform some calculations on their own.

Let us consider the current state of our program: lock A has been acquired by thread A, and lock B has been acquired by thread B. After their respective calculation processes are complete, thread A will then try to acquire lock B, and thread B will try to acquire lock A. We can easily see that this is the beginning of our deadlock situation: since lock B is already being held by thread B, and cannot be acquired by thread A, thread B, for the same reason, cannot acquire lock A.

Both of the threads will now wait infinitely, in order to acquire their respective second lock. However, the only way a lock can be released is for a thread to continue its execution instructions and release all of the locks it has at the end. Our program will therefore be stuck in its execution at this point, and no further progress will be made.

The following diagram further illustrates the process of how the deadlock unfolds, in sequence:

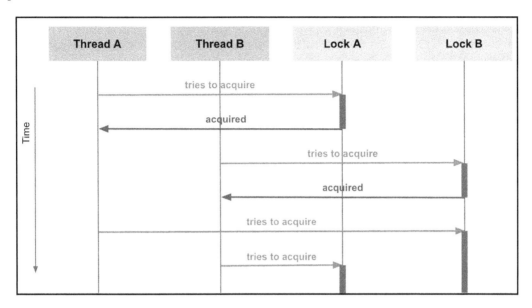

Deadlock sequence diagram

Now, let's see the deadlock that we have created in action. Run the script, and you should obtain the following output:

```
> python example1.py
Thread A is starting...
Thread A waiting to acquire lock A.
Thread B is starting...
Thread A has acquired lock A, performing some calculation...
Thread B waiting to acquire lock B.
Thread B has acquired lock B, performing some calculation...
Thread A waiting to acquire lock B.
Thread B waiting to acquire lock A.
```

As we discussed, since each thread is trying to acquire a lock that is currently held by the other thread, and the only way for a lock to be released is for a thread to continue its execution. This is a deadlock, and your program will hang infinitely, never reaching the final print statement in the last line of the program.

Approaches to deadlock situations

As we have seen, deadlock can lead our concurrent programs to an infinite hang, which is undesirable in every way. In this section, we will be discussing potential approaches to prevent deadlocks from occurring. Intuitively, each approach looks to eliminate one of the four Coffman conditions from our program, in order to prevent deadlocks.

Implementing ranking among resources

From both the Dining Philosophers problem and our Python example, we can see that the last condition of the four Coffman conditions, circular wait, is at the heart of the problem of deadlock. It specifies that the different processes (or threads) in our concurrent program wait for resources held by other processes (or threads) in a circular manner. Giving this a closer look, we can see that the root cause for this condition is the order (or lack thereof) in which the processes (or threads) access the resources.

In the Dining Philosophers problem, each philosopher is instructed to pick up the fork on their left side first, while in our Python example, the threads always try to acquire the locks with the same name before performing any calculations. As you have seen, when the philosophers want to start eating at the same time, they will pick up their respective left forks, and will be stuck in an infinite wait; similarly, when the two threads start their execution at the same time, they will acquire their individual locks, and, again, they will wait for the other locks infinitely.

The conclusion that we can infer from this is that if, instead of accessing the resources arbitrarily, the processes (or threads) were to access them in a predetermined, static order, the circular nature of the way that they acquire and wait for the resources will be eliminated. So, for our two-lock Python example, instead of having thread A try to acquire lock A and thread B try to acquire lock B in their respective execution instructions, we will require that both threads try to acquire the locks in the same order. For example, both threads will now try to acquire lock A first, perform some calculations, try to acquire lock B, perform further calculations, and finally, release both threads.

This change is implemented in the `Chapter12/example2.py` file, as follows:

```
# Chapter12/example2.py

import threading
import time

def thread_a():
    print('Thread A is starting...')
```

```
    print('Thread A waiting to acquire lock A.')
    lock_a.acquire()
    print('Thread A has acquired lock A, performing some calculation...')
    time.sleep(2)

    print('Thread A waiting to acquire lock B.')
    lock_b.acquire()
    print('Thread A has acquired lock B, performing some calculation...')
    time.sleep(2)

    print('Thread A releasing both locks.')
    lock_a.release()
    lock_b.release()

def thread_b():
    print('Thread B is starting...')

    print('Thread B waiting to acquire lock A.')
    lock_a.acquire()
    print('Thread B has acquired lock A, performing some calculation...')
    time.sleep(5)

    print('Thread B waiting to acquire lock B.')
    lock_b.acquire()
    print('Thread B has acquired lock B, performing some calculation...')
    time.sleep(5)

    print('Thread B releasing both locks.')
    lock_b.release()
    lock_a.release()

lock_a = threading.Lock()
lock_b = threading.Lock()

thread1 = threading.Thread(target=thread_a)
thread2 = threading.Thread(target=thread_b)

thread1.start()
thread2.start()

thread1.join()
thread2.join()

print('Finished.')
```

This version of the script is now able to finish its execution, and should produce the following output:

```
> python3 example2.py
Thread A is starting...
Thread A waiting to acquire lock A.
Thread A has acquired lock A, performing some calculation...
Thread B is starting...
Thread B waiting to acquire lock A.
Thread A waiting to acquire lock B.
Thread A has acquired lock B, performing some calculation...
Thread A releasing both locks.
Thread B has acquired lock A, performing some calculation...
Thread B waiting to acquire lock B.
Thread B has acquired lock B, performing some calculation...
Thread B releasing both locks.
Finished.
```

This approach efficiently eliminates the problem of deadlock in our two-lock example, but how well does it hold up for the Dining Philosophers problem? To answer this question, let's try to simulate the problem and the solution in Python by ourselves. The Chapter12/example3.py file contains the implementation of the Dining Philosophers problem in Python, as follows:

```
# Chapter12/example3.py

import threading

# The philosopher thread
def philosopher(left, right):
    while True:
        with left:
            with right:
                print(f'Philosopher at {threading.currentThread()}
                    is eating.')

# The chopsticks
N_FORKS = 5
forks = [threading.Lock() for n in range(N_FORKS)]

# Create all of the philosophers
phils = [threading.Thread(
    target=philosopher,
    args=(forks[n], forks[(n + 1) % N_FORKS])
) for n in range(N_FORKS)]

# Run all of the philosophers
```

```
for p in phils:
    p.start()
```

Here, we have the `philospher()` function as the underlying logic for our separate threads. It takes in two `Threading.Lock` objects and simulates the previously discussed eating procedure, with two context managers. In our main program, we create a list of five lock objects, named `forks`, and a list of five threads, named `phils`, with the specification that the first thread will take in the first and second locks, the second thread will take in the second and third locks, and so on; and the fifth thread will take in the fifth and first locks (in order). Finally, we start all five threads simultaneously.

Run the script, and it can easily be observed that deadlock occurs almost immediately. The following is my output, up until the program hangs infinitely:

```
> python3 example3.py
Philosopher at <Thread(Thread-1, started 123145445048320)> is eating.
Philosopher at <Thread(Thread-1, started 123145445048320)> is eating.
Philosopher at <Thread(Thread-1, started 123145445048320)> is eating.
Philosopher at <Thread(Thread-1, started 123145445048320)> is eating.
Philosopher at <Thread(Thread-1, started 123145445048320)> is eating.
Philosopher at <Thread(Thread-1, started 123145445048320)> is eating.
Philosopher at <Thread(Thread-3, started 123145455558656)> is eating.
Philosopher at <Thread(Thread-1, started 123145445048320)> is eating.
Philosopher at <Thread(Thread-3, started 123145455558656)> is eating.
Philosopher at <Thread(Thread-3, started 123145455558656)> is eating.
Philosopher at <Thread(Thread-3, started 123145455558656)> is eating.
Philosopher at <Thread(Thread-3, started 123145455558656)> is eating.
Philosopher at <Thread(Thread-5, started 123145466068992)> is eating.
Philosopher at <Thread(Thread-3, started 123145455558656)> is eating.
Philosopher at <Thread(Thread-3, started 123145455558656)> is eating.
```

The question that naturally follows is: how can we implement an order in which the locks are acquired in the `philosopher()` function? We will be using the built-in `id()` function in Python, which returns the unique, constant identity of the parameter, as the keys to sort the lock objects. We will also implement a custom context manager, in order to factor out this sorting logic in a separate class. Navigate to `Chapter12/example4.py` for this specific implementation, as follows:

```
# Chapter12/example4.py

class acquire(object):
    def __init__(self, *locks):
        self.locks = sorted(locks, key=lambda x: id(x))

    def __enter__(self):
        for lock in self.locks:
```

```
                lock.acquire()

    def __exit__(self, ty, val, tb):
        for lock in reversed(self.locks):
            lock.release()
        return False

# The philosopher thread
def philosopher(left, right):
    while True:
        with acquire(left,right):
            print(f'Philosopher at {threading.currentThread()}
                is eating.')
```

With the main program remaining in the same, this script will produce an output showing that this solution of ranking can effectively address the Dining Philosophers problem.

However, there is a problem with this approach when it is applied to some particular cases. Keeping the high-level idea of concurrency in mind, we know that one of our main goals when applying concurrency to our programs is to improve the speed. Let us go back to our two-lock example and examine the execution time of our program with resource ranking implemented. Take a look at the `Chapter12/example5.py` file; it is simply the two-lock program with ranked (or ordered) locking implemented, combined with a timer that is added to keep track of how much time it takes for the two threads to finish executing.

After running the script, your output should look similar to the following:

```
> python3 example5.py
Thread A is starting...
Thread A waiting to acquire lock A.
Thread B is starting...
Thread A has acquired lock A, performing some calculation...
Thread B waiting to acquire lock A.
Thread A waiting to acquire lock B.
Thread A has acquired lock B, performing some calculation...
Thread A releasing both locks.
Thread B has acquired lock A, performing some calculation...
Thread B waiting to acquire lock B.
Thread B has acquired lock B, performing some calculation...
Thread B releasing both locks.
Took 14.01 seconds.
Finished.
```

You can see that the combined execution of both threads took around 14 seconds. However, if we take a closer look at the specific instructions in the two threads, we can see that aside from interacting with the locks, thread A would take around 4 seconds to do its calculations (simulated by two `time.sleep(2)` commands), while thread B would take around 10 seconds (two `time.sleep(5)` commands).

Does this mean that our program is taking as long as it would if we were to execute the two threads sequentially? We will test this theory with our `Chapter12/example6.py` file, in which we specify that each thread should execute its instructions one at a time, in our main program:

```
# Chapter12/example6.py

lock_a = threading.Lock()
lock_b = threading.Lock()

thread1 = threading.Thread(target=thread_a)
thread2 = threading.Thread(target=thread_b)

start = timer()

thread1.start()
thread1.join()

thread2.start()
thread2.join()

print('Took %.2f seconds.' % (timer() - start))
print('Finished.')
```

Run this script, and you will see that this sequential version of our two-lock program will take the same amount of time as its concurrent counterpart:

```
> python3 example6.py
Thread A is starting...
Thread A waiting to acquire lock A.
Thread A has acquired lock A, performing some calculation...
Thread A waiting to acquire lock B.
Thread A has acquired lock B, performing some calculation...
Thread A releasing both locks.
Thread B is starting...
Thread B waiting to acquire lock A.
Thread B has acquired lock A, performing some calculation...
Thread B waiting to acquire lock B.
Thread B has acquired lock B, performing some calculation...
Thread B releasing both locks.
Took 14.01 seconds.
```

`Finished.`

This interesting phenomenon is a direct result of the heavy requirements that we have placed on the locks in the program. In other words, since each thread has to acquire both locks to complete its execution, each lock cannot be acquired by more than one thread at any given time, and finally, the locks are required to be acquired in a specific order, and the execution of individual threads cannot happen simultaneously. If we were to go back and examine the output produced by the `Chapter12/example5.py` file, it would be apparent that thread B could not start its calculations after thread A released both locks at the end of its execution.

It is quite intuitive, then, to arrive at the conclusion that if you placed enough locks on the resources of your concurrent program, it would become entirely sequential in its execution, and, combined with the overhead of concurrent programming functionalities, it would have an even worse speed than the purely sequential version of the program. However, we did not see in the Dining Philosophers problem (simulated in Python) this sequentiality created by locks. This is because in the two-thread problem, two locks were enough to sequentialize the program execution, while five were not enough to do the same for the Dining Philosophers problem.

We will explore another instance of this phenomenon in `Chapter 14`, *Race Conditions*.

Ignoring locks and sharing resources

Locks are undoubtedly an important tool in synchronization tasks, and in concurrent programming in general. However, if the use of locks leads to an undesirable situation, such as a deadlock, then it is quite natural for us to explore the option of simply not using locks in our concurrent programs. By ignoring locks, our program's resources effectively become shareable among different processes/threads in a concurrent program, thus eliminating the first of the four Coffman conditions: mutual exclusion.

This approach to the problem of deadlock can be straightforward to implement; let us try with the two preceding examples. In the two-lock example, we simply remove the code specifying any interaction with the lock objects both inside the thread functions and in the main program. In other words, we are not utilizing a locking mechanism anymore. The `Chapter12/example7.py` file contains the implementation of this approach, as follows:

```
# Chapter12/example7.py

import threading
import time
from timeit import default_timer as timer
```

```
def thread_a():
    print('Thread A is starting...')

    print('Thread A is performing some calculation...')
    time.sleep(2)

    print('Thread A is performing some calculation...')
    time.sleep(2)

def thread_b():
    print('Thread B is starting...')

    print('Thread B is performing some calculation...')
    time.sleep(5)

    print('Thread B is performing some calculation...')
    time.sleep(5)

thread1 = threading.Thread(target=thread_a)
thread2 = threading.Thread(target=thread_b)

start = timer()

thread1.start()
thread2.start()

thread1.join()
thread2.join()

print('Took %.2f seconds.' % (timer() - start))

print('Finished.')
```

Run the script, and your output should look similar to the following:

```
> python3 example7.py
Thread A is starting...
Thread A is performing some calculation...
Thread B is starting...
Thread B is performing some calculation...
Thread A is performing some calculation...
Thread B is performing some calculation...
Took 10.00 seconds.
Finished.
```

It is clear that since we are not using locks to restrict access to any calculation processes, the executions of the two threads have now become entirely independent of one another, and the threads were therefore run completely in parallel. For this reason, we also obtained a better speed: since the threads ran in parallel, the total time that the whole program took was the same as the time that the longer task of the two threads took (in other words, thread B, with 10 seconds).

What about the Dining Philosophers problem? It seems that we can also conclude that without locks (the forks), the problem can be solved easily. Since the resources (food) are unique to each philosopher (in other words, no philosopher should eat another philosopher's food), it should be the case that each philosopher can proceed with their execution without worrying about the others. By ignoring the locks, each can be executed in parallel, similar to what we saw in our two-lock example.

Doing this, however, means that we are completely misunderstanding the problem. We know that locks are utilized so that processes and threads can access the shared resources in a program in a systematic, coordinated way, to avoid mishandling the data. Therefore, removing any locking mechanisms in a concurrent program means that the likelihood of the shared resources, which are now free from access limitations, being manipulated in an uncoordinated way (and therefore, becoming corrupted) increases significantly.

So, by ignoring locks, it is relatively likely that we will need to completely redesign and restructure our concurrent program. If the shared resources still need to be accessed and manipulated in an organized way, other synchronization methods will need to be implemented. The logic of our processes and threads might need to be altered to appropriately interact with this new synchronization method, the execution time might be negatively affected by this change in the structure of the program, and other potential synchronization problems might also arise.

An additional note about locks

While the approach of dismissing locking mechanisms in our program to eliminate deadlocks might raise some questions and concerns, it does effectively reveal a new point for us about lock objects in Python: it is possible for an element of a concurrent program to completely bypass the locks when accessing a given resource. In other words, lock objects only prevent different processes/threads from accessing and manipulating a shared resource if those processes or threads actually acquire the lock objects.

Locks, then, do not actually lock anything. They are simply flags that help to indicate whether a resource should be accessed at a given time; if a poorly instructed, or even malicious, process/thread attempts to access that resource without checking the lock object exists, it will most likely be able to do that without difficulty. In other words, locks are not at all connected to the resources that they are supposed to lock, and they most certainly do not block processes/threads from accessing those resources.

The simple use of locks is therefore inefficient to design and implement a secure, dynamic, concurrent data structure. To achieve that, we would need to either add more concrete links between the locks and their corresponding resources, or utilize a different synchronization tool altogether (for example, atomic message queues).

Concluding note on deadlock solutions

You have seen two of the most common approaches to the problem of deadlock. Each addresses one of the four Coffman conditions, and, while both (somewhat) successfully prevent deadlocks from occurring in our examples, each raises different, additional problems and concerns. It is therefore important to truly understand the nature of your concurrent programs, in order to know which of the two is applicable, if either of them are.

It is also possible that some programs, through deadlock, are revealed to us as unsuitable to be made concurrent; some programs are better left sequential, and will be made worse with forced concurrency. As we have discussed, while concurrency provides significant improvements in many areas of our applications, some are inherently inappropriate for the application of concurrent programming. In situations of deadlock, developers should be ready to consider different approaches to designing a concurrent program, and should not be reluctant to implement another method when one concurrent approach does not work.

The concept of livelock

The concept of livelock is connected to deadlock; some even consider it an alternate version of deadlock. In a livelock situation, the processes (or threads) in the concurrent program are able to switch their states; in fact, they switch states constantly. Yet, they simply switch back and forth infinitely, and no progress is made. We will now consider an actual scenario of livelock.

Suppose that a pair of spouses are eating dinner together at a table. They only have one fork to share with each other, so only one of them can eat at any given point. Additionally, the spouses are really polite to each other, so even if one spouse is hungry and wants to eat their food, they will leave the fork on the table if their partner is also hungry. This specification is at the heart of creating a livelock for this problem: when both spouses are hungry, each will wait for the other to eat first, creating a infinite loop in which each spouse switches between wanting to eat and waiting for the other spouse to eat.

Let's simulate this problem in Python. Navigate to `Chapter12/example8.py`, and take a look at the `Spouse` class:

```
# Chapter12/example8.py

class Spouse(threading.Thread):

    def __init__(self, name, partner):
        threading.Thread.__init__(self)
        self.name = name
        self.partner = partner
        self.hungry = True

    def run(self):
        while self.hungry:
            print('%s is hungry and wants to eat.' % self.name)

            if self.partner.hungry:
                print('%s is waiting for their partner to eat first...'
                    % self.name)
            else:
                with fork:
                    print('%s has stared eating.' % self.name)
                    time.sleep(5)

                    print('%s is now full.' % self.name)
                    self.hungry = False
```

This class inherits from the `threading.Thread` class and implements the logic that we discussed previously. It takes in a name for the `Spouse` instance and another `Spouse` object as its partner; when initialized, a `Spouse` object is also always hungry (the `hungry` attribute is always set to `True`). The `run()` function in the class specifies the logic when the thread is started: as long as the `Spouse` object's `hungry` attribute is set to `True`, the object will attempt to use the fork, which is a lock object, to eat. However, it always checks to see whether its partner also has its `hungry` attribute set to `True`, in which case, it will not proceed to acquire the lock, and will instead wait for its partner to do it.

In our main program, we create the fork as a lock object first; then, we create two Spouse thread objects, which are each other's partner attributes. Finally, we start both threads, and run the program until both threads finish executing:

```
# Chapter12/example8.py

fork = threading.Lock()

partner1 = Spouse('Wife', None)
partner2 = Spouse('Husband', partner1)
partner1.partner = partner2

partner1.start()
partner2.start()

partner1.join()
partner2.join()

print('Finished.')
```

Run the script, and you will see that, as we discussed, each thread will go into an infinite loop, switching between wanting to eat and waiting for its partner to eat; the program will run forever, until Python is interrupted. The following code shows the first few lines of the output that I obtained:

```
> python3 example8.py
Wife is hungry and wants to eat.
Wife is waiting for their partner to eat first...
Husband is hungry and wants to eat.
Wife is hungry and wants to eat.
Husband is waiting for their partner to eat first...
Wife is waiting for their partner to eat first...
Husband is hungry and wants to eat.
Wife is hungry and wants to eat.
Husband is waiting for their partner to eat first...
Wife is waiting for their partner to eat first...
Husband is hungry and wants to eat.
Wife is hungry and wants to eat.
Husband is waiting for their partner to eat first...
...
```

Summary

In the field of computer science, deadlock refers to a specific situation in concurrent programming, in which no progress is made and the program is locked in its current state. In most cases, this phenomenon is caused by a lack of, or mishandled, coordination between different lock objects, and it can be illustrated with the Dining Philosophers problem.

Potential approaches to preventing deadlocks from occurring include imposing an order for the lock objects and sharing non-shareable resources by ignoring lock objects. Each solution addresses one of the four Coffman conditions, and, while both solutions can successfully prevent deadlocks, each raises different, additional problems and concerns.

Connected to the concept of deadlock is livelock. In a livelock situation, processes (or threads) in the concurrent program are able to switch their states, but they simply switch back and forth infinitely, and no progress is made. In the next chapter, we will discuss another common problem in concurrent programming: starvation.

Questions

- What can lead to a deadlock situation, and why is it undesirable?
- How is the Dining Philosophers problem related to the problem of deadlock?
- What are the four Coffman conditions?
- How can resource ranking solve the problem of deadlock? What other problems can occur when this is implemented?
- How can ignoring locks solve the problem of deadlock? What other problems can occur when this is implemented?
- How is livelock related to deadlock?

Further reading

For more information, you can refer to the following links:

- *Parallel Programming with Python*, by Jan. Palach, Packt Publishing Ltd, 2014
- *Python Parallel Programming Cookbook*, by Giancarlo Zaccone, Packt Publishing Ltd, 2015
- *Python Thread Deadlock Avoidance* (`dabeaz.blogspot.com/2009/11/python-thread-deadlock-avoidance_20`)

13
Starvation

In this chapter, we will discuss the concept of starvation and its potential causes in concurrent programming. We will cover a number of readers-writers problems, which are prime examples of starvation, and we will simulate them in example Python code. This chapter will also cover the relationship between deadlock and starvation, as well as some potential solutions for starvation.

The following topics will be covered in this chapter:

- The basic idea behind starvation, its root causes, and some more relevant concepts
- A detailed analysis of the readers-writers problem, which is used to illustrate the complexity of starvation in a concurrent system

Technical requirements

The following is a list of prerequisites for this chapter:

- Ensure that you have Python 3 installed on your computer
- Download the GitHub repository at `https://github.com/PacktPublishing/Mastering-Concurrency-in-Python`
- During this chapter, we will be working with the subfolder titled `Chapter13`
- Check out the following video to see the Code in Action: `http://bit.ly/2r3caw8`

The concept of starvation

Starvation is a problem in concurrent systems, in which a process (or a thread) cannot gain access to the necessary resources in order to proceed with its execution and, therefore, cannot make any progress. In this section, we will look into the characteristics of a starvation situation, analyze the most common causes of starvation, and finally, consider a sample program that exemplifies starvation.

What is starvation?

It is quite common for a concurrent program to implement some sort of ordering between the different processes in its execution. For example, consider a program that has three separate processes, as follows:

- One is responsible for handling extremely pressing instructions that need to be run as soon as the necessary resources become available
- Another process is responsible for other important executions, which are not as essential as the tasks in the first process
- The last one handles miscellaneous, very infrequent tasks

Furthermore, these three process need to utilize the same resources in order to execute their respective instructions.

Intuitively, we have every reason to implement a specification that allows the first process to have the highest priority of execution and access to resources, then the second process, and then the last process, with the lowest priority. However, imagine situations in which the first two processes (with higher priorities) run so often that the third process cannot execute its instructions; anytime the third process needs to run, it checks to see whether the resources are available to be used and finds out that one of the other, higher-priority processes is using them.

This is a situation of starvation: the third process is given no opportunity to execute and, therefore, no progress can be made with that process. In a typical concurrent program, it is quite common to have more than three processes at different priority levels, yet the situation is fundamentally similar: some processes are given more opportunities to run and, therefore, they are constantly executing. Others have lower priorities and cannot access the necessary resources to execute.

Scheduling

In the next few subsections, we will be discussing the potential candidates that cause starvation situations. Most of the time, a poorly coordinated set of scheduling instructions is the main cause of starvation. For example, a considerably naive algorithm that deals with three separate tasks might implement constant communication and interaction between the first two tasks.

This setup leads to the fact that the execution flow of the algorithm switches solely between the first and second tasks, while the third finds itself idle and unable to make any progress with its execution; in this case, because it is starved of CPU execution flow. Intuitively, we can identify the root of the problem as the fact that the algorithm allows the first two tasks to always dominate the CPU, and hence, effectively prevents any other task to also utilize the CPU. A characteristic of a good scheduling algorithm is the ability to distribute the execution flow and allocate the resources equally and appropriately.

As mentioned previously, many concurrent systems and programs implement a specific order of priority, in terms of process and thread execution. This implementation of ordered scheduling may very likely lead to the starvation of processes and threads of lower priorities and can result in a condition called **priority inversion**.

Suppose that, in your concurrent program, you have process A of the highest priority, process B of a medium priority, and finally, process C of the lowest priority; process C would most likely be put in the situation of starvation. Additionally, if the execution of process A, the prioritized process, is dependent on the completion of process C, which is already in starvation, then process A might never be able to complete its execution, either, even though it is given the highest priority in the concurrent program.

The following diagram further illustrates the concept of priority inversion: a high-priority task running from the time **t2** to **t3** needs to access some resources, which are being utilized by a low-priority task:

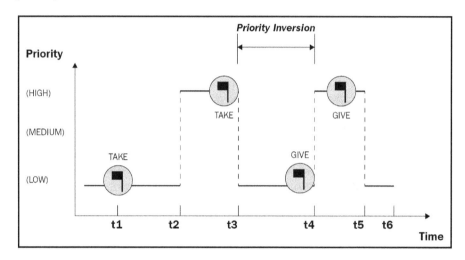

Diagram of priority inversion

To reiterate, combining starvation and priority inversion can lead to a situation where even the high-priority tasks are unable to execute their instructions.

Causes of starvation

With the complexity of designing a scheduling algorithm in mind, let us discuss the specific causes of starvation. The situations that we described in the preceding section indicate some potential causes of the situation of starvation. However, starvation can arise from a number of sources, as follows:

- Processes (or threads) with high priorities dominate the execution flow in the CPU, and hence, low-priority processes (or threads) are not given the opportunity to execute their own instructions.
- Processes (or threads) with high priorities dominate the usage of non-shareable resources, and hence, low-priority processes (or threads) are not given the opportunity to execute their own instructions. This situation is similar to the first one, but addresses the priority of accessing resources, instead of the priority of the execution itself.

- Processes (or threads) with low priorities are waiting for resources to execute their instructions, but, as soon as the resources become available, other processes (or threads) with higher priorities are immediately given access to them, so the low-priority processes (or threads) wait infinitely.

There are other causes of starvation, as well, but the preceding are the most common root causes.

Starvation's relationship to deadlock

Interestingly, deadlock situations can also lead to starvation, as the definition of starvation states that if there is a process (or a thread) that is unable to make any progress because it cannot gain access to the necessary process, the process (or thread) is experiencing starvation.

Recall our example of deadlock, the Dining Philosophers problem, illustrated as follows:

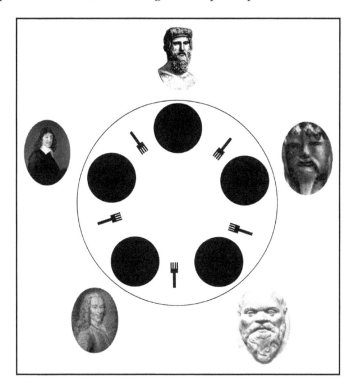

An illustration of the Dining Philosophers problem

When deadlock occurs for this situation, no philosopher can obtain the necessary resources to execute their instructions (each philosopher is required to have two forks to start eating). Each philosopher that is in a deadlock is therefore also in a state of starvation.

The readers-writers problem

The readers-writers problem is one of the classic and most complex examples in the field of computer science, illustrating problems that might occur in a concurrent program. Throughout the analysis of the different variations of the readers-writers problem, we will reveal more about starvation, as well as its common causes. We will also simulate the problem in Python, so that a deeper understanding of the problem can be gained.

Problem statement

In a readers-writers problem, first and foremost, we have a shared resource, which, in most cases, is a text file. Different threads interact with that text file; each is either a reader or a writer. A **reader** is a thread that simply accesses the shared resource (the text file) and reads in the data included in that file, while a **writer** is a thread that accesses, and possibly mutates, the contents of the text file.

We know that writers and readers cannot access the shared resources simultaneously since if a thread is writing data to the file, no other thread should be accessing the file to read any data from it. The goal of the readers-writers problem is therefore to find a correct and efficient way to design and coordinate the scheduling of these reader and writer thread. A successful implementation of that goal is not only that the program as a whole executes in the most optimized way, but also that all threads are given sufficient opportunity to execute their instructions and no starvation can occur. Additionally, the shared resource (the text file) needs to be handled appropriately, so that no data will be corrupted.

The following diagram further illustrates the setup of the readers-writers problem:

Diagram of readers-writers problem

The first readers-writers problem

As we mentioned, the problem asks us to come up with a scheduling algorithm, so that readers and writers can access the text file appropriately and efficiently, without mishandling/corrupting the data that is included. A naive solution to this problem is to impose a lock on the text file, so that it becomes a non-shareable resource; this means that only one thread (either a reader or a writer) can access (and potentially manipulate) the text file at any given time.

Yet, this approach simply equates to a sequential program: if the shared resource can be utilized by only one thread at a given time, none of the processing time between different threads can be overlapped, and effectively, the execution becomes sequential. Therefore, this is not an optimal solution, as it is taking advantage of concurrent programming.

One insight regarding the reader threads can lead to a more optimal solution to this problem: since readers simply read in the text file and do not alter the data in it, multiple readers can be allowed to access the text file simultaneously. Indeed, even if more than one reader is fetching data from the text file at the same time, the data is not being changed in any way, and the consistency and accuracy of the data is therefore maintained.

Following this approach, we will implement a specification in which no reader will be kept waiting if the shared resource is being opened for reading by another reader. Specifically, in addition to a lock on the shared resource, we will also have a counter for the number of readers currently accessing the resource. If, at any point in the program, that counter goes from zero to one (in other words, at least one reader is starting to access the resource), we will lock the resource from the writers; similarly, whenever the counter decreases to zero (in other words, no reader is asking for access to the resource), we will release the lock on the resource, so that writers can access it.

This specification is efficient for the readers, in the sense that, once the first reader has accessed the resource and placed a lock on it, no writers can access it, and the subsequent readers will not have to re-lock it until the last reader finishes reading the resource.

Let us try to implement this solution in Python. If you have already downloaded the code for this book from the GitHub page, go ahead and navigate to the `Chapter13` folder. Let us take a look at the `Chapter13/example1.py` file; specifically, the `writer()` and `reader()` functions, as follows:

```
# Chapter13/example1.py

def writer():
    global text

    while True:
        with resource:
            print(f'Writing being done by
                    {threading.current_thread().name}.')
            text += f'Writing was done by
                    {threading.current_thread().name}. '

def reader():
    global rcount

    while True:
        with rcounter:
            rcount += 1
            if rcount == 1:
                resource.acquire()
```

```
print(f'Reading being done by
        {threading.current_thread().name}:')
print(text)

with rcounter:
    rcount -= 1
    if rcount == 0:
        resource.release()
```

In the preceding script, the `writer()` function, which is to be called by a `threading.Thread` instance (in other words, a separate thread), specifies the logic of the writer threads that we discussed previously: accessing the shared resource (in this case, the global variable, `text`, which is simply a Python string) and writing some data to the resource. Note that we are putting all of its instructions inside a `while` loop, to simulate the constant nature of the application (writers and readers constantly try to access the shared resource).

We can also see the reader logic in the `reader()` function. Before asking for access to the shared resource, each reader will increment a counter for the number of readers that are currently active and trying to access the resource. Similarly, after reading data off the file, each reader needs to decrement the number of readers. During this process, if a reader is the first reader to access the file (in other words, when the counter is one), it will put a lock on the file, so that no writers can access it; conversely, when a reader is the last reader to read the file, it has to release that lock.

One note about the handling of that counter of readers: you might have noticed that we are using a lock object named `rcounter` when incrementing/decrementing the counter variable (`rcount`). This is a method that is used to avoid a race condition, which is another common concurrency-related problem, for the counter variable; specifically, without the lock, multiple threads can be accessing and altering the counter variable at the same time, but the only way to ensure the integrity of the data is for this counter variable to be handled sequentially. We will discuss race conditions (and the practice that is used to avoid them) in more detail in the next chapter.

Going back to our current script, in the main program, we will set up the `text` variable, the counter for readers, and two lock objects (for the reader counter and the shared resource, respectively). We are also initializing and starting three reader threads and two writer threads, as follows:

```
# Chapter13/example1.py

text = 'This is some text. '
rcount = 0
```

```
rcounter = threading.Lock()
resource = threading.Lock()

threads = [threading.Thread(target=reader) for i in range(3)] +
[threading.Thread(target=writer) for i in range(2)]

for thread in threads:
    thread.start()
```

It is important to note that, since the instructions of the reader and writer threads are both wrapped in `while` loops, the script, when started, will run infinitely. You should cancel the Python execution after around 3-4 seconds, when enough output has been produced so that the general behavior of the program can be observed.

The following code shows the first few lines of output that I obtained after running the script:

```
> python3 example1.py
Reading being done by Thread-1:
This is some text.
Reading being done by Thread-2:
Reading being done by Thread-1:
This is some text.
This is some text.
Reading being done by Thread-2:
Reading being done by Thread-1:
This is some text.
This is some text.
Reading being done by Thread-3:
Reading being done by Thread-1:
This is some text.
This is some text.
...
```

As you can see, there is a specific pattern in the preceding output: all of the threads that were accessing the shared resource were readers. In fact, throughout my entire output, no writer was able to access the file, and therefore, the `text` variable only contains the initial string, `This is some text.`, and was not altered in any way. The output that you obtain should also have the same pattern (the shared resource not being altered).

In this case, the writers are experiencing starvation, as none of them are able to access and use the resource. This is a direct result of our scheduling algorithm; since multiple readers are allowed to access the text file simultaneously, if there are multiple readers accessing the text file frequently enough, it will create a continuous stream of readers going through the text file, giving no room for a writer to attempt to access the file.

This scheduling algorithm inadvertently gives priority to the readers over the writers, and is therefore called **readers-preference**. So, this design is undesirable.

The second readers-writers problem

The problem with the first approach is that, when a reader is accessing the text file and a writer is waiting for the file to be unlocked, if another reader starts its execution and wants to access the file, it will be given priority over the writer that has already been waiting. Additionally, if more and more readers keep requesting access to the file, the writer will be waiting infinitely, and that was what we observed in our first code example.

To address this problem, we will implement the specification that, once a writer makes a request to access the file, no reader should be able to jump in line and access the file before that writer. To do this, we will have an additional lock object in our program, to specify whether a writer is waiting for the file, and consequently, whether a reader thread can attempt to read the file; we will call this lock `read_try`.

Similar to how the first of the readers accessing the text file always locks it from the writers, we will now have the first writer of the multiple that are waiting to access the file lock `read_try`, so that no reader can, again, jump in line before those writers that requested access before it. As we discussed in reference to the readers, since we are keeping track of the number of writers waiting for the text file, we will need to implement a counter for the number of writers, and its corresponding lock, in our program.

The `Chapter13/example2.py` file contains the code for this implementation, as follows:

```
# Chapter13/example2.py

import threading

def writer():
    global text
    global wcount

    while True:
        with wcounter:
            wcount += 1
            if wcount == 1:
                read_try.acquire()

        with resource:
            print(f'Writing being done by
                    {threading.current_thread().name}.')
            text += f'Writing was done by
```

```
                        {threading.current_thread().name}. '

            with wcounter:
                wcount -= 1
                if wcount == 0:
                    read_try.release()

    def reader():
        global rcount

        while True:
            with read_try:
                with rcounter:
                    rcount += 1
                    if rcount == 1:
                        resource.acquire()

                print(f'Reading being done by
                        {threading.current_thread().name}:')
                print(text)

                with rcounter:
                    rcount -= 1
                    if rcount == 0:
                        resource.release()

    text = 'This is some text. '
    wcount = 0
    rcount = 0

    wcounter = threading.Lock()
    rcounter = threading.Lock()
    resource = threading.Lock()
    read_try = threading.Lock()

    threads = [threading.Thread(target=reader) for i in range(3)] +
              [threading.Thread(target=writer) for i in range(2)]

    for thread in threads:
        thread.start()
```

Compared to our first solution to the problem, the main program remains relatively the same (except for the initialization of the read_try lock, the wcount counter, and its lock, wcounter), but in our writer() function, we are locking read_try as soon as there is at least one writer waiting to access the file; when the last writer finishes its execution, it will release the lock, so that any reader waiting for the file can now access it.

Again, to see the output produced by the program, we will have it run for 3-4 seconds, and then cancel the execution, as the program would otherwise run forever. The following is the output that I obtained via this script:

```
> python3 example2.py
Reading being done by Thread-1:
This is some text.
Reading being done by Thread-1:
This is some text.
Writing being done by Thread-4.
Writing being done by Thread-5.
Writing being done by Thread-4.
Writing being done by Thread-4.
Writing being done by Thread-4.
Writing being done by Thread-5.
Writing being done by Thread-4.
...
```

It can be observed that, while some readers were able to access the text file (indicated by the first four lines of my output), once a writer gained access to the shared resource, no reader was able to access it anymore. The rest of my output included messages about writing instructions: `Writing being done by`, and so on. As opposed to what we saw in the first solution of the readers-writers problem, this solution is giving priority to writers, and, as a consequence, the readers are starved. This is therefore called **writers-preference**.

The priority that writers were given over readers resulted from the fact that, while only the first and the last writers have to acquire and release the `read_try` lock, respectively, each and every reader wanting to access the text file have to interact with that lock object individually. Once `read_try` is locked by a writer, no reader can even attempt to execute its instructions, let alone try to access the text file.

There are cases in which some readers are able to gain access to the text file, if the readers are initialized and executed before the writers (for example, in our program, the readers were the first three elements, and the writers were the last two, in our list of threads). However, once a writer is able to access the file and acquire the `read_try` lock during its execution, starvation will most likely occur for the readers.

This solution is also not desirable, as it gives higher priority to the writer threads in our program.

The third readers-writers problem

You have seen that both of the solutions that we tried to implement can result in starvation, by not giving equal priorities to the separate threads; one can starve the writers, and the other can starve the readers. A balance between these two approaches might give us an implementation with equal priorities among the readers and writers, and hence, solve the problem of starvation.

Recall this: in our second approach, we are placing a lock on a reader's attempt to access the text file, requiring that no writer will be starved once it starts waiting for the file. In this solution, we will implement a lock that also utilizes this logic, but is then applied to both readers and writers. All of the threads will then be subjected to the constraints of the lock, and equal priority will hence be achieved among the separate threads.

Specifically, this is a lock that specifies whether a thread will be given access to the text file at a given moment; we will call this the **service lock**. Each writer or reader has to try to acquire this service lock before executing any of its instructions. A writer, having obtained this service lock, will also attempt to obtain the resource lock and release the service lock immediately thereafter. The writer will then execute its writing logic and finally release the resource lock at the end of its execution.

Let us take a look at the `writer()` function in the `Chapter13/example3.py` file for our implementation in Python, as follows:

```python
# Chapter13/example3.py

def writer():
    global text

    while True:
        with service:
            resource.acquire()

        print(f'Writing being done by
            {threading.current_thread().name}.')
        text += f'Writing was done by
            {threading.current_thread().name}. '

        resource.release()
```

A reader, on the other hand, will also need to acquire the service lock first. Since we are still allowing multiple readers to access the resource at the same time, we are implementing the reader counter and its corresponding lock.

The reader will acquire the service lock and the counter lock, increment the reader counter (and potentially, lock the resource), and then release the service lock and counter lock, sequentially. Now, it will actually read data off the text file, and finally, it will decrement the reader counter, and will potentially release the resource lock, if it is the last reader to access the file at that time.

The `reader()` function contains this specification, as follows:

```
# Chapter13/example3.py

def reader():
    global rcount

    while True:
        with service:
            rcounter.acquire()
            rcount += 1
            if rcount == 1:
                resource.acquire()
        rcounter.release()

        print(f'Reading being done by
            {threading.current_thread().name}:')
        #print(text)

        with rcounter:
            rcount -= 1
            if rcount == 0:
                resource.release()
```

Finally, in our main program, we initialize the text string, the reader counter, all of the necessary locks, and the reader and writer threads, as follows:

```
# Chapter13/example3.py

text = 'This is some text. '
rcount = 0

rcounter = threading.Lock()
resource = threading.Lock()
service = threading.Lock()

threads = [threading.Thread(target=reader) for i in range(3)] +
[threading.Thread(target=writer) for i in range(2)]

for thread in threads:
    thread.start()
```

Note that, we are commenting the code that prints out the current content of the text file in the `reader()` function for readability for our output later on. Run the program for 3-4 seconds, and then cancel it. The following output is what I obtained on my personal computer:

```
> python3 example3.py
Reading being done by Thread-3:
Writing being done by Thread-4.
Reading being done by Thread-1:
Writing being done by Thread-5.
Reading being done by Thread-2:
Reading being done by Thread-3:
Writing being done by Thread-4.
. . .
```

The pattern that we have with this current output is that the readers and writers are able to access the shared resource cooperatively and efficiently; all of the readers and writers are executing their instructions, and no thread is being starved by this scheduling algorithm.

Note that as you work with a reader-writer problem in your concurrent program, you do not have to reinvent the wheel regarding the approaches that we just discussed. PyPI actually has an external library called `readerwriterlock` that contains the implementation of the three approaches in Python, as well as supports for timeouts. Navigate to `https://pypi.org/project/readerwriterlock/` to find out more about the library and its documentation.

Solutions to starvation

Through an analysis of different approaches to the readers-writers problem, you have seen the key to solving starvation: since some threads will be starved if they are not given a high priority in accessing the shared resources, implementing fairness in the execution of all of the threads will prevent starvation from occurring. Fairness, in this case, does not require a program to forgo any order or priority that it has imposed on the different threads; but to implement fairness, a program needs to ensure that all threads are given sufficient opportunities to execute their instructions.

Keeping this idea in mind, we can potentially address the problem of starvation by implementing one (or a combination) of the following approaches:

- **Increasing the priority of low-priority threads**: As we did with the writer threads in the second approach and the reader threads in the third approach to the readers-writers problem, prioritizing the threads that would otherwise not have any opportunity to access the shared resource can successfully eliminate starvation.
- **First-in-first-out thread queue**: To ensure that a thread that started waiting for the shared resource before another thread will be able to acquire the resource before the other thread, we can keep track of the threads requesting access in a first-in-first-out queue.
- **Other methods**: Several methods can also be implemented to balance the selection frequency of different threads. For example, a priority queue that also gives gradually increasing priority to threads that have been waiting in the queue for a long time, or if a thread has been able to access the shared resource for many times, it will be given less priority, and so on.

Solving starvation in your concurrent program can be a rather complex and involved process, and a deep understanding of its scheduling algorithm, combined with an understanding of how processes and threads interact with the shared resources, is necessary during the process. As you saw in the example of the readers-writers problem, it can also take several implementations and revisions of different approaches to arrive at a good solution to starvation.

Summary

Starvation is a problem in concurrent systems in which a process (or thread) cannot gain access to the necessary resources to proceed with its execution and, therefore, cannot make any progress. Most of the time, a poorly coordinated set of scheduling instructions is the main cause of starvation; deadlock situations can also lead to starvation.

The readers-writers problem is one of the classic and most complex examples in the field of computer science, illustrating problems that might occur in a concurrent program. Through an analysis of different approaches to the readers-writers problem, you have gained insight regarding how starvation can be solved with different scheduling algorithms. Fairness is an essential element of a good scheduling algorithm, and, by making sure that the priority is distributed appropriately among different processes and threads, starvation can be eliminated.

In the next chapter, we will discuss the last of the three common problems of concurrent programming: race conditions. We will cover the basic foundation and causes of race conditions, relevant concepts, and the connection of race conditions to other concurrency-related problems.

Questions

- What is starvation, and why is it undesirable in a concurrent program?
- What are the underlying causes of starvation? What are the common high-level causes of starvation that can manifest from the underlying cause?
- What is the connection between deadlock and starvation?
- What is the readers-writers problem?
- What is the first approach to the readers-writers problem? Why does starvation arise in that situation?
- What is the second approach to the readers-writers problem? Why does starvation arise in that situation?
- What is the third approach to the readers-writers problem? Why does it successfully address starvation?
- What are some common solutions to starvation?

Further reading

- *Parallel Programming with Python*, by Jan Palach, Packt Publishing Ltd, 2014
- *Python Parallel Programming Cookbook*, by Giancarlo Zaccone, Packt Publishing Ltd, 2015
- *Starvation and Fairness* (`tutorials.jenkov.com/java-concurrency/starvation-and-fairness`), by Jakob Jenkov
- *Faster Fair Solution for the Reader-Writer Problem*, V.Popov and O.Mazonka

14
Race Conditions

In this chapter, we will discuss the concept of race conditions and their potential causes in the context of concurrency. The definition of critical section, which is a concept highly relevant to race conditions and concurrent programming, will also be covered. We will use some example code in Python to simulate race conditions and the solutions commonly used to address them. Finally, real-life applications that commonly deal with race conditions will be discussed.

The following topics will be covered in this chapter:

- The basic concept of a race condition, and how it occurs in concurrent applications, along with the definition of critical sections
- A simulation of a race condition in Python and how to implement race condition solutions
- The real-life computer science concepts that commonly interact and work with race conditions

Technical requirements

Following is the list of prerequisites needed for this chapter:

- Ensure that you have Python 3 installed on your computer
- Download the GitHub repository at `https://github.com/PacktPublishing/Mastering-Concurrency-in-Python`
- During this chapter, we will be working with the subfolder titled `Chapter14`
- Check out the following video to see the Code in Action: `http://bit.ly/2AdYWRj`

The concept of race conditions

A race condition is typically defined as a phenomenon during which the output of a system is indeterminate and dependent on the scheduling algorithm and the order in which tasks are scheduled and executed. When the data becomes mishandled and corrupted during this process, a race condition becomes a bug in the system. Given the nature of this problem, it is quite common for a race condition to occur in concurrent systems, which emphasize scheduling and coordinating independent tasks.

A race condition can occur in both an electronic hardware system and a software application; in this chapter, we will only be discussing race conditions in the context of software development—specifically, concurrent software applications. This section will cover the theoretical foundations of race conditions and their root causes and the concept of critical sections.

Critical sections

Critical sections indicate shared resources that are accessed by multiple processes or threads in a concurrent application, which can lead to unexpected, and even erroneous, behavior. We have seen that there are multiple methods to protect the integrity of the data contained in these resources, and we call these protected sections **critical sections**.

As you can imagine, the data in these critical sections, when interacted with and altered concurrently or in parallel, can become mishandled or corrupted. This is especially true when the threads and processes interacting with it are poorly coordinated and scheduled. The logical conclusion, therefore, is to not allow multiple agents to go into a critical section at the same time. We call this concept **mutual exclusion**.

We will discuss the relationship between critical sections and the causes of race conditions in the next subsection.

How race conditions occur

Let's consider a simple concurrent program, in order to understand what can give rise to a race condition. Suppose that the program has a shared resource and two separate threads (thread 1 and thread 2) that will access and interact with that resource. Specifically, the shared resource is a number and, as per their respective execution instructions, each thread is to read in that number, increment it by 1, and finally, update the value of the shared resource with the incremented number.

Suppose that the shared number is originally 2, and then, thread 1 accesses and interacts with the number; the shared resource then becomes 3. After thread 1 successfully alters and exits the resource, thread 2 begins to execute its instructions, and the shared resource that is a number is updated to 4. Throughout this process, the number was originally 2, was incremented twice (each time by a separate thread), and held a value of 4 at the end. The shared number was not mishandled and corrupted in this case.

Imagine, then, a scenario in which the shared number is still 2 at the beginning, yet both of the threads access the number at the same time. Now, each of the threads reads in the number 2 from the shared resource, each increments the number 2 to 3 individually, and then, each writes the number 3 back to the shared resource. Even though the shared resource was accessed and interacted with by a thread twice, it only held a value of 3 at the end of the process.

This is an example of a race condition occurring in a concurrent program: since the second thread to access a shared resource does it before the first thread finishes its execution (in other words, writing the new value to the shared resource), the second thread fails to take in the updated resource value. This leads to the fact that, when the second thread writes to the resource, the value that is processed and updated by the first thread is overwritten. At the end of the execution of the two threads, the shared resource has technically only been updated by the second thread.

The following diagram further illustrates the contrast between a correct data handling process and a situation with a race condition:

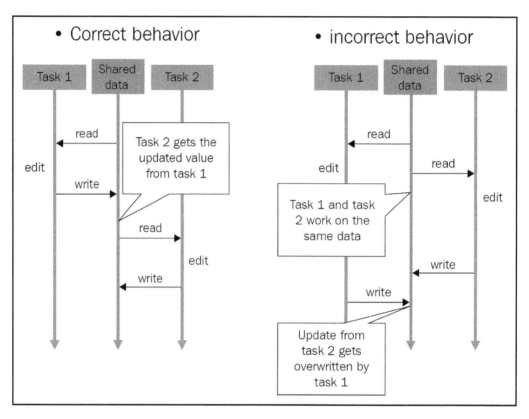

Mishandling shared data

Intuitively, we can see that a race condition can result in the mishandling and corruption of data. In the preceding example, we can see that a race condition can occur with only two separate threads accessing a common resource, causing the shared resource to be updated incorrectly and hold an incorrect value at the end of the program. We know that most real-life concurrent applications contain significantly more threads and processes and more shared resources, and the more threads/processes that interact with the shared resource, the more likely it is that a race condition will occur.

Simulating race conditions in Python

Before we discuss a solution that we can implement to solve the problem of race conditions, let's try to simulate the problem in Python. If you have already downloaded the code for this book from the GitHub page, go ahead and navigate to the `Chapter14` folder. Let's take a look at the `Chapter14/example1.py` file—specifically, the `update()` function, as follows:

```python
# Chapter14/example1.py

import random
import time

def update():
    global counter

    current_counter = counter # reading in shared resource
    time.sleep(random.randint(0, 1)) # simulating heavy calculations
    counter = current_counter + 1 # updating shared resource
```

The goal of the preceding `update()` function is to increment a global variable called `counter`, and it is to be called by a separate thread in our script. Inside the function, we are interacting with a shared resource—in this case, `counter`. We then assign the value of `counter` to another local variable, called `current_counter` (this is to simulate the process of reading data from more complex data structures for the shared resources).

Next, we will pause the execution of the function by using the `time.sleep()` method. The length of the period during which the program will pause is pseudo-randomly chosen between 0 and 1, generated by the function call, `random.randint(0, 1)`, so the program will either pause for one second or not at all. Finally, we assign the newly computed value of `current_counter` (which is its one-increment) to the original shared resource (the `counter` variable).

Now, we can move on to our main program:

```python
# Chapter14/example1.py

import threading

counter = 0

threads = [threading.Thread(target=update) for i in range(20)]

for thread in threads:
    thread.start()
```

```
for thread in threads:
    thread.join()

print(f'Final counter: {counter}.')
print('Finished.')
```

Here, we are initializing the `counter` global variable with a set of `threading.Thread` objects, in order to execute the `update()` function concurrently; we are initializing twenty thread objects, to increment our shared counter twenty times. After starting and joining all of the threads that we have, we can finally print out the end value of our shared `counter` variable.

Theoretically, a well-designed concurrent program will successfully increment the share counter twenty times in total, and, since its original value is 0, the end value of the counter should be 20 at the end of the program. However, as you run this script, the `counter` variable that you obtain will most likely not hold an end value of 20. The following is my own output, obtained from running the script:

```
> python3 example1.py
Final counter: 9.
Finished.
```

This output indicates that the counter was only successfully incremented nine times. This is a direct result of a race condition that our concurrent program has. This race condition occurs when a specific thread spends time reading in and processing the data from the shared resource (specifically, for one second, using the `time.sleep()` method), and another thread reads in the current value of the `counter` variable, which, at this point, has not been updated by the first thread, since it has not completed its execution.

Interestingly, if a thread does not spend anytime processing the data (in other words, when 0 is chosen by the pseudo-random `random.randint()` method), the value of the shared resource can potentially be updated just in time for the next thread to read and process it. This phenomenon is illustrated by the fact that the end value of the counter varies within different runs of the program. For example, the following is the output that I obtained after running the script three times. The output from the first run is as follows:

```
> python3 example1.py
Final counter: 9.
Finished.
```

The output from the second run is as follows:

```
> python3 example1.py
Final counter: 12.
Finished.
```

The output from the third run is as follows:

```
> python3 example1.py
Final counter: 5.
Finished.
```

Again, the final value of the counter is dependent on the number of threads that spend one second pausing and the number of threads not pausing at all. Since these two numbers are, in turn, dependent on the `random.randint()` method, the final value of the counter changes between different runs of the program. We will still have a race condition in our program, except for when we can ensure that the final value of the counter is always `20` (the counter being successfully incremented twenty times, in total).

Locks as a solution to race conditions

In this section, we will discuss the most common solution to race conditions: locks. Intuitively, since the race conditions that we observed arose when multiple threads or processes accessed and wrote to a shared resource simultaneously, the key idea to solving race conditions is to isolate the executions of different threads/processes, especially when interacting with a shared resource. Specifically, we need to make sure that a thread/process can only access the shared resource after any other threads/processes interacting with the resource have finished their interactions with that resource.

The effectiveness of locks

With locks, we can turn a shared resource in a concurrent program into a critical section, whose integrity of data is guaranteed to be protected. A critical section guarantees the mutual exclusion of a shared resource, and cannot be accessed concurrently by multiple processes or threads; this will prevent any protected data from being updated or altered with conflicting information, resulting from race conditions.

In the following diagram, **Thread B** is blocked from accessing the shared resource—the critical section, named `var`—by a mutex (mutual exclusion) lock, because **Thread A** is already accessing the resource:

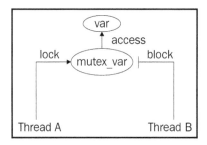

Locks prevent simultaneous access to a critical section

Now, we will specify that, in order to gain access to a critical section in a concurrent program, a thread or process needs to acquire a lock object that is associated with the critical section; similarly, that thread or process also needs to release that lock upon leaving the critical section. This setup will effectively prevent multiple accesses to the critical section, and will therefore prevent race conditions. The following diagram illustrates the execution flow of multiple threads interacting with multiple critical sections, with the implementation of locks in place:

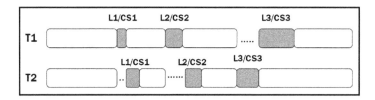

Locks and critical sections in multiple threads

As you can see in the diagram, threads **T1** and **T2** both interact with three critical sections in their respective execution instructions: **CS1**, **CS2**, and **CS3**. Here, **T1** and **T2** attempt to access **CS1** at almost the same time, and, since **CS1** is protected with lock **L1**, only **T1** is able to acquire lock **L1**, and hence, access/interact with the critical section, while **T2** has to spend time waiting for **T1** to exit out of the critical section and release the lock before accessing the section itself. Similarly, for the critical sections, **CS2** and **CS3**, although both threads require access to a critical section at the same time, only one can process it, while the other has to wait to acquire the lock associated with the critical section.

Implementation in Python

Now, let's implement the specification in the preceding example, in order to solve the problem of race conditions. Navigate to the Chapter14/example2.py file and consider our corrected update() function, as follows:

```
# Chapter14/example2.py

import random
import time

def update():
    global counter

    with count_lock:
        current_counter = counter # reading in shared resource
        time.sleep(random.randint(0, 1)) # simulating heavy calculations
        counter = current_counter + 1
```

You can see that all of the execution instructions of a thread specified in the update() function are under the context manager of a lock object named count_lock. So, every time a thread is called to run the function, it will have to first acquire the lock object, before any instructions can be executed. In our main program, we simply create the lock object in addition to what we already had, as follows:

```
# Chapter14/example2.py

import threading

counter = 0
count_lock = threading.Lock()

threads = [threading.Thread(target=update) for i in range(20)]

for thread in threads:
    thread.start()
for thread in threads:
    thread.join()

print(f'Final counter: {counter}.')
print('Finished.')
```

Run the program, and your output should look similar to the following:

```
> python3 example2.py
Final counter: 20.
Finished.
```

You can see that the counter was successfully incremented twenty times and held the correct value at the end of the program. Furthermore, no matter how many times the script is executed, the final value of the counter will always be **20**. This is the advantage of using locks to implement critical sections in your concurrent programs.

The downside of locks

In Chapter 12, *Deadlock*, we covered an interesting phenomenon, in which the use of locks can lead to undesirable results. Specifically, we found out that, with enough locks implemented in a concurrent program, the whole program can become sequential. Let's analyze this concept with our current program. Consider the Chapter14/example3.py file, as follows:

```python
# ch14/example3.py

import threading
import random; random.seed(0)
import time

def update(pause_period):
    global counter

    with count_lock:
        current_counter = counter # reading in shared resource
        time.sleep(pause_period) # simulating heavy calculations
        counter = current_counter + 1 # updating shared resource

pause_periods = [random.randint(0, 1) for i in range(20)]

###############################################################################

counter = 0
count_lock = threading.Lock()

start = time.perf_counter()
for i in range(20):
    update(pause_periods[i])

print('--Sequential version--')
```

```
print(f'Final counter: {counter}.')
print(f'Took {time.perf_counter() - start : .2f} seconds.')

###################################################################

counter = 0

threads = [threading.Thread(target=update, args=(pause_periods[i],)) for i
in range(20)]

start = time.perf_counter()
for thread in threads:
    thread.start()
for thread in threads:
    thread.join()

print('--Concurrent version--')
print(f'Final counter: {counter}.')
print(f'Took {time.perf_counter() - start : .2f} seconds.')

###################################################################

print('Finished.')
```

Turning a concurrent program sequential

The goal of this script is to compare the speed of our current concurrent program with its sequential version. Here, we are still using the same update() function, with locks, and we are running it twenty times, both sequentially and concurrently, like we did earlier. We are also creating a list of determined periods of pausing, so that these periods are consistent between when we simulate the sequential version and when we simulate the concurrent version (for this reason, the update() function now takes in a parameter that specifies the period of pausing each time it is called):

```
pause_periods = [random.randint(0, 1) for i in range(20)]
```

During the next step of the program, we simply call the update() function inside a for loop, with twenty iterations, keeping track of the time it takes for the loop to finish. Note that, even though this is to simulate the sequential version of the program, the update() function still needs the lock object to be created prior, so we are initializing it here:

```
counter = 0
count_lock = threading.Lock()

start = time.perf_counter()
```

```
for i in range(20):
    update(pause_periods[i])

print('--Sequential version--')
print(f'Final counter: {counter}.')
print(f'Took {time.perf_counter() - start : .2f} seconds.')
```

The last step is to reset the counter and run the concurrent version of the program that we already implemented. Again, we need to pass in the corresponding pause period while initializing each of the threads that run the update() function. We are also keeping track of the time it takes for this concurrent version of the program to run:

```
counter = 0

threads = [threading.Thread(target=update, args=(pause_periods[i],)) for i in range(20)]

start = time.perf_counter()
for thread in threads:
    thread.start()
for thread in threads:
    thread.join()

print('--Concurrent version--')
print(f'Final counter: {counter}.')
print(f'Took {time.perf_counter() - start : .2f} seconds.')
```

Now, after you have run the script, you will observe that both the sequential version and the concurrent version of our program took the same amount of time to run. Specifically, the following is the output that I obtained; in this case, they both took approximately 12 seconds. The actual time that your program takes might be different, but the speed of the two versions should still be equal:

```
> python3 example3.py
--Sequential version--
Final counter: 20.
Took 12.03 seconds.
--Concurrent version--
Final counter: 20.
Took 12.03 seconds.
Finished.
```

So, our concurrent program is taking just as much time as its sequential version, which negates one of the biggest purposes of implementing concurrency in a program: improving speed. But why would concurrent and traditional sequential applications with the same sets of instructions and elements also have the same speed? Should the concurrent program always produce a faster speed than the sequential one?

Recall that, in our program, the critical section is being protected by a lock object, and no multiple threads can access it at the same time. Since all of the execution of the program (incrementing the counter for twenty times) depends on a thread accessing the critical section, the placement of the lock object on the critical section means that only one thread can be executing at a given time. With this specification, the executions of any two threads cannot overlap with each other, and no additional speed can be gained from this implementation of concurrency.

This is the phenomenon that we encountered when analyzing the problem of deadlock: if enough locks are placed in a concurrent program, that program will become entirely sequential. This is a reason why locks are sometimes undesirable solutions to problems in concurrent programming. However, this situation only happens if all of the execution of the concurrent program is dependent upon interacting with the critical section. Most of the time, reading and manipulating the data of a shared resource is only a portion of the entire program and, therefore, concurrency still provides the intended additional speed for our program.

Locks do not lock anything

An additional aspect of locks is the fact that they do not actually lock anything. The only way that a lock object is utilized, with respect to a specific shared resource, is for the threads and processes interacting with that resource to also interact with the lock. In other words, if those threads and processes choose to not check with the lock before accessing and altering the shared resource, the lock object itself cannot stop them from doing so.

In our examples, you have seen that, to implement the acquiring/releasing process of a lock object, the instructions of a thread or process will be wrapped around by a lock context manager; this specification is dependent on the implementation of the thread/process execution logic and not the resource. That is because the lock objects that we have seen are not connected to the resources that they are supposed to protect in any way. So, if the thread/process execution logic does not require any interaction with the lock object associated with the shared resource, that thread or process can simply gain access to the resource without difficulty, potentially resulting in the mismanipulation and corruption of data.

This is not only true in the scope of having multiple threads and processes in a single concurrent program. Suppose that we have a concurrent system consisting of multiple components that all interact and manipulate the data of a resource shared across the system, and this resource is associated with a lock object; it follows that, if any of these components fail to interact with that lock, it can simply bypass the protection implemented by the lock and access the shared resource. More importantly, this characteristic of locks also has implications regarding the security of a concurrent program. If an outside, malicious agent is connected to the system (say, a malicious client interacting with a server) and intends to corrupt the data shared across the system, that agent can be instructed to simply ignore the lock object and access that data in an intrusive way.

The view that locks don't lock anything was popularized by Raymond Hettinger, a Python core developer who worked on the implementation of various elements in Python concurrent programming. It is argued that using lock objects alone does not guarantee a secure implementation of concurrent data structures and systems. Locks need to be concretely linked to the resources that they are to protect, and nothing should be able to access a resource without first acquiring the lock that is associated with it. Alternatively, other concurrent synchronization tools, such as atomic message queues, can provide a solution to this problem.

Race conditions in real life

You have now learned about the concept of race conditions, how they are caused in concurrent systems, and how to effectively prevent them. In this section, we will provide an overarching view of how race conditions can occur in real-life examples, within the various sub-fields of computer science. Specifically, we will be discussing the topics of security, file management, and networking.

Security

Concurrent programming can have significant implications in terms of the security of the system in question. Recall that a race condition arises between the process of reading and altering the data of a resource; a race condition in an authenticating system can cause the corruption of data between the **time of check** (when the credentials of an agent are checked) and the **time of use** (when the agent can utilize the resource). This problem is also known as a **Time-Of-Check-To-Time-Of-Use** (**TOCTTOU**) bug, which is undoubtedly detrimental to security systems.

Careless protection of shared resources when handling race conditions, as we briefly touched upon during the last section, can provide external agents with access to those supposedly protected resources. Those agents can then change the data of the resources to create **privilege escalation** (in simple terms, to give themselves more illegal access to more shared resources), or they can simply corrupt the data, causing the whole system to malfunction.

Interestingly, race conditions can also be used to implement computer security. As race conditions result from the uncoordinated access of multiple threads/processes to a shared resources, the specification in which a race condition occurs is significantly random. For example, in our own Python example, you saw that, when simulating a race condition, the final value of the counter varies between different executions of the program; this is (partly) because of the unpredictable nature of the situation, in which multiple threads are running and accessing the shared resources. (I say partly, since the randomness also results from the random pausing periods that we generate in each execution of the program.) So, race conditions are sometimes intentionally provoked, and the information obtained when the race condition occurs can be used to generate digital fingerprints for security processes—this information, again, is significantly random, and is therefore valuable for security purposes.

Operating systems

Race conditions can occur in the context of file and memory management in an operating system, when two separate programs attempt to access the same resource, such as memory space. Imagine a situation where two processes from different programs have been running for a significant amount of time, and, even though they were originally initialized apart from each other in terms of memory space, enough data has been accumulated and the stack of execution of one process now collides with that of the other process. This can lead to the two processes sharing the same portion of memory space and can ultimately result in unpredictable consequences.

Another aspect of the complexity of race conditions is illustrated by the Unix version 7 operating system—specifically, in the `mkdir` command. Typically, the `mkdir` command is used to create a new directory in the Unix operating system; this is done by calling the `mknod` command to create the actual directory and the `chown` command to specify the owner of that directory. Because there are two separate commands to be run and a definite gap exists between when the first command is finished and the second is called, this can cause a race condition.

During the gap between the two commands, if someone can delete the new directory created by the `mknod` command and link the reference to another file, when the `chown` command is run, the ownership of that file will be changed. By exploiting this vulnerability, someone can theoretically change the ownership of any file in an operating system so that someone can create a new directory. The following diagram further illustrates this exploitation:

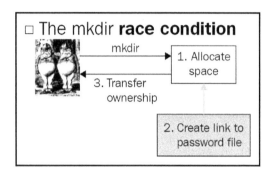

Diagram of mkdir race condition

Networking

In networking, race conditions can take the form of giving multiple users unique privileges in a network. Specifically, say a given server should only have exactly one user with admin privileges. If two users, who are both eligible to become the server admin, request access to those privileges at the same time, then it is possible for both of them to gain that access. This is because, at the point when both of the user requests are received by the server, neither of the users have been granted admin privileges yet, and the server thinks that admin privileges can still be given out.

This form of a race condition is quite common when a network is highly optimized for parallel processing (for example, non-blocking sockets), without a careful consideration of the resources shared across the network.

Summary

A race condition is defined as a phenomenon during which the output of a system is indeterminate and is dependent on the scheduling algorithm and the order in which tasks are scheduled and executed. Critical sections indicate shared resources that are accessed by multiple processes or threads in a concurrent application, which can lead to unexpected, and even erroneous, behavior. A race condition occurs when two or more threads/processes access and alter a shared resource simultaneously, resulting in mishandled and corrupted data. Race conditions also have significant implications in real-life applications, such as security, operating systems, and networking.

Since the race conditions that we observed arose when multiple threads or processes accessed and wrote to a shared resource simultaneously, the key idea for solving race conditions is to isolate the execution of different threads/processes, especially when interacting with a shared resource. With locks, we can turn a shared resource in a concurrent program into a critical section, whose integrity of data is guaranteed to be protected. However, there are a number of disadvantages to using locks: with enough locks implemented in a concurrent program, the whole program might become sequential; locks don't lock anything.

In the next chapter, we will consider one of the biggest problems in Python concurrent programming: the infamous **Global Interpreter Lock (GIL)**. You will learn about the basic idea behind the GIL, its purposes, and how to effectively work with it in concurrent Python applications.

Questions

- What is a critical section?
- What is a race condition and why is it undesirable in a concurrent program?
- What is the underlying cause of race conditions?
- How can locks solve the problem of race conditions?
- Why are locks sometimes undesirable in a concurrent program?
- What is the significance of race conditions in real-life systems and applications?

Further reading

For more information, you can refer to the following links:

- *Parallel Programming with Python*, by Jan Palach, Packt Publishing Ltd, 2014
- *Python Parallel Programming Cookbook*, by Giancarlo Zaccone, Packt Publishing Ltd, 2015
- *Race Conditions and Critical Sections* (tutorials.jenkov.com/java-concurrency/race-conditions-and-critical-sections), by Jakob Jenkov
- *Race conditions, files, and security flaws; or the tortoise and the hare redux*, by Matt Bishop, Technical Report CSE-95-98(1995)
- *Computer and Information Security, Chapter 11, Software Flaws and Malware 1 Illustration* (slideplayer.com/slide/10319860/)

15
The Global Interpreter Lock

One of the major players in Python concurrent programming is the **Global Interpreter Lock (GIL)**. In this chapter, we will cover the definition and purposes of the GIL, and how it affects concurrent Python applications. The problems that the GIL poses for Python concurrent systems and the controversy around its implementation will also be discussed. Finally, we will mention some thoughts on how Python programmers and developers should think about, and interact with, the GIL.

The following topics will be covered in this chapter:

- A brief introduction to the GIL: what gave rise to it, and the problems it causes
- Efforts in removing/fixing the GIL in Python
- How to effectively work with the GIL in Python concurrent programs

Technical requirements

The following is a list of prerequisites for this chapter:

- Ensure that you have Python 3 installed on your computer
- Download the GitHub repository at `https://github.com/PacktPublishing/Mastering-Concurrency-in-Python`
- During this chapter, we will be working with the subfolder named `Chapter15`
- Check out the following video to see the Code in Action: `http://bit.ly/2DFDYhC`

An introduction to the Global Interpreter Lock

The GIL is quite popular in the Python concurrent programming community. Designed as a lock that will only allow one thread to access and control the Python interpreter at any given time, the GIL in Python is often known as the infamous GIL that prevents multithreaded programs from reaching their fully optimized speed. In this section, we will discuss the concept behind the GIL, and its goals: why it was designed and implemented, and how it affected multithreaded programming in Python.

An analysis of memory management in Python

Before we jump into the specifics of the GIL and its effects, let's consider the problems that Python core developers encountered during the early days of Python, and that gave rise to a need for the GIL. Specifically, there is a significant difference between Python programming and programming in other popular languages, in terms of managing objects in the memory space.

For example, in the programming language C++, a variable is actually a location in the memory space where a value will be written. This setup leads to the fact that, when a non-pointer variable is assigned with a specific value, the programming language will effectively copy that specific value to the memory location (that is, the variable). Additionally, when a variable is assigned with another variable (which is not a pointer), the memory location of the latter will be copied to that of the former; no further connection between these two variables will be maintained after the assignment.

On the other hand, Python considers a variable as simply a name, while the actual values of its variables are isolated in another region in the memory space. When a value is assigned to a variable, the variable is effectively given a reference to the location in the memory space of the value (even though the term referencing is not used in the same sense as C++ referencing). Memory management in Python is therefore fundamentally different from the model of putting a value into a memory space that we see in C++.

This means that when an assignment instruction is executed, Python simply interacts with references and switches them around—not the actual values themselves. Also, for this reason, multiple variables can be referenced by the same value, and the changes made by one variable will be reflected throughout all of the other associated variables.

Let's analyze this feature in Python. If you have already downloaded the code for this book from the GitHub page, go ahead and navigate to the `Chapter15` folder. Let's take a look at the `Chapter15/example1.py` file, as follows:

```
# Chapter15/example1.py

import sys

print(f'Reference count when direct-referencing: {sys.getrefcount([7])}.')

a = [7]
print(f'Reference count when referenced once: {sys.getrefcount(a)}.')

b = a
print(f'Reference count when referenced twice: {sys.getrefcount(a)}.')

######################################################################

a[0] = 8
print(f'Variable a after a is changed: {a}.')
print(f'Variable b after a is changed: {b}.')

print('Finished.')
```

In this example, we are looking at the management of the value `[7]` (a list of one element: the integer 7). We mentioned that values in Python are stored independently of variables, and value management in Python simply references variables to the appropriate values. The `sys.getrefcount()` method in Python takes in an object and returns the counter of all references that the value associated to that object has. Here, we are calling `sys.getrefcount()` three times: on the actual value, `[7]`; the variable a that is assigned with the value; and finally, the variable b that is assigned with the variable a.

Additionally, we are exploring the process of mutating the value by using a variable referenced with it and the resulting values of all of the variables associated to that value. Specifically, we are mutating the first element of the list via variable a, and printing out the values of both a and b. Run the script, and your output should be similar to the following:

```
> python3 example1.py
Reference count when direct-referencing: 1.
Reference count when referenced once: 2.
Reference count when referenced twice: 3.
Variable a after a is changed: [8].
Variable b after a is changed: [8].
Finished.
```

As you can see, this output is consistent with what we discussed: for the first `sys.getrefcount()` function call, there is only one reference count for the value [7], which is created when we directly reference it; when we assign the list to variable a, the value has two references, since a is now associated with the value; finally, when a is assigned to b, [7] is additionally referenced by b, and the reference count is now three.

In the output of the second part of the program, we can see that, when we changed the value of which variable a references, [7] was mutated instead of the variable a. As a result, variable b, which was referencing the same value as a, also had its value changed.

The following diagram illustrates this process. In Python programs, variables (a and b) simply make references to the actual values (objects), and an assignment statement between two variables (for example, a = b) instructs Python to have the two variables reference the same object (as opposed to copying the actual value to another memory location, like in C++):

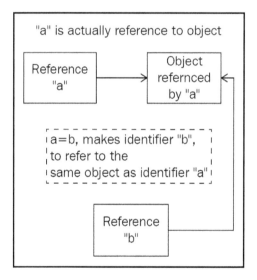

Diagram of Python's referencing scheme

The problem that the GIL addresses

Keeping Python's implementation of memory and variable management in mind, we can see that references to a given value in Python are constantly changing in a program, and keeping track of the reference count for a value is therefore highly important.

Now, applying what you learned in Chapter 14, *Race Conditions*, you should know that in a Python concurrent program, this reference count is a shared resource that needs protection from race conditions. In other words, this reference count is a critical section, which, if handled carelessly, will result in an incorrect interpretation of how many variables are referencing a particular value. This will cause memory leaks that will make Python programs significantly inefficient, and may even release a memory that is actually being referenced by some variables, losing that value forever.

As you learned in the previous chapter, a solution to making sure that race conditions will not occur with regard to a particular shared resource is to place a lock on that resource, effectively allowing one thread, at the most, to access the resource at any given time within a concurrent program. We also discussed that, if enough locks are placed in a concurrent program, that program will become entirely sequential, and no additional speed will be gained by implementing concurrency.

The GIL is a solution to the combination of the two preceding problems, being one single lock on the entire execution of Python. The GIL must first be acquired by any Python instruction that wants to be executed (CPU-bound tasks), preventing a race condition from occurring for any reference count.

In the early days of the development of the Python language, other solutions to the problem described here were also proposed, but the GIL was the most efficient and simple to implement, by far. Since the GIL is a lightweight, overarching lock for the entire execution of Python, no other lock needs to be implemented to guarantee the integrity of other critical sections, keeping the performance overhead of Python programs at a minimum.

Problems raised by the GIL

Intuitively, with a lock guarding all CPU-bound tasks in Python, a concurrent program will not be able to become fully multithreading. The GIL effectively prevents CPU-bound tasks from being executed in parallel across multiple threads. To understand the effect of this feature of the GIL, let's consider an example in Python; navigate to Chapter15/example2.py, as follows:

```python
# Chapter15/example2.py

import time
import threading

COUNT = 50000000

def countdown(n):
    while n > 0:
        n -= 1

###########################################################################

start = time.time()
countdown(COUNT)

print('Sequential program finished.')
print(f'Took {time.time() - start : .2f} seconds.')

###########################################################################

thread1 = threading.Thread(target=countdown, args=(COUNT // 2,))
thread2 = threading.Thread(target=countdown, args=(COUNT // 2,))

start = time.time()
thread1.start()
thread2.start()
thread1.join()
thread2.join()

print('Concurrent program finished.')
print(f'Took {time.time() - start : .2f} seconds.')
```

In this example, we are comparing the speed of executing a particular program in Python sequentially and concurrently, via multithreading. Specifically, we have a function named `countdown()` that simulates a heavy CPU-bound task, which takes in a number, n, and decrements it until it becomes zero or negative. We then call `countdown()` on 50,000,000 once, as a sequential program. Finally, we call the function twice, each in a separate thread, on 25,000,000, which is exactly half of 50,000,000; this is the multithreading version of the program. We are also keeping track of the time it takes for Python to run both the sequential program and the multithreading program.

Theoretically, the multithreading version of the program should take half as long as the sequential version, as the task is effectively being split in half and run in parallel, via the two threads that we created. However, the output produced by the program would suggest otherwise. The following output is what I obtained through running the script:

```
> python3 example2.py
Sequential program finished.
Took 2.80 seconds.
Concurrent program finished.
Took 2.74 seconds.
```

Contrary to what we predicted, the concurrent version of the countdown took almost as long as the sequential version; multithreading did not offer any considerable speedup for our program. This is a direct effect of having the GIL guarding CPU-bound tasks, as multiple threads are not allowed to run simultaneously. Sometimes, a multithreading program can take even longer to complete its execution than its sequential counterpart, since there is also the overhead of acquiring and releasing the GIL.

This is undoubtedly a significant problem for multithreading, and for concurrent programming in Python in general, because as long as a program contains CPU-bound instructions, those instructions will, in fact, be sequential in the execution of the program. However, instructions that are not CPU-bound happen outside the GIL, and thus, they are not affected by the GIL (for example, I/O-bound instructions).

The potential removal of the GIL from Python

You have learned that the GIL sets a significant constraint on our multithreading programs in Python, especially those with CPU-bound tasks. For this reason, many Python developers have come to view the GIL in a negative light, and the term *"the infamous GIL"* has started to become popular; it is not surprising that some have even advocated the complete removal of the GIL from the Python language.

In fact, multiple attempts to remove the GIL have been made by prominent Python users. However, the GIL is so deeply implanted in the implementation of the language, and the execution of most libraries and packages that are not thread-safe is so significantly dependent on the GIL, that the removal of the GIL will actually engender bugs as well as backward incompatibility issues for your Python programs. A number of Python developers and researchers tried to completely omit the GIL from Python execution, and most existing C extensions, which depend heavily on the functionalities of the GIL, stopped working.

Now there are other viable solutions to address the problems that we have discussed; in other words, the GIL is in every way replaceable. However, most of these solutions contain so many complex instructions that they actually decrease the performance of sequential and I/O-bound programs, which are not affected by the GIL. So, these solutions will slow down single-threaded or multithreaded I/O programs, which actually make up a large percentage of existing Python applications. Interestingly, the creator of Python, Guido van Rossum, also commented on this topic in his article, *It isn't Easy to Remove the GIL*:

> *"I'd welcome a set of patches into Py3k only if the performance for a single-threaded program (and for a multi-threaded but I/O-bound program) does not decrease."*

Unfortunately, this request has not been achieved by any of the proposed alternatives to the GIL. The GIL remains an integral part of the Python language.

How to work with the GIL

There are a few ways to deal with the GIL in your Python applications, which will be addressed as follows.

Implementing multiprocessing, rather than multithreading

This is perhaps the most popular and easiest method to circumvent the GIL and achieve optimal speed in a concurrent program. As the GIL only prevents multiple threads from executing CPU-bound tasks simultaneously, processes executing over multiple cores of a system, each having its own memory space, are completely immune to the GIL.

Specifically, considering the preceding countdown example, let's compare the performance of that CPU-bound program when it is sequential, multithreading, and multiprocessing. Navigate to the `Chapter15/example3.py` file; the first part of the program is identical to what we saw earlier, but at the end we add in an implementation of a multiprocessing solution for the problem of counting down from 50,000,000, using two separate processes:

```
# Chapter15/example3.py

import time
import threading
from multiprocessing import Pool

COUNT = 50000000

def countdown(n):
    while n > 0:
        n -= 1

if __name__ == '__main__':

    ###################################################################
    # Sequential

    start = time.time()
    countdown(COUNT)

    print('Sequential program finished.')
    print(f'Took {time.time() - start : .2f} seconds.')
    print()

    ###################################################################
    # Multithreading

    thread1 = threading.Thread(target=countdown, args=(COUNT // 2,))
    thread2 = threading.Thread(target=countdown, args=(COUNT // 2,))

    start = time.time()
    thread1.start()
```

```
thread2.start()
thread1.join()
thread2.join()

print('Multithreading program finished.')
print(f'Took {time.time() - start : .2f} seconds.')
print()

##################################################################
# Multiprocessing

pool = Pool(processes=2)
start = time.time()
pool.apply_async(countdown, args=(COUNT//2,))
pool.apply_async(countdown, args=(COUNT//2,))
pool.close()
pool.join()

print('Multiprocessing program finished.')
print(f'Took {time.time() - start : .2f} seconds.')
```

After running the program, my output was as follows:

```
> python3 example3.py
Sequential program finished.
Took 2.95 seconds.

Multithreading program finished.
Took 2.69 seconds.

Multiprocessing program finished.
Took 1.54 seconds.
```

There is still a minimal difference in speed between the sequential and multithreading versions of the program. However, the multiprocessing version was able to cut that speed by almost half in its execution; as discussed in earlier chapters; since processes are fairly heavy weight, multiprocessing instructions contain significant overhead, which is the reason why the speed of the multiprocessing program was not exactly half of the sequential program.

Getting around the GIL with native extensions

There are Python native extensions that are written in C/C++, and are therefore able to avoid the limitations that the GIL sets out; one example is the most popular Python scientific computing package, NumPy. Within these extensions, manual releases of the GIL can be made, so that the execution can simply bypass the lock. However, these releases need to be implemented carefully and accompanied by the reassertion of the GIL before the execution goes back to the main Python execution.

Utilizing a different Python interpreter

The GIL only exists in CPython, which is the most common interpreter for the language by far, and is built in C. However, there are other interpreters for Python, such as Jython (written in Java) and IronPython (written in C++), that can be used to avoid the GIL and its affects on multithreading programs. Keep in mind that these interpreters are not as widely used as CPython, and some packages and libraries might not be compatible with one or both of them.

Summary

While the GIL in Python offers a simple and intuitive solution to one of the more difficult problems in the language, it also raises a number of problems of its own, concerning the ability to run multiple threads in a Python program to process CPU-bound tasks. Multiple attempts have been made to remove the GIL from the main implementation of Python, but none have been able to achieve it while maintaining the effectiveness of processing non-CPU-bound tasks, which are affected by the GIL.

In Python, multiple methods are available to provide options for working with the GIL. All in all, while it possesses considerable notoriety among the Python programming community, the GIL only affects a certain portion of the Python ecosystem, and can be seen as a necessary evil that is too essential to remove from the language. Python developers should learn to coexist with the GIL, and work around it in their concurrent programs.

In the last four chapters, we discussed some of the most well-known and common problems in concurrent programming in Python. In the last section of the book, we will be looking at some of the more advanced functionalities of concurrency that Python provides. In the next chapter, you will learn about the design of lock-free and lock-based concurrent data structures.

Questions

- What are the differences in memory management between Python and C++?
- What problem does the GIL solve for Python?
- What problem does the GIL create for Python?
- What are some of the approaches to circumventing the GIL in Python programs?

Further reading

For more information, you can refer to the following links:

- *What is the Python Global Interpreter Lock (GIL)?* (`realpython.com/python-gil/`), Abhinav Ajitsaria
- *The Python GIL Visualized* (`dabeaz.blogspot.com/2010/01/python-gil-visualized`), Dave Beazley
- *Copy Operations in Python* (`pythontic.com/modules/copy/introduction`)
- *It isn't Easy to Remove the GIL* (`www.artima.com/weblogs/viewpost.jsp?thread=214235`), Guido Van Rossum
- *Parallel Programming with Python*, by Jan Palach, Packt Publishing Ltd, 2014
- *Learning Concurrency in Python: Build highly efficient, robust, and concurrent applications*, Elliot Forbes (2017)

16
Designing Lock-Based and Mutex-Free Concurrent Data Structures

In this chapter, we will analyze the detailed process of designing and implementing two common types of data structure in concurrent programming: lock-based and mutex-free. The principal differences between the two data structures, as well as their respective usages in concurrent programming, will be discussed. Throughout the chapter, an analysis of the trade-off between the accuracy and speed of concurrent programs is also supplied. Through this analysis, readers will be able to apply the same trade-off analysis for their own concurrent applications.

The following topics will be covered in this chapter:

- Common problems with lock-based data structures, and how to address them
- A detailed analysis of how to implement a lock-based data structure
- The idea behind mutex-free data structures, along with their advantages and disadvantages, as compared to lock-based data structures
- A detailed analysis of how to implement a mutex-free data structure

Technical requirements

The following is a list of prerequisites for this chapter:

- Ensure that you have Python 3 installed on your computer
- Download the GitHub repository at `https://github.com/PacktPublishing/Mastering-Concurrency-in-Python`
- Throughout this chapter, we will be working with the subfolder named `Chapter16`
- Check out the following video to see the Code in Action: `http://bit.ly/2QhT3MS`

Lock-based concurrent data structures in Python

In previous chapters that covered the usage of locks, you learned that locks don't lock anything; an insubstantial locking mechanism implemented on a data structure does not actually prevent external programs from accessing the data structure at the same time, by simply bypassing the lock imposed. One solution to this problem is to embed the lock into the data structure, so that it is impossible for the lock to be ignored by external entities.

In the first section of this chapter, we will consider the theories behind the preceding specific use of locks and lock-based data structures. Specifically, we will analyze the process of designing a concurrent counter that can be safely executed by different threads, using locks (or mutex) as the synchronization mechanism.

LocklessCounter and race conditions

First, let's simulate the problem encountered with a naive, lockless implementation of a counter class in a concurrent program. If you have already downloaded the code for this book from the GitHub page, go ahead and navigate to the `Chapter16` folder.

Let us take a look at the `Chapter16/example1.py` file—specifically, the implementation of the `LocklessCounter` class:

```
# Chapter16/example1.py

import time

class LocklessCounter:
    def __init__(self):
        self.value = 0

    def increment(self, x):
        new_value = self.value + x
        time.sleep(0.001) # creating a delay
        self.value = new_value

    def get_value(self):
        return self.value
```

This is a simple counter that has an attribute called `value`, which contains the current value of the counter, assigned with 0 when the counter instance is first initialized. The `increment()` method of the class takes in an argument, `x`, and increases the current value of the calling `LocklessCounter` object by x. Notice that we are creating a small delay inside the `increment()` function, between the process of computing the new value of the counter and the process of assigning that new value to the counter object. The class also has a method called `get_value()`, which returns the current value of the calling counter.

It is quite obvious why this implementation of the `LocklessCounter` class can create a race condition in a concurrent program: while a thread is in the middle of incrementing a shared counter, another thread also might access the counter to execute the `increment()` method, and the change to the counter value made by the first thread might be overwritten by the one made by the second thread.

As a refresher, the following diagram shows how a race condition can occur in situations where multiple processes or threads access and mutate a shared resource at the same time:

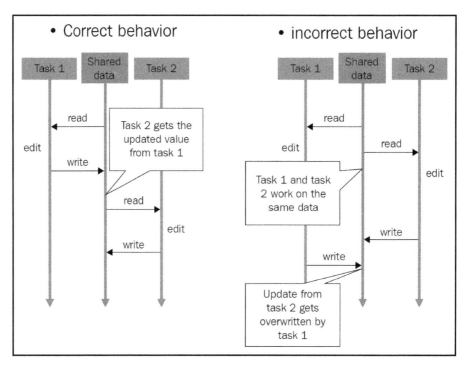

Diagram of a race condition

To simulate this race condition, in our main program we are including a total of three threads, to increment a shared counter by 300 times:

```
# Chapter16/example1.py

from concurrent.futures import ThreadPoolExecutor

counter = LocklessCounter()
with ThreadPoolExecutor(max_workers=3) as executor:
    executor.map(counter.increment, [1 for i in range(300)])

print(f'Final counter: {counter.get_value()}.')
print('Finished.')
```

The `concurrent.futures` module offers us an easy and high-level way to schedule a task through a pool of threads. Specifically, after initializing a shared counter object, we declare the variable `executor` as a pool of three threads (use a context manager), and that executor calls the `increment()` method on the shared counter 300 times, each time incrementing the value of the counter by `1`.

These tasks are to be executed among the three threads in the pool, using the `map()` method of the `ThreadPoolExecutor` class. At the end of the program, we simply print out the final value of the counter object. The following code shows my own output after running the script:

```
> python3 example1.py
Final counter: 101.
Finished.
```

While it is possible to obtain a different value for the counter when executing the script on your own system, it is extremely unlikely that the final value of the counter will actually be 300, which is the correct value. Additionally, if you were to run the script over and over again, it would be possible to obtain different values for the counter, illustrating the non-deterministic nature of the program. Again, as some threads were overwriting the changes made by other threads, some increments got lost during the execution, resulting in the fact that the counter was only successfully incremented `101` times, in this case.

Embedding locks in the data structure of the counter

The goal of a good lock-based concurrent data structure is to have its locks internally implemented within its class attributes and methods, so that external functions and programs cannot bypass those locks and access a shared concurrent object simultaneously. For our counter data structure, we will be adding an additional attribute for the class, which will hold the `lock` object that corresponds to the value of the counter. Consider the following new implementation of the data structure in the `Chapter16/example2.py` file:

```
# Chapter16/example2.py

import threading
import time

class LockedCounter:
    def __init__(self):
        self.value = 0
        self.lock = threading.Lock()
```

```
    def increment(self, x):
        with self.lock:
            new_value = self.value + x
            time.sleep(0.001) # creating a delay
            self.value = new_value

    def get_value(self):
        with self.lock:
            value = self.value

        return value
```

In this implementation of our counter data structure, a `lock` object is also initialized as an attribute of a `LockedCounter` instance, when that instance is initialized. Additionally, any time the value of the counter is accessed by a thread, whether for reading (the `get_value()` method) or updating (the `increment()` method), that `lock` attribute has to be acquired, to ensure that no other thread is also accessing it. This is done by using a context manager with the `lock` attribute.

Theoretically, this implementation should solve the problem of the race condition for us. In our main program, we are implementing the same thread pool that was used in the previous example. A shared counter will be created, and it will be incremented 300 times (each time by one unit), across three different threads:

```
# Chapter16/example2.py

from concurrent.futures import ThreadPoolExecutor

counter = LockedCounter()
with ThreadPoolExecutor(max_workers=3) as executor:
    executor.map(counter.increment, [1 for i in range(300)])

print(f'Final counter: {counter.get_value()}.')
print('Finished.')
```

Run the script, and the output produced by the program should be similar to the following:

```
> python3 example2.py
Final counter: 300.
Finished.
```

As you can see, the problem of the race condition has been addressed successfully: the final value of the counter is `300`, which corresponds perfectly to the number of increments that were executed. Furthermore, no matter how many times the program is run again, the value of the counter will always remain `300`. What we currently have is a working, correct data structure for concurrent counters.

The concept of scalability

One aspect of programming that is essential to the application of concurrency is **scalability**. By scalability, we mean the changes in performance when the number of tasks to be processed by the program increases. Andre B. Bondi, founder and president of Software Performance and Scalability Consulting, LLC, defines the term scalability as *"the capability of a system, network, or process to handle a growing amount of work, or its potential to be enlarged to accommodate that growth."*

In concurrent programming, scalability is an important concept that always needs to be taken into account; the amount of work that grows in concurrent programming is typically the number of tasks to be executed, as well as the number of processes and threads active to execute those tasks. For example, the designing, implementing, and testing phases of a concurrent application usually involve fairly small amounts of work, to facilitate efficient and fast development. This means that a typical concurrent application will handle significantly more work in real-life situations than it did during the development stage. This is why an analysis of scalability is crucial in well-designed concurrent applications.

Since the execution of a process or thread is independent of the process execution of another, as long as the amount of work a single process/thread is responsible for remains the same, we would like changes in the number of processes/threads to not affect the performance of the general program. This characteristic is called **perfect scalability**, and is a desirable characteristic for a concurrent program; if the amount of work for a given perfectly scalable concurrent program increases, the program can simply create more active processes or threads, in order to absorb the increased amount of work. Its performance can then stay stable.

However, perfect scalability is virtually impossible to achieve most of the time, due to the overhead in creating threads and processes. That being said, if the performance of a concurrent program does not considerably worsen as the number of active processes or threads increases, then we can accept the scalability. The term **considerably worsen** is highly dependent on the types of task that the concurrent program is responsible for executing, as well as how large a decrease in program performance is permitted.

In this kind of analysis, we will consider a two-dimensional graph, representing the scalability of a given concurrent program. The x axis denotes the number of active threads or processes (again, each is responsible for executing a fixed amount of work throughout the program); the y axis denotes the speed of the program, with different numbers of active threads or processes. The graph under consideration will have a generally increasing trend; the more processes/threads the program has, the more time it will (most likely) take for the program to execute. Perfect scalability, on the other hand, will translate to a horizontal line, as no additional time is needed when the number of threads/processes increases.

The following diagram is an example of such a graph, for scalability analysis:

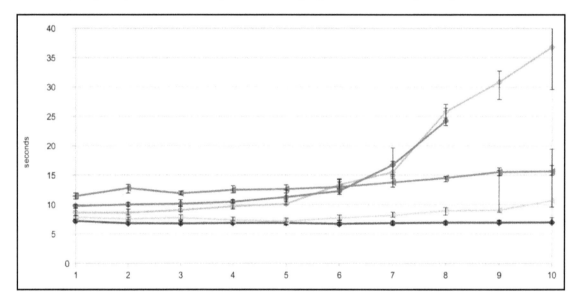

Example of scalability analysis (Source: stackoverflow.com/questions/10660990/c-sharp-server-scalability-issue-on-linux)

In the preceding graph, the x axis indicates the number of executing threads/processes, and the y axis indicates the running time (in seconds, in this case). The different graphs indicate the scalability of specific setups (the operating system combined with multiple cores).

The steeper the slope of a graph is, the worse the corresponding concurrent model scales with an increasing number of threads/processes. For example, a horizontal line (the dark blue and lowest graph in this case) signifies perfect scalability, while the yellow (upper most) graph indicates an undesirable scalability.

Analysis of the scalability of the counter data structure

Now, let's consider the scalability of our current counter data structure—specifically, with changing numbers of active threads. We had three threads increment a shared counter for a total of 300 times; so, in our scalability analysis, we will have each of the active threads increment a shared counter 100 times, while changing the number of active threads in our program. Following the aforementioned specification of scalability, we will look at how the performance (speed) of the program that uses the counter data structure changes when the number of threads increases.

Consider the `Chapter16/example3.py` file, as follows:

```
# Chapter16/example3.py

import threading
from concurrent.futures import ThreadPoolExecutor
import time
import matplotlib.pyplot as plt

class LockedCounter:
    def __init__(self):
        self.value = 0
        self.lock = threading.Lock()

    def increment(self, x):
        with self.lock:
            new_value = self.value + x
            time.sleep(0.001) # creating a delay
            self.value = new_value

    def get_value(self):
        with self.lock:
            value = self.value

        return value

n_threads = []
times = []
for n_workers in range(1, 11):
    n_threads.append(n_workers)

    counter = LockedCounter()

    start = time.time()
```

```
    with ThreadPoolExecutor(max_workers=n_workers) as executor:
        executor.map(counter.increment,
                        [1 for i in range(100 * n_workers)])

    times.append(time.time() - start)

    print(f'Number of threads: {n_workers}')
    print(f'Final counter: {counter.get_value()}.')
    print(f'Time taken: {times[-1] : .2f} seconds.')
    print('-' * 40)

plt.plot(n_threads, times)
plt.xlabel('Number of threads'); plt.ylabel('Time in seconds')
plt.show()
```

In the preceding script, we are still using the same implementation of the `LockedCounter` class that we used in the previous example. In our main program, we are testing this class against various numbers of active threads; specifically, we are iterating over a `for` loop, to have the number of active threads go from 1 to 10. In each iteration, we initialize a shared counter and create a pool of threads to process an appropriate number of tasks—in this case, incrementing the shared counter 100 times for each thread.

We are also keeping track of the number of active threads, as well as the time it took for the pool of threads to finish its tasks in each iteration. This is our data for the scalability analysis process. We are printing this data out and plotting a scalability graph similar to what we saw in the preceding sample graph.

The following code shows my output from running the script:

```
> python3 example3.py
Number of threads: 1
Final counter: 100.
Time taken: 0.15 seconds.
----------------------------------------
Number of threads: 2
Final counter: 200.
Time taken: 0.28 seconds.
----------------------------------------
Number of threads: 3
Final counter: 300.
Time taken: 0.45 seconds.
----------------------------------------
Number of threads: 4
Final counter: 400.
Time taken: 0.59 seconds.
----------------------------------------
Number of threads: 5
```

```
Final counter: 500.
Time taken: 0.75 seconds.
------------------------------------------
Number of threads: 6
Final counter: 600.
Time taken: 0.87 seconds.
------------------------------------------
Number of threads: 7
Final counter: 700.
Time taken: 1.01 seconds.
------------------------------------------
Number of threads: 8
Final counter: 800.
Time taken: 1.18 seconds.
------------------------------------------
Number of threads: 9
Final counter: 900.
Time taken: 1.29 seconds.
------------------------------------------
Number of threads: 10
Final counter: 1000.
Time taken: 1.49 seconds.
------------------------------------------
```

Additionally, the scalability graph that I obtained is shown as follows:

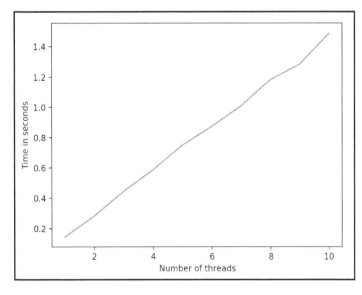

Scalability of lock-based counter data structures

Even if your own output varies in the specific duration of each iteration, the scalability trend should be relatively the same; in other words, your scalability graph should have the same slope as the preceding graph. As you can see from the kinds of output that we have, even though the counter in each iteration had the correct value, the current scalability of our counter data structure is highly undesirable: as more threads are added to the program to execute more tasks, the performance of the program decreases, almost linearly. Recall that the desired perfect scalability requires the performance to remain stable across different numbers of threads/processes. Our counter data structure increases the execution time of the program that we have by an amount that is proportional to the increase in the number of active threads.

Intuitively, this constraint in scalability results from our locking mechanism: since only one thread can access and increment the shared counter at any given time, the more increments the program has to execute, the longer it will take to finish all increment tasks. Of the biggest disadvantages to using locks as a synchronization mechanism, this is the second: locks can execute a concurrent program (again, the first disadvantage is the fact that locks don't actually lock anything).

Approximate counters as a solution for scalability

Given the complexity of designing and implementing a correct, yet fast, lock-based concurrent data structure, developing efficiently scalable locking mechanisms is a popular topic of research in computer science, and many approaches to solving the problem that we are facing have been proposed. In this section, we will discuss one of them: **approximate counters**.

The idea behind approximate counters

Let's think back to our current program and the reason why the locks are preventing us from achieving good performance in terms of speed: all of the active threads in our program interact with the same shared counter, which can only interact with one thread at a time. The solution to this problem is to isolate the interactions with a counter of separate threads. Specifically, the value of the counter that we are keeping track of will not be represented by only a single, shared counter object anymore; instead, we will use many **local counters**, one per thread/process, in addition to the shared **global counter** that we originally had.

The basic idea behind this approach is to distribute the work (incrementing the shared global counter) across other low-level counters. When an active thread executes and wants to increment the global counter, first it has to increment its corresponding local counter. Interacting with individual local counters, unlike doing it with a single, shared counter, is highly scalable, as only one thread accesses and updates each local counter; in other words, there is no contention between different threads in interacting with the individual local counters.

As each thread interacts with its corresponding local counter, the local counters have to interact with the global counter. Specifically, each local counter will periodically acquire the lock for the global counter and increment it with respect to its current value; for example, if a local counter holding the value of six wants to increment the global counter, it will do it by six units, and set its own value back to zero. This is because all increments reported from the local counters are relative to the value of the global counter, meaning that, if a local counter holds the value of x, the global counter should increment its value by x.

You can think of this design as a simple network, with the global counter being at the center node, and each local counter being a rear node. Each rear node interacts with the center node by sending its value to the center node and consequently resetting its value back to zero. The following diagram further illustrates this design:

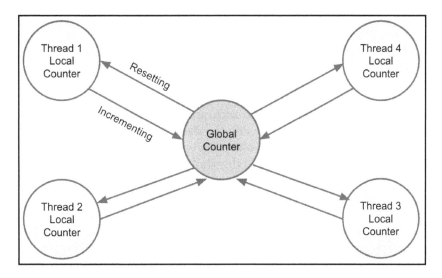

Diagram of four-thread approximate counters

As discussed previously, if all of the active threads were to interact with the same lock-based counter, no additional speed could be gained from making the program concurrent, since the execution between separate threads cannot be overlapped. Now, with one separate counter object for each thread, the threads can update their corresponding local counters independently and simultaneously, creating overlaps that will result in better performance in speed for our program, making the program more scalable.

The name of the technique, **approximate counters**, comes from the fact that the value of the global counter is simply an approximation of the correct value. Specifically, the value of the global counter is calculated solely via the values of the local counters, and it becomes more accurate each time the global counter is incremented by one of the local counters.

There is, however, a specification in this design that deserves great consideration. How often should the local counters interact with the global counter and update its value? Surely it cannot be at the rate of every increment (incrementing the global counter every time a local counter is incremented), as that would be equivalent to using one shared lock, with even more over overhead (from the local counters).

A quantity called **threshold S** is used to denote the frequency in question; specifically, threshold S is defined as the upper boundary of the value of a local counter. So, if a local counter is incremented such that its value is greater than threshold S, it should update the global counter and reset its value to zero. The smaller threshold S is, the more frequently the local counters will update the global counter, and the less scalable our program will be, but the value of the global counter will be more up-to-date. Conversely, the larger threshold S is, the less frequently the value of the global counter will be updated, but the better the performance of our program will be.

There is, therefore, a trade-off between the accuracy of an approximate counter object and the scalability of a concurrent program using the data structure. Similar to other common trade-offs in computer science and programming, only through personal experimentation and testing can one determine the optimal threshold S for one's approximate counter data structure. In the next section, when we implement our own design for an approximate counter data structure, we will arbitrarily set the value of threshold S to 10.

Implementing approximate counters in Python

With the concept of approximate counters in mind, let's try to implement the data structure in Python, building on our previous design for the lock-based counter. Consider the following `Chapter16/example4.py` file—specifically, the `LockedCounter` class and the `ApproximateCounter` class:

```
# Chapter16/example4.py
```

```
import threading
import time

class LockedCounter:
    def __init__(self):
        self.value = 0
        self.lock = threading.Lock()

    def increment(self, x):
        with self.lock:
            new_value = self.value + x
            time.sleep(0.001) # creating a delay
            self.value = new_value

    def get_value(self):
        with self.lock:
            value = self.value

        return value

class ApproximateCounter:
    def __init__(self, global_counter):
        self.value = 0
        self.lock = threading.Lock()
        self.global_counter = global_counter
        self.threshold = 10

    def increment(self, x):
        with self.lock:
            new_value = self.value + x
            time.sleep(0.001) # creating a delay
            self.value = new_value

            if self.value >= self.threshold:
                self.global_counter.increment(self.value)
                self.value = 0

    def get_value(self):
        with self.lock:
            value = self.value

        return value
```

While the `LockedCounter` class remains the same as in our previous example (this class will be used to implement our global counter objects), the `ApproximateCounter` class, which contains the implementation of the approximate counter logic that we discussed previously, is of interest. A newly initialized `ApproximateCounter` object will be given a starting value of 0, and it will also have a lock, as it is also a lock-based data structure. The important attributes of an `ApproximateCounter` object are the global counter that it needs to report to and the threshold that specifies the rate at which it reports to its corresponding global counter. As mentioned previously, here, we are simply choosing 10 as an arbitrary value for the threshold.

In the `increment()` method of the `ApproximateCounter` class, we can also see the same increment logic: the method takes in a parameter named x and increments the value of the counter by x while holding the lock of the calling approximate counter object. Additionally, the method also has to check whether the newly incremented value of the counter is past its threshold; if so, it will increment the value of its global counter by an amount that is equal to the current value of the local counter, and that value of the local counter will be set back to 0. The `get_value()` method that is used to return the current value of the counter in this class is the same as what we saw previously.

Now, let's test and compare the scalability of the new data structure in our main program. First, we will regenerate the data for the scalability of our old single-lock counter data structure:

```python
# Chapter16/example4.py

from concurrent.futures import ThreadPoolExecutor

# Previous single-lock counter

single_counter_n_threads = []
single_counter_times = []
for n_workers in range(1, 11):
    single_counter_n_threads.append(n_workers)

    counter = LockedCounter()

    start = time.time()

    with ThreadPoolExecutor(max_workers=n_workers) as executor:
        executor.map(counter.increment,
                    [1 for i in range(100 * n_workers)])

    single_counter_times.append(time.time() - start)
```

Just like in our previous example, we are using a `ThreadPoolExecutor` object to process tasks concurrently, in separate threads, while keeping track of the time it took for each iteration to finish; there is nothing surprising here. Next, we will generate the same data with a corresponding number of active threads in the iterations of the `for` loop, as follows:

```
# New approximate counters

def thread_increment(counter):
    counter.increment(1)

approx_counter_n_threads = []
approx_counter_times = []
for n_workers in range(1, 11):
    approx_counter_n_threads.append(n_workers)

    global_counter = LockedCounter()

    start = time.time()

    local_counters = [ApproximateCounter(global_counter) for i in
range(n_workers)]
    with ThreadPoolExecutor(max_workers=n_workers) as executor:
        for i in range(100):
            executor.map(thread_increment, local_counters)

    approx_counter_times.append(time.time() - start)

    print(f'Number of threads: {n_workers}')
    print(f'Final counter: {global_counter.get_value()}.')
    print('-' * 40)
```

Let's take some time to analyze the preceding code. First, we have an external `thread_increment()` function that takes in a counter and increments it by 1; this function will be used as refactored code later on, to individually increment our local counters.

Again, we will be iterating through a `for` loop to analyze the performance of this new data structure with a changing number of active threads. Inside each iteration, we first initialize a `LockedCounter` object as our global counter, together with a list of local counters, which are instances of the `ApproximateCounter` class. All of them are associated with the same global counter (which was passed in the initialization method), as they need to report to the same counter.

Next, similar to what we have been doing to schedule tasks for multiple threads, we are using a context manager to create a thread pool, inside of which we will be distributing the tasks (incrementing the local counters) via a nested `for` loop. The reason we are looping through another `for` loop is to simulate the number of tasks consistent with what we implemented in the previous example, and also to distribute those tasks across all of the local counters concurrently. We are also printing out the final value of the global counter in each iteration, to ensure that our new data structure is working correctly.

Finally, in our main program, we will be plotting the data points that are generated from the two `for` loops, to compare the scalability of the two data structures via their respective performances:

```
# Chapter16/example4.py
import matplotlib.pyplot as plt

# Plotting

single_counter_line, = plt.plot(
    single_counter_n_threads,
    single_counter_times,
    c = 'blue',
    label = 'Single counter'
)
approx_counter_line, = plt.plot(
    approx_counter_n_threads,
    approx_counter_times,
    c = 'red',
    label = 'Approximate counter'
)
plt.legend(handles=[single_counter_line, approx_counter_line], loc=2)
plt.xlabel('Number of threads'); plt.ylabel('Time in seconds')
plt.show()
```

Run the script, and the first output that you will receive will include the individual final values of the global counters in our second `for` loop, as follows:

```
> python3 example4.py
Number of threads: 1
Final counter: 100.
----------------------------------------
Number of threads: 2
Final counter: 200.
----------------------------------------
Number of threads: 3
Final counter: 300.
----------------------------------------
```

```
Number of threads: 4
Final counter: 400.
----------------------------------------
Number of threads: 5
Final counter: 500.
----------------------------------------
Number of threads: 6
Final counter: 600.
----------------------------------------
Number of threads: 7
Final counter: 700.
----------------------------------------
Number of threads: 8
Final counter: 800.
----------------------------------------
Number of threads: 9
Final counter: 900.
----------------------------------------
Number of threads: 10
Final counter: 1000.
----------------------------------------
```

As you can see, the final values that we obtained from the global counters are all correct, proving that our data structure is working as intended. Additionally, you will obtain a graph similar to the following:

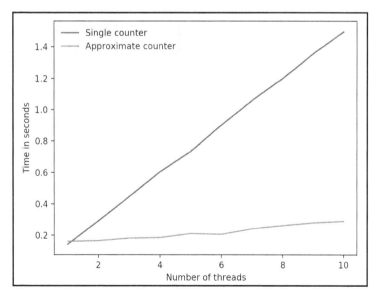

Scalability of single-lock counter and approximate counters

The blue line indicates the changes in speed of the single-lock counter data structure, while the red line indicates those of the approximate counter data structure. As you can see, even though the performance of the approximate counter does worsen somewhat as the number of threads increases (due to overheads such as creating individual local counters and distributing an increasing number of increment tasks), our new data structure is highly scalable, especially in comparison to our previous single-lock counter data structure.

A few considerations for approximate counter designs

One thing that you may have noticed is that, even though only a single thread interacts with a single local counter, the data structure still has a `lock` attribute in its initialization. This is because it is, in fact, possible for multiple threads to share the same local counters. There are situations in which it is inefficient to create one local counter for every active thread, so the developer can have two or more share the same local counter instead, and individual counters can still report to the same global counter.

For example, suppose that there are 20 threads executing in a concurrent counter program; we can only have 10 local counters reporting to one global counter. From what we have seen, this setup will have a lower level of scalability than one with an individual local counter for each thread, but the advantage of this approach that it uses less memory space and avoids the overhead of creating more local counters.

There is another possible variation to the way in which a program that utilizes approximate counters can be designed. Instead of having only one layer of local counters, we can also implement semi-global counters that local counters report to, which, in turn, report to the global counters that are one level higher than themselves. When using the approximate counter data structure, the developer not only has to find, as discussed previously, an appropriate threshold of reporting, but he or she also needs to optimize the number of threads associated with one single local counter, as well as the number of layers in our design.

Mutex-free concurrent data structures in Python

The previous subsection concluded our discussion of designing a lock-based concurrent data structure in Python, and the complexities involved therein. We will now move on to one approach to the theoretical design of mutex-free concurrent data structures.

The term **mutex-free** in concurrent data structures indicates the lack of a locking mechanism to protect the integrity of the data structure. This does not mean that the data structure simply disregards the protection of its data; instead, the data structure has to employ other synchronization mechanisms. In this section, we will analyze one such mechanism, known as **read-copy-update**, and discuss how to apply it to a Python data structure.

The impossibility of being lock-free in Python

The opposite of a lock-based data structure is a lock-free one. Here we will be discussing its definition and the reason why the characteristic of being lock-free is actually impossible in Python, and why the closest we can get to it is being mutex-free.

Unlike a lock-based data structure, a data structure that is lock-free not only does not employ any locking mechanism (like mutex-free data structures), but also requires that any given thread or process cannot be waiting to execute indefinitely. This means that, if a lock-free data structure is successfully implemented, applications utilizing that data structure will never encounter the problems of deadlock and starvation. For this reason, lock-free data structures are widely considered a more advanced technique in concurrent programming, and consequently, they are significantly more difficult to implement.

The characteristic of being lock-free, however, is actually impossible to implement in Python (or in the CPython interpreter, to be more specific). As you have probably guessed, this is due to the existence of the GIL, which prevents more than one thread from executing in the CPU at any given time. To learn more about the GIL, navigate to `Chapter 15`, *The Global Interpreter Lock*, and read the in-depth analysis on the GIL, if you have not already. All in all, having a purely lock-free data structure implemented in CPython is a logical impossibility.

However, this does not mean that concurrent programs in Python cannot benefit from the design of lock-free data structures. As mentioned previously, mutex-free Python data structures (which can be considered a subset of lock-free data structures) are entirely possible to implement. In fact, mutex-free data structures still result in the successful avoidance of deadlock and starvation problems. However, they cannot fully take advantage of the purely lock-free execution that would result in better speed.

In the next subsections, we will take a look at a custom data structure in Python, analyze the problem that it raises if used concurrently, and, finally, try to apply a mutex-free logic to the underlying data structure.

Introduction to the network data structure

The data structure that we are implementing resembles a network of nodes, one of which is the primary node. Additionally, each node contains a key and a value for the node. You can think of this data structure as a Python dictionary (in other words, a set of keys and values respectively paired together), but one of these key and value pairs is called the primary node of the network.

A good way to visualize this data structure is to analyze a situation in which the data structure is utilized. Suppose that you have been asked to implement the request handling logic of a popular website, which is also, unfortunately, a common target for **denial of service (DoS)** attacks. Since it is highly possible that the website will be taken down fairly frequently, despite the efforts of the cybersecurity team, an approach that you could take to guarantee that clients of the website will still be able to access it is to keep more than one working copy of the website, in addition to the main website, on the server.

These copies are equivalent to the main website in every way, and the main website can therefore be completely replaced by any of the copies at any time. Now, if and when the main website is taken down by a DoS attack, you, as the server administrator, can simply allow the main website to go down and switch the address of the new main website to one of the copies that you have ready. The clients of the website will therefore experience no difficulty or inconsistency when accessing the data from the website, since the copies are identical to the main website that was taken down. Servers that do not implement this mechanism, on the other hand, will most likely have to spend some time recovering from a DoS attack (isolating the attack, building back the interrupted or corrupted data, and so on).

At this point, a connection between this method of web administration and the aforementioned network data structure can be made. In fact, the network data structure is, in essence, a high-level abstraction of the method; the data structure is a set of nodes or pairs of values (the website address and the data, in the preceding case), while keeping track of a primary node that can also be replaced by any other node (clients accessing the website are directed to a new website when the main website is attacked). We will call this processing **refreshing the primary** in our data structure, which is illustrated in the following diagram:

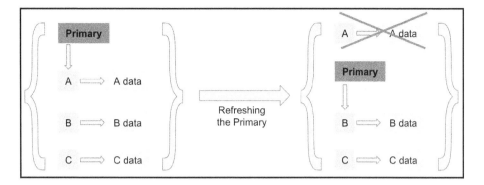

Diagram of network primary refreshing

In the preceding diagram, we have three separate notes of data in our network data structure (visualized as a dictionary, denoted by a pair of curly braces): key **A,** pointing to some data; key **B,** pointing to its own data; and, finally, key **C,** also pointing to its own data. Additionally, we have a pointer indicating the primary key of our dictionary network, pointing to key **A.** As the primary refresh process takes place, we will stop keeping track of key **A** (which is the primary key) and its own, and then have the primary pointer pointing to another node in the network (in this case, key **B**).

Implementing a simple network data structure in Python and race conditions

Let's consider a starting implementation of this data structure in Python. Navigate to the Chapter16/network.py file, as follows:

```
# Chapter16/network.py

import time
from random import choice

class Network:
    def __init__(self, primary_key, primary_value):
        self.primary_key = primary_key
        self.data = {primary_key: primary_value}

    def __str__(self):
        result = '{\n'
        for key in self.data:
            result += f'\t{key}: {self.data[key]};\n'
```

```
            return result + '}'

    def add_node(self, key, value):
        if key not in self.data:
            self.data[key] = value
            return True

        return False
    # precondition: the object has more than one node left
    def refresh_primary(self):
        del self.data[self.primary_key]
        self.primary_key = choice(list(self.data))

    def get_primary_value(self):
        primary_key = self.primary_key
        time.sleep(1) # creating a delay
        return self.data[primary_key]
```

This file contains the `Network` class, which implements the logic that we discussed previously. Upon initialization, each instance of this class will have at least one node in its network (stored in the `data` attribute) that is its primary node; we are also using Python's dictionary data structure to implement this network design. Each object also has to keep track of the key of its primary data, stored in its `primary_key` attribute.

In this class, we also have an `add_node()` method that is used to add a new node of data to a network object; note that each node has to have a key and a value. Recall our web administration example—this corresponds to an internet address and the data that the website has. The class also has a `refresh_primary()` method that simulates refreshing the primary process (which deletes the reference to the previous primary data and pseudo-randomly selects a new primary node from the remaining nodes). Keep in mind that the precondition for this method is that the calling network object has to have at least two nodes left .

Finally, we have an accessor method, called `get_primary_value()`, that returns the value that the primary key of the calling network object points to. Here, we add in a slight delay in the execution of the method, to simulate the race condition that will occur from using this naive data structure. (Additionally, we are overwriting the default `__str__()` method, for easy debugging.)

Now, let's turn our attention to the `Chapter16/example5.py` file, where we import this data structure and use it in a concurrent program:

```
# Chapter16/example5.py

from network import Network
import threading

def print_network_primary_value():
    global my_network

    print(f'Current primary value: {my_network.get_primary_value()}.')

my_network = Network('A', 1)
print(f'Initial network: {my_network}')
print()

my_network.add_node('B', 1)
my_network.add_node('C', 1)
print(f'Full network: {my_network}')
print()

thread1 = threading.Thread(target=print_network_primary_value)
thread2 = threading.Thread(target=my_network.refresh_primary)

thread1.start()
thread2.start()

thread1.join()
thread2.join()

print(f'Final network: {my_network}')
print()

print('Finished.')
```

First of all, we implement a function called `print_network_primary_value()`, which accesses and obtains the primary data of a network object that is also a global variable, using the aforementioned `get_primary_value()` method. In our main program, we then initialize a network object with a starting node, with A as the node key and 1 as the node data (this node also automatically becomes the primary node). We then add two more nodes to this network: B, pointing to 1, and C, pointing to 1, respectively.

Now, two threads are initialized and started, the first of which calls the print_network_primary_value() function to print out the current primary data of the network. The second calls the refresh_primary() method from the network object. We are also printing out the current state of the network object at various points throughout the program.

It is quite easy to spot the race condition that will likely occur here: since the first thread is trying to access the primary data while the second thread is trying to refresh the data of the network (in essence, deleting the current primary data at that time), the first thread will most likely cause an error in its execution. Specifically, the following is my output after running the script:

```
> python3 example5.py
Initial network: {
  A: 1;
}

Full network: {
  A: 1;
  B: 1;
  C: 1;
}

Exception in thread Thread-1:
Traceback (most recent call last):
  File
"/Library/Frameworks/Python.framework/Versions/3.7/lib/python3.7/threading.
py", line 917, in _bootstrap_inner
    self.run()
  File
"/Library/Frameworks/Python.framework/Versions/3.7/lib/python3.7/threading.
py", line 865, in run
    self._target(*self._args, **self._kwargs)
  File "example5.py", line 7, in print_network_primary_value
    print(f'Current primary value: {my_network.get_primary_value()}.')
  File
"/Users/quannguyen/Documents/python/mastering_concurrency/ch16/network.py",
line 30, in get_primary_value
    return self.data[primary_key]
KeyError: 'A'

Final network: {
  B: 1;
  C: 1;
}

Finished.
```

Just like we discussed, we encountered a `KeyError` that resulted from the fact that, by the time the first thread obtained the primary key, that key and the primary data had already been deleted from the data structure by its execution in the second thread. The following diagram further illustrates this point:

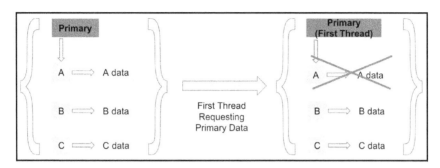

Race condition with network data structure

As you saw in previous chapters, we are using the `time.sleep()` function in the source code of the data structure, to ensure that the race condition will occur. Most of the time, the execution will be fast enough that an error will not occur, yet the race condition will still be there, and this is a problem in our current data structure that we need to address.

RCU as a solution

The root of the race condition that we are encountering is, as we know, the fact that the network object that we are working with is being shared between different threads, which are mutating and reading the data from the data structure simultaneously. Specifically, the second thread in our program was mutating the data (by calling the `refresh_primary()` method), while the first thread was reading from the same data.

Obviously, we can simply apply locking as the synchronization mechanism for this data structure. However, we know that the tasks of acquiring and releasing locks involve a slight cost that will become substantial as the data structure is widely used across a system. As popular websites and systems (namely, MongoDB) use this abstraction to design and structure their servers, a considerably high level of traffic will make the cost of using locks apparent, and cause the performance to decrease. Implementing a variation of an approximate data structure could help with this issue, but the complexity of the implementation might prove to be too difficult to follow through.

Thus, we arrive at the goal of using a mutex-free approach as our synchronization mechanism—in this case, **read-copy-update** (**RCU**). To protect the integrity of your data structure, RCU is, in essence, a synchronization mechanism that creates and maintains another version of the data structure when a thread or process requests read or write access to it. By isolating the interaction between the data structure and threads/processes within a separate copy, RCU ensures that no conflicting data can occur. As a thread or a process has mutated the information in the copy of the data structure that it is assigned to, that update can then be reported to the original data structure.

In short, when a shared data structure has threads or processes requesting access to it (the read process), it needs to return a copy of itself, instead of letting the threads/processes access its own data (the copy process); finally, if there are any changes in the copies of the data structure, they will need to be updated back to the shared data structure (the update process).

RCU is particularly useful for data structures that have to handle a single updater and multiple readers at the same time, which is the typical case of the server network that we discussed previously (multiple clients constantly accessing and requesting data, but only occasional, periodic attacks). But how would this apply to our current network data structure? Theoretically, the accessor method of our data structure (the get_primary_value() method), which is, again, the root of the race condition, needs to create a copy of the data structure before reading the data from a thread. This specification is implemented in the accessor method, in the Chapter16/concurrent_network.py file, as follows:

```
# Chapter16/concurrent_network.py

from copy import deepcopy
import time

class Network:
    [...]

    def get_primary_value(self):
        copy_network = deepcopy(self)

        primary_key = copy_network.primary_key
        time.sleep(1) # creating a delay
        return copy_network.data[primary_key]
```

Here, we are using the built-in `deepcopy` method from the copy module, which returns a separate copy of our network in a different memory location. Then, we only read the data from this copy of the network object, and not the original object itself. This process is illustrated in the following diagram:

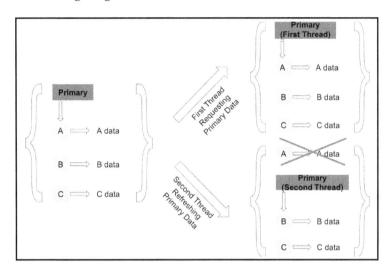

RCU addressing the race condition

In the preceding diagram, we can see that no conflict will occur in terms of data, as the two threads now deal with different copies of the data structure. Let us see this implementation in action in the `Chapter16/example6.py` file, which contains the same instructions as the previous `example5.py` file (initializing a network object, calling two threads at the same time—one to access the primary data of the network, the other to refresh the same primary data), only now the program is using our new data structure from the `concurrent_network.py` file.

After running the script, your output should be the same as the following:

```
> python3 example6.py
Initial network: {
  A: 1;
}

Full network: {
  A: 1;
  B: 1;
  C: 1;
}
```

```
Current primary value: 1.
Final network: {
  B: 1;
  C: 1;
}

Finished.
```

As you can see, not only does the program obtain the correct value of the primary data in the first thread without evoking any errors, it also holds the correct network at the end of the program (without the previously deleted node, with the key A). The RCU method does, indeed, solve the problem of the race condition, without the use of any locking mechanisms.

One thing that you might have also noticed is that RCU could also be applied for our counter example in the previous section. It is true that both RCU and approximate counters are reasonable approaches to the counter problem, and the question of which one is the better solution for a specific concurrent problem can only be answered by empirical, hands-on analysis such as scalability analysis.

Building on simple data structures

Throughout this chapter, we have worked with a number of simple, concurrent data structures, such as counters and networks. For this reason, we were able to truly get to the bottom of the problems that we encountered in the concurrent programs that utilize these data structures, and were able perform in-depth analyses of how to improve their structures and design.

As you work on more complex concurrent data structures in your work and projects, you will see that their designs and structures, and the problems that accompany them, are, in fact, fundamentally similar to those that we saw in the data structures we analyzed. By truly understanding the underlying architecture of the data structures, as well as the root of problems that can occur in the programs that use them, you can build on this knowledge and design data structures that are more complex in instruction but equivalent in logic.

Summary

In this chapter, we studied the theoretical differences between lock-based and mutex-free data structures: a lock-based data structure uses a locking mechanism to protect the integrity of its data, while a mutex-free one does not. We analyzed the problem of race conditions that can occur in poorly-designed data structures, and looked at how to address it in both situations.

In our example of the concurrent lock-based counter data structure, we considered the design of approximate counters, as well as the improved scalability that the design can offer. In our analysis of the concurrent network data structure, we studied the RCU technique, which isolates reading instructions from updating instructions, with the goal of maintaining the integrity of the concurrent data structure.

In the next chapter, we will look at another set of advanced concepts in Python concurrent programming: memory models and operations on atomic types. You will learn more about Python memory management, as well as the definition and uses of atomic types.

Questions

- What is the main approach to solving the problem that locks don't lock anything?
- Describe the concept of scalability in the context of concurrent programming
- How does a naive locking mechanism affect the scalability of a concurrent program?
- What are approximate counters, and how do they help with the problem of scalability in concurrent programming?
- Are lock-free data structures possible in Python? Why or why not?
- What is a mutex-free concurrent data structure, and how is it different from a concurrent lock-based one?
- What is the RCU technique, and what problem does it solve for mutex-free concurrent data structures?

Further reading

For more information, you can refer to the following links:

- *Operating systems: Three easy pieces*. Vol. 151. Wisconsin: Arpaci-Dusseau Books, 2014, by Arpaci-Dusseau, Remzi H. and Andrea C. Arpaci-Dusseau
- *The Secret Life of Concurrent Data Structures* (`addthis.com/blog/2013/04/25/the-secret-life-of-concurrent-data-structures/`), by Michael Spiegel
- *What is RCU, fundamentally?* Linux Weekly News (LWN. net) (2007), McKenney, Paul E. and Jonathan Walpole
- *Wasp's Nest: The Read-Copy-Update Pattern in Python* (`emptysqua.re/blog/wasps-nest-read-copy-update-python/`), Davis, A. Jesse Jiryu
- *Characteristics of scalability and their impact on performance*, proceedings of the second international **workshop on software and performance (WOSP)** '00. p. 195, André B

17
Memory Models and Operations on Atomic Types

The considerations that need to be made during concurrent programming processes, and the problems that follow, are all connected to the way in which Python manages its memory. A deep understanding of how variables and values are stored and referenced in Python, therefore, would not only help to pinpoint the low-level bugs that cause the concurrent program to malfunction but also helps to optimize the concurrent codes. In this chapter, we will take an in-depth look into the Python memory model as well as its atomic types, specifically their places in the Python concurrency ecosystem.

The following topics will be covered in this chapter:

- The Python memory model, its components that support memory allocation on various levels, and the general philosophy in managing memory in Python
- The definition of atomic operations, the roles they play in concurrent programming, and how to use them in Python

Technical requirements

The following are the technical requirements for this chapter:

- Have Python 3 installed on your computer
- Download the GitHub repository at `https://github.com/PacktPublishing/Mastering-Concurrency-in-Python`
- During this chapter, we will be working with the subfolder titled `Chapter17`
- Check out the following video to see the Code in Action: `http://bit.ly/2AiToVy`

Python memory model

You might remember the brief discussion on the method of memory management in Python in Chapter 15, *The Global Interpreter Lock*. In this section, we will look at the Python memory model in greater depth by comparing its memory management mechanism to those of Java and C++ and discuss how it relates to the practices of concurrent programming in Python.

The components of Python memory manager

Data in Python is stored in memory in a particular way. To gain an in-depth understanding on a high level, regarding how data is handled in concurrent programs, we first need to dive deep into the theoretical structure of Python memory allocation. In this section, we will discuss how data is allocated in a private heap, and the handling of this data via the **Python memory manager**—an overarching entity that ensures the integrity of the data.

The Python memory manager consists of a number of components that interact with different entities and support different functionalities. For example, one component handles the allocation of memory at a low level by interacting with the memory manager of the operating system that Python is running on; it is called the **raw memory allocator**.

On the higher levels, there are also a number of other memory allocators that interact with the aforementioned private heap of objects and values. These components of the Python memory manager handle object-specific allocations that execute memory operations that are specific to the given data and object types: integers have to be handled and managed by a different allocator to one that manages strings, or one for dictionaries or tuples. As storing and reading instructions varies between these data types, these different object-specific memory allocators are implemented to gain additional speed while sacrificing some processing space.

One step lower than the aforementioned raw memory allocator are the system allocators from the standard C library (assuming that the Python interpreter under consideration is CPython). Sometimes known as general-purpose allocators, these written-in-C entities are responsible for helping the raw memory allocator interact with the memory manager of the operating system.

The entire model of the Python memory manager described previously can be illustrated by the following diagram:

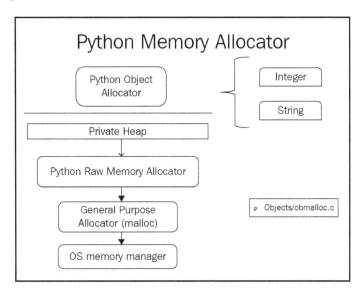

Python memory manager components

Memory model as a labeled directed graph

We have learned about the general process of memory allocation in Python, so in this section, let's think about how data is stored and referenced in Python. Many programmers often think about the memory model in Python as one object graph with a label at each node and the edges are directed—in short, it is a labeled directed object graph. This memory model was first put into use with the second oldest computer programming language, **Lisp** (previously known as LISP).

It is often thought of as a directed graph because its memory model keeps track of its data and variables via nothing but pointers: the value of every variable is a pointer, and this point can be pointing to a symbol, a number, or a subroutine. So, these pointers are the directed edges in the object graph, and the actual values (symbols, numbers, subroutines) are the nodes in the graph. The following diagram is a simplification of the Lisp memory model in its early stages:

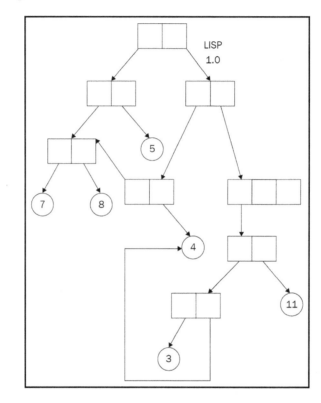

Lisp memory model as an object graph

With this object-graph memory model come a number of advantageous characteristics for memory management. First of all, the model offers a significant degree of flexibility in terms of reusability; it is possible, and in fact quite easy, to write a data structure or a set of instructions for one kind of data type or object and then also reuse it on other kinds. In contrast, C is a programming language that utilizes a different memory model that does not offer this flexibility, and its programmers are usually required to spend a significant amount of time rewriting the same data structures and algorithms for different kinds of data types and objects.

Another form of flexibility that this memory model provides is the fact that every object can be referenced by any number of pointers (or ultimately variables) and therefore be mutated by any of them. We have already seen the effect of this characteristic in a sample Python program in `Chapter 15`, *The Global Interpreter Lock*, if two variables reference the same (mutable) object (achieved when one variable is assigned to another) and one successfully mutates the object via its reference, then the change will also be reflected through the reference of the second variable.

As also discussed in `Chapter 15`, *The Global Interpreter Lock*, this is not similar to the memory management in C++. For example, as when a variable (that is not a pointer or a reference) is assigned with a specific value, the programming language will copy that specific value to the memory location that contains the original variable. Additionally, when a variable is assigned with another variable, the memory location of the latter will be copied to that of the former; no further connection between these two variables is maintained after the assignment.

However, some argue that this can, in fact, be a disadvantage in programming, especially concurrent programming, as uncoordinated attempts to mutate a shared object can lead to undesirable results. As experienced Python programmers, you might have also noticed that type errors (when a variable expected to be one specific type is referencing an object of a different, noncompatible type) are quite common in Python programming. This is also a direct result of this memory model, because, again, a reference pointer can point to anything.

In the context of concurrency

With the theoretical basics of the Python memory model in mind, how can we expect it to affect the ecosystem of Python concurrent programming? Fortunately, the Python memory model works in favor of concurrent programming in the sense that it allows thinking and reasoning about concurrency that is easier and more intuitive. Specifically, Python implements its memory model and executes its program instructions in the same way that we conventionally expect it to.

To understand this advantage that Python possesses, let's first consider concurrency in the Java programming language. To achieve better performance in terms of speed in concurrent programs (specifically multithreading programs), Java allows CPUs to rearrange the order in which given operations included in Java code are to be executed. The rearrangement, however, is made in an arbitrary way so that we cannot easily reason the order of execution from just the sequential ordering of the code when multiple threads are executing. This leads to the fact that if a concurrent program in Java executes in a way that is not intended, the developer would need to spend a significant amount of time determining the order of execution of the program to pinpoint the bug in their program.

Unlike Java, Python has its memory model structured in a way that maintains the sequential consistency of its instructions. This means that the order in which the instructions are arranged in the Python code specifies the order of their execution—no arbitrary rearrangement of the code and, therefore, no surprising behavior from the concurrent programs. However, since the rearrangement in Java concurrency is implemented in order to achieve better speed for the programs, this means that Python is sacrificing its performance to keep its execution simpler and more intuitive.

Atomic operations in Python

Another important topic regarding memory management is atomic operations. In this subsection, we will be exploring the definition of being atomic in programming, the roles that atomic operations have in the context of concurrent programming, and finally how to use atomic operations in Python programs.

What does it mean to be atomic?

Let's first examine the actual characteristic of being atomic. If an operation is atomic in a concurrent program, then it cannot be interrupted by other entities in the program during its execution; an atomic operation can also be called linearizable, indivisible, or uninterruptible. Given the nature of race conditions and how common they are in concurrent programs, it is quite intuitive to conclude that atomicity is a desirable characteristic of a program, as it guarantees the integrity of the shared data, and protects it from uncoordinated mutations.

The term "atomic" refers to the fact that an atomic operation appears instantaneous to the rest of the program that it is in. This means that the operation has to be executed in a continuous, uninterrupted manner. The most common method of implementing atomicity, as you could probably guess, is via mutual exclusion, or locks. Locks, as we have seen, require interactions with a shared resource to take place one thread or process at a time, thus protecting those interactions of one thread/process from being interrupted and potentially corrupted by other competing threads or processes.

If a programmer allows some of the operations in their concurrent program to be nonatomic, they would also need to allow those operations to be careful and flexible (in the sense of interacting and mutating data) enough so that no errors should result from them being interrupted by other operations. If, however, irregular and erroneous behaviors were to take place when these operations are interrupted during their execution, it would be quite difficult for the programmer to actually reproduce and debug those behaviors.

The GIL reconsidered

One of the major elements in the context of Python atomic operations is, of course, the GIL; there are additionally common misconceptions as well as complexities regarding the role the GIL plays in atomic operations.

For example, as reading about the definition of atomic operations, some tend to argue that all operations in Python are actually atomic, as the GIL actually requires threads to execute in a coordinated manner, with only one being able to run at any given point. This is, in fact, a false statement. The requirement of the GIL that only one thread can execute Python code at a given time does not lead to the atomicity of all Python operations; one operation can still be interrupted by another, and errors can still result from the mishandling and corruption of shared data.

At a lower level, the Python interpreter handles the switching between threads in a Python concurrent program. This process is done with respect to bytecode instructions, which are compiled Python code that are interpretable and executable by machines. Specifically, Python maintains a fixed frequency specifying how often the interpreter should switch between one active thread to another and this frequency can be set using the built-in `sys.setswitchinterval()` method. Any nonatomic operation can be interrupted during its execution by this thread switching event.

In Python 2, the default value for this frequency is 1,000 bytecode instructions, which means that after a thread has successfully executed 1,000 bytecode instructions, the Python interpreter will look for other active threads that are waiting to be executed. If there is at least one other waiting thread, the interpreter will have the currently running thread to release the GIL and have the waiting thread acquire it and thus start the execution of the latter thread.

In Python 3, the frequency is fundamentally different. The unit used for the frequency is now time-based, specifically in seconds. With the default value of 15 milliseconds, this frequency specifies that if a thread has been executing for at least the amount of time equal to the threshold, then the thread switching event (together with the releasing and acquiring of the GIL) will take place as soon as the thread finishes the execution of the current bytecode instruction.

Innate atomicity in Python

As mentioned previously, an operation can be interrupted during its execution if the thread executing it has passed its executing limit (for example, 15 milliseconds in Python 3 by default), at which point the operation has to finish its current bytecode instruction and give back the GIL to another thread that is waiting. This means that the thread-switching event only takes place between bytecode instructions.

There are operations in Python that can be executed in one single bytecode instruction and are therefore atomic in nature without the help of external mechanisms, such as mutual exclusion. Specifically, if an operation in a thread completes its execution in one single bytecode, it cannot be interrupted by the thread-switching event as the event only takes place after the current bytecode instruction is completed. This characteristic of innate atomicity is very useful, as it allows the operations that have it to execute their instructions freely even if no synchronization method is being utilized, while still guaranteeing that they will not be interrupted and have their data corrupted.

Atomic versus nonatomic

It is important to note that it can be surprising for programmers to learn which operations in Python are atomic and which are not. Some might assume that since simple operations take less bytecode than complex ones, the simpler an operation is, the more likely it is to be innately atomic. However, this is not the case, and the only way to determine with certainty which operations are atomic in nature is to perform further analyses.

According to the documentation of Python 3 (which can be found via this link: `docs.python.org/3/faq/library.html#what-kinds-of-global-value-mutation-are-thread-safe`), some examples of innately atomic operations include the following:

- Appending a predefined object to a list
- Extending a list with another list
- Fetching an element from a list
- "Popping" from a list
- Sorting a list
- Assigning a variable to another variable
- Assigning a variable to an attribute of an object
- Creating a new entry for a dictionary
- Updating a dictionary with another dictionary

Some operations that are not innately atomic include the following:

- Incrementing an integer, including using +=
- Updating an element in a list by referencing another element in that list
- Updating an entry in a dictionary via referencing another entry in that dictionary

Simulation in Python

Let's analyze the difference between an atomic operation and a nonatomic one in an actual Python concurrent program. If you already have the code for this book downloaded from the GitHub page, go ahead and navigate to the `Chapter17` folder. For this example, we are considering the `Chapter17/example1.py` file:

```
# Chapter17/example1.py

import sys; sys.setswitchinterval(.000001)
import threading

def foo():
    global n
    n += 1

n = 0

threads = []
for i in range(1000):
    thread = threading.Thread(target=foo)
    threads.append(thread)
```

```
for thread in threads:
    thread.start()

for thread in threads:
    thread.join()

print(f'Final value: {n}.')

print('Finished.')
```

First of all, we are resetting the thread-switching frequency of the Python interpreter to 0.000001 seconds—this is to have the thread switching event take place more often than usual and thus amplify any race condition that might be in our program.

The gist of the program is to increment a simple global counter (n) with 1,000 separate threads, each incrementing the counter once via the foo() function. Since the counter was originally initialized as 0, if the program executed correctly, we would have that counter holding the value of 1,000 at the end of the program. However, we know that the increment operator that we are using in the foo() function (+=) is not an atomic operation, which means it can be interrupted by a thread-switching event when applied on a global variable.

After running the script multiple times, we can observe that there is, in fact, a race condition existing in our code. This is illustrated by incorrect values of the counter that are less than 1,000. For example, the following is an output I obtained:

```
> python3 example1.py
Final value: 998.
Finished.
```

This is consistent with what we have previously discussed, that is, since the += operator is not atomic, it would need other synchronization mechanisms to ensure the integrity of the data that it interacts with from multiple threads concurrently. Let's now simulate the same experiment with an operation that we know is atomic, specifically **appending a predefined object to a list**.

In the Chapter17/example2.py file, we have the following code:

```
# Chapter17/example2.py

import sys; sys.setswitchinterval(.000001)
import threading

def foo():
    global my_list
    my_list.append(1)
```

```
my_list = []

threads = []
for i in range(1000):
    thread = threading.Thread(target=foo)
    threads.append(thread)

for thread in threads:
    thread.start()

for thread in threads:
    thread.join()

print(f'Final list length: {len(my_list)}.')

print('Finished.')
```

Instead of a global counter, we now have a global list that was originally empty. The new `foo()` function now takes this global list and appends the integer `1` to it. In the rest of the program, we are still creating and running 1,000 separate threads, each of which calls the `foo()` function once. At the end of the program, we will print out the length of the global list to see if the list has been successfully mutated 1,000 times. Specifically, if the length of the list is less than 1,000, we will know that there is a race condition in our code, similar to what we saw in the previous example.

As the `list.append()` method is an atomic operation, however, it is guaranteed that there is no race condition when the threads call the `foo()` function and interact with the global list. This is illustrated by the length of the list at the end of the program. No matter how many times we run the program, the list will always have a length of 1,000:

```
> python3 example2.py
Final list length: 1000.
Finished.
```

Even though some operations in Python are innately atomic, it can be quite difficult to tell whether a given operation is atomic on its own or not. Since the application of nonatomic operations on shared data can lead to race conditions and thus erroneous results, it is always recommended that programmers utilize synchronization mechanisms to ensure the integrity of the shared data within a concurrent program.

Summary

In this chapter, we have examined the underlying structure of the Python memory model, as well as how the language manages its values and variables in a concurrent programming context. Given the way memory management in Python is structured and implemented, the reasoning for the behaviors of a concurrent program can be significantly easier than doing the same in another programming language. The ease in understanding and debugging concurrent programs in Python, however, also comes with a decrease in performance.

Atomic operations are instructions that cannot be interrupted during their execution. Atomicity is a desirable characteristic of concurrent operations, as it guarantees the safety of data shared across different threads. While there are operations in Python that are innately atomic, synchronization mechanisms such as locking are always recommended to guarantee the atomicity of a given operation.

In the next chapter, we will be looking into how to build a concurrent server from scratch. Through this process, we will learn more about implementing communication protocols as well as applying concurrency to an existing Python application.

Questions

- What are the main components of the Python memory manager?
- How does the Python memory model resemble a labeled directed graph?
- What are the advantages and disadvantages of the Python memory model in terms of developing concurrent applications in Python?
- What is an atomic operation, and why is it desirable in concurrent programming?
- Give three examples of innately atomic operations in Python.

Further reading

For more information you can refer the following links:

- *The memory models that underlie programming languages* (`http://canonical.org/~kragen/memory-models/`), K. J. Sitaker
- *Grok the GIL: How to write fast and thread-safe Python* (`opensource.com/article/17/4/grok-gil`), A. Jesse Jiryu Davis
- *Thread Synchronization Mechanisms in Python* (`http://effbot.org/zone/thread-synchronization.htm#atomic-operations`), Fredrik Lundh
- *Memory Management* (`https://docs.python.org/3/c-api/memory.html`), Python Documentation
- *Concurrency* (`jython.org/jythonbook/en/1.0/Concurrency`), Jython Documentation
- *Memory management in Python* (`anubnair.wordpress.com/2014/09/30/memory-management-in-python/`), Anu B Nair

18
Building a Server from Scratch

In this chapter, we will analyze a more advanced application of concurrent programming: building a working non-blocking server from scratch. We will cover complex uses of the `socket` module, such as isolating the user business logic from callbacks and writing the callback logic with inline generators, both instances designed to run concurrently. We will also discuss the use of the `await` and `yield` keywords, using an example.

The following topics will be covered in this chapter:

- Using a comprehensive API from the `socket` module to build a server from scratch
- Basic information on Python generators and asynchronous generators
- How to use inline generators with the `await` and `yield` keywords to convert a blocking server to a non-blocking one

Technical requirements

The following is a list of prerequisites for this chapter:

- Ensure that you have Python 3 installed on your computer
- Ensure that you have `telnet` installed on your computer
- Download the GitHub repository at `https://github.com/PacktPublishing/Mastering-Concurrency-in-Python`
- During this chapter, we will be working with the subfolder named `Chapter18`
- Check out the following video to see the Code in Action: `http://bit.ly/2KrgWwh`

Low-level network programming via the socket module

In this chapter, we will be using the `socket` module, which is a built-in library in Python, to build our working server. The `socket` module is one of the modules that are most frequently used to implement low-level communication protocols, while providing intuitive options to control those protocols. In this section, we will introduce the process of implementing the underlying low-level architecture of a server, as well as the key methods and functionalities of the module that will be used in our examples later on.

Note that in order to successfully follow the examples in this chapter, you will need to install the telnet program on your system. Telnet is a program that provides terminal commands that facilitate protocols for bidirectional, interactive, text-based communication. We covered the installation of telnet in `Chapter 11`, *Building Communication Channels with asyncio*; if you do not already have Telnet installed on your system, simply navigate to (and follow the directions in) that chapter.

Note that macOS systems have a preinstalled alternative to Telnet, called Netcat. If you do not want Telnet installed on your macOS computer, simply use the command `nc` instead of `telnet` in the following examples, and you will achieve the same effect.

The theory of server-side communication

In `Chapter 11`, *Building Communication Channels with asyncio,* you encountered brief examples of implementing asynchronous communication channels at a higher level, using the `aiohttp` module. In this section, we will dive deeper into the programming structure of a server-side communication channel, and how it can interact with its clients in an efficient way.

In the field of network programming, a **socket** is defined as a theoretical endpoint within a node of a specific computer network. The socket is responsible for receiving or sending data from the node that it is in. The fact that the socket is unique to the node that owns it means that other nodes in the same computer network are theoretically unable to interact with the socket. In other words, the socket is only available to its corresponding node.

To open a communication channel from the server-side, a network programmer must first create a socket and bind it to a specific address. This address is typically a pair of values, containing information about the host and a port for the server. Then, through the socket, the server begins to listen to any potential communication request created by its clients in the network. Any request from a client to connect to the server will thus need to be through the created socket.

Upon receiving a request to connect from a potential client, the server can decide whether to accept that request. A connection will then be established between the two systems in the network, which means that they can start to communicate and share data with each other. As the client sends a message to the server via the communication channel, the server then processes the message and eventually sends a response back to the client through the same channel; this process continues until the connection between them ends, either through one of them quitting the connection channel or through some external factors.

The preceding is the basic process of creating a server and establishing connections with potential clients. There are multiple security measures implemented at each stage of the process, though they are not our concern and will not be discussed here. The following diagram also maps out the process that was just described:

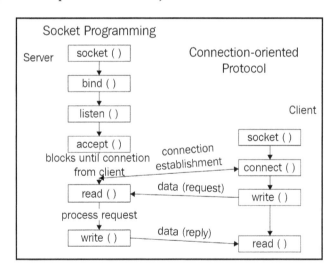

Network programming with sockets

Note that in order to create a request to connect to the server, a potential client also has to initialize its own socket for the communication channel (as shown in the preceding diagram). Again, we are only interested in the server-side theory of this process, and thus, we are not discussing client-side elements here.

The API of the socket module

In this section, we will explore the key API provided by the `socket` module to achieve the same functionalities in the process described previously. As we have mentioned, the `socket` module comes built-in in any Python 3 distribution, so we can simply import the module into our program without having to run installation commands.

To create a socket, we will use the `socket.socket()` method, which returns a socket object. This object is what we will be working with during most of the process of implementing various communication protocols. Additionally, socket methods have the following methods that help us control the communication protocols:

- `socket.bind()`: This method binds the calling socket to the address that is passed to the method. In our examples, we will be passing in a tuple containing the address of the host and the port for the communication channel.
- `socket.listen()`: This method allows the server that we create to accept connections from potential clients. Another optional positive-integer parameter can be passed to the method, to specify the number of allowed unaccepted connections before the server refuses new connections. We will be using 5 as an arbitrary number for this method in our later examples.
- `socket.accept()`: This method, as the name suggests, accepts a specific connection that the calling socket object has. This calling object has to first be bound to an address and listening for connections to call this method. In other words, this method is to be called after the two preceding methods. The method also returns a pair of values, `(conn, address)`, with `conn` being the new socket object that has accepted the connection and is able to send and receive data, and `address` being the address on the other end of the connection (the client address).
- `socket.makefile()`: This method returns a `file` object that is associated with the calling `socket` object. We will be using this method to create a file that contains the data sent from the accepted clients of our server. This `file` object will also need to be closed appropriately, using the `close()` method.
- `socket.sendall()`: This method sends the data passed as a parameter to the calling `socket` object. We will use this method to send data back to the clients connected to our server. Note that this method takes in data in bytes, so we will be passing byte strings to this method in our examples.
- `socket.close()`: This method marks the calling `socket` object as closed. After this point, all operations applied on the `socket` object will fail. This is to be used when we terminate our server.

Building a simple echo server

The best way to truly understand the use of the methods and functions described previously is to see them in action in a sample program. In this section, we will build an echo server as our starting example. This server, as the term suggests, sends whatever it received from each client back to the client. Through this example, you will learn how to set up a functional server, as well as how to handle client connections and data from it, and we will build more complex servers in later sections.

Before we jump into the code, however, let's discuss the structure of the program that will implement the communication logic for this server. First, we will have what is called the **reactor**, which sets up the server itself and provides the logic whenever a new connection is requested from potential clients. Specifically, once the server has been set up, this reactor will go through an infinite loop and handle all connection requests that the server receives.

If you have read the previous chapters on asynchronous programming, it is also possible to think of this reactor as an event loop. This event loop goes through all of the events that are to be processed (in this case, they are requests), and handles them one by one, using an event handler. The following diagram further illustrates this process:

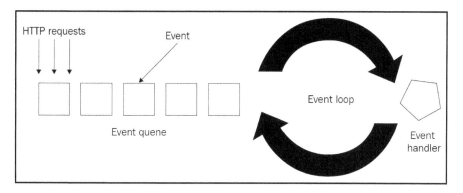

An event loop in network programming

The second part of our program, then, is the event handler in the event loop analogy, which contains the user business logic: how to process the data received from clients, and what to send back to each of them. For our current example, since it is an echo server, we are only sending back whatever each client sent to our server (if the data is valid).

With that structure in mind, let's move on to the actual implementation of this server. Download the code for this chapter from the GitHub page, then go ahead and navigate to the `Chapter18` folder. The script that we are interested in is in the `Chapter18/example1.py` file, as follows:

```python
# Chapter18/example1.py

import socket

# Main event loop
def reactor(host, port):
    sock = socket.socket()
    sock.bind((host, port))
    sock.listen(5)
    print(f'Server up, running, and waiting for call on {host} {port}')

    try:
        while True:
            conn, cli_address = sock.accept()
            process_request(conn, cli_address)

    finally:
        sock.close()

def process_request(conn, cli_address):
    file = conn.makefile()

    print(f'Received connection from {cli_address}')

    try:
        while True:
            line = file.readline()
            if line:
                line = line.rstrip()
                if line == 'quit':
                    conn.sendall(b'connection closed\r\n')
                    return

                print(f'{cli_address} --> {line}')
                conn.sendall(b'Echoed: %a\r\n' % line)
    finally:
        print(f'{cli_address} quit')
        file.close()
        conn.close()

if __name__ == '__main__':
    reactor('localhost', 8080)
```

The program is structured in the same way that we discussed previously: a reactor and a user business logic handler (the `process_request()` function). First, the reactor sets up the server (by creating a socket, binding it to the parametric host and port address, and calling the `listen()` method). It then goes into an infinite loop and facilitates any potential connection with a client, first accepting the connection by calling the `accept()` method on the `socket` object, and then calling the `process_request()` function. The reactor is also responsible for closing the `socket` object if an error occurs during the preceding process.

The `process_request()` function, on the other hand, will first create a `file` object associated with the socket that is passed to it. Again, this `file` object is used by our server to read data from its client that is connected via that specific socket. Specifically, after making the `file` object, the function will go into another infinite loop that keeps reading from the `file` object, using the `readline()` function. If the data read from the file is valid, we will send back the same data, using the `sendall()` method.

We are also printing out what the server receives from each of its clients as the server output, by including the line `print(f'{cli_address} --> {line}')`. One more specification is that, if the data read from the file is equal to the string `quit`, then we will close the connection with that specific client. After a connection is closed, we will need to carefully handle the `socket` object itself, and the `file` object associated with it, using the `close()` method for both.

Finally, at the end of our program, we simply call the `reactor()` function and pass it information about our server. In this case, we simply use the loopback interface of our server, at port `8080`. Now, we will execute the script to initialize our local server. Your output should be similar to the following:

```
> python3 example1.py
Server up, running, and waiting for call on localhost 8080
```

At this point, our server is up and running (as indicated in the output). Now, we would like to create some clients for this server. To do this, open another Terminal window and use the Telnet program to connect to the running server, by running `telnet localhost 8080`. Your output should be similar to the following:

```
> telnet localhost 8080
Trying 127.0.0.1...
Connected to localhost.
```

This output means that the Telnet client has successfully connected to the server that we created. Now, we can test whether the server can handle its requests the way that we intended it to. Specifically, enter some data and hit *return* or *Enter* to send it to the server, and you will see that the client will receive an echoed message from the server, in the way that we implemented in the preceding `process_request()` function. Again, a client can stop its connection to this server by sending the string `quit` to the server.

The following code shows my output when entering a few different phrases:

```
> telnet localhost 8080
Trying 127.0.0.1...
Connected to localhost.
Escape character is '^]'.
hello
Echoed: 'hello'
nice
Echoed: 'nice'
fdkgsnas
Echoed: 'fdkgsnas'
quit
connection closed
Connection closed by foreign host.
```

Looking at the output of our server, you can also see what was happening during this connection:

```
> python3 example1.py
Server up, running, and waiting for call on localhost 8080
Received connection from ('127.0.0.1', 59778)
('127.0.0.1', 59778) --> hello
('127.0.0.1', 59778) --> nice
('127.0.0.1', 59778) --> fdkgsnas
('127.0.0.1', 59778) quit
```

The server, as mentioned, is designed to run forever in the reactor as an event loop, which can be stopped by a `KeyboardInterrupt` exception.

We have successfully implemented our first echo server, using low-level methods provided by the `socket` module. In the next section, we will implement a more advanced functionality for our server and analyze the process of converting it to a non-blocking server that can handle multiple clients at the same time.

Building a calculator server with the socket module

The functionality that we are trying to implement is to have a simple request handler that calculates either the sum or the product of a list of integers, and that is included in the data sent from the clients. Specifically, if a client sends the string 1, 2 ,4 to our server, then the server should send back 7 if it is to calculate sums, or 8 if it is to calculate products.

Every server implements some form of data processing, in addition to handling requests coming in from clients and sending the results of that data processing task to those clients. This prototype will therefore serve as a first building block for more extensive servers, with further complex functionalities.

The underlying calculation logic

We will be using the split() method for Python strings to extract elements that are separated by a specific character in a string. Therefore, we will require all data coming from clients to be formatted this way (integers separated by commas), and, if a client sends in something that is not in this format, we will simply send back an error message and require them to make a new message.

The basic calculation logic is included in the Chapter18/example2.py file, as follows:

```
# Chapter18/example2.py

from operator import mul
from functools import reduce

try:
    while True:
        line = input('Please enter a list of integer, separated by commas:
')
        try:
            nums = list(map(int, line.split(',')))
        except ValueError:
            print('ERROR. Enter only integers separated by commas')
            continue

        print('Sum of input integers', sum(nums))
        print('Product of input integers', reduce(mul, nums, 1))

except KeyboardInterrupt:
    print('\nFinished.')
```

Again, we are using the `split()` method, with the `','` argument, to extract out the individual numbers in a specific string. The `sum()` function is used to calculate, evidently, the sum of the parametric list of numbers. To calculate the aggregated product, we need to import the `mul()` method (for multiplication) from the `operator` module, as well as the `reduce()` method from the `functools` module, to apply the multiplication on each of the elements in the list of numbers under consideration.

As a side note, the third argument passed to the `reduce()` method (the number 1) is the starting value for the reduction process. To learn more about reduction operations, read through `Chapter 7`, *Reduction Operators in Processes*, if you have not done so already.

As for our actual server, we will also keep track of the **mode of calculation**. The mode of calculation, whose default is to execute summation, dictates whether the server should perform summation and multiplication on the input list of numbers. The mode is also unique to each client connection, and can be switched around by that client. Specifically, if the data sent by a specific client is the string `sum`, then we will switch the mode of calculation to summation, and the same goes for the string `product`.

Implementing the calculator server

Now, let's take a look at the full implementation of this server in the `Chapter18/example3.py` file:

```
# Chapter18/example3.py

import socket
from operator import mul
from functools import reduce

# Main event loop
def reactor(host, port):
    sock = socket.socket()
    sock.bind((host, port))
    sock.listen(5)
    print(f'Server up, running, and waiting for call on {host} {port}')

    try:
        while True:
            conn, cli_address = sock.accept()
            process_request(conn, cli_address)

    finally:
        sock.close()
```

```
def process_request(conn, cli_address):
    file = conn.makefile()

    print(f'Received connection from {cli_address}')
    mode = 'sum'

    try:
        conn.sendall(b'<welcome: starting in sum mode>\n')
        while True:
            line = file.readline()
            if line:
                line = line.rstrip()
                if line == 'quit':
                    conn.sendall(b'connection closed\r\n')
                    return

                if line == 'sum':
                    conn.sendall(b'<switching to sum mode>\r\n')
                    mode = 'sum'
                    continue
                if line == 'product':
                    conn.sendall(b'<switching to product mode>\r\n')
                    mode = 'product'
                    continue

                print(f'{cli_address} --> {line}')
                try:
                    nums = list(map(int, line.split(',')))
                except ValueError:
                    conn.sendall(
                        b'ERROR.
                        Enter only integers separated by commas\n')
                    continue

                if mode == 'sum':
                    conn.sendall(b'Sum of input numbers: %a\r\n'
                        % str(sum(nums)))
                else:
                    conn.sendall(b'Product of input numbers: %a\r\n'
                        % str(reduce(mul, nums, 1)))
    finally:
        print(f'{cli_address} quit')
        file.close()
        conn.close()

if __name__ == '__main__':
    reactor('localhost', 8080)
```

The reactor component of our server remains the same as our previous example, since the event loop handles the same type of logic. In our user business logic part (the `process_request()` function), we are still using `file` objects returned from the `makefile()` method to obtain data sent by the clients of the server. If a client sends in the string `quit`, the connection between that client and the server will still be stopped.

The first new thing in this program is the local variable `mode` in the `process_request()` function. This variable specifies the mode of calculation that we discussed earlier, and has the default value of the string `sum`. As you can see, at the very end of the `try` block in the `process_request()` function, this variable decides what kind of data is to be sent back to the current client:

```
if mode == 'sum':
    conn.sendall(b'Sum of input numbers: %a\r\n'
        % str(sum(nums)))
else:
    conn.sendall(b'Product of input numbers: %a\r\n'
        % str(reduce(mul, nums, 1)))
```

Additionally, if data sent from a client is equal to the string `sum`, then the `mode` variable will be set to `sum`, and the same applies for the string `product`. The client will also receive a message announcing that the mode of calculation has been changed. This logic is included in the following portion of the code:

```
if line == 'sum':
    conn.sendall(b'<switching to sum mode>\r\n')
    mode = 'sum'
    continue
if line == 'product':
    conn.sendall(b'<switching to product mode>\r\n')
    mode = 'product'
    continue
```

Now, let's look at how this server performs in a real experiment. Execute the program to run the server, and you will see output similar to that of the previous example:

```
> python3 example3.py
Server up, running, and waiting for call on localhost 8080
```

Again, we will be using Telnet to create clients for this server. As you are connected to the server through a Telnet client, try to enter some data to test out the server logic that we implemented. The following code shows what I obtained with various types of input:

```
> telnet localhost 8080
Trying 127.0.0.1...
Connected to localhost.
```

```
Escape character is '^]'.
<welcome: starting in sum mode>
1,2
Sum of input numbers: '3'
4,9
Sum of input numbers: '13'
product
<switching to product mode>
0,-3
Product of input numbers: '0'
5,-9,10
Product of input numbers: '-450'
hello
ERROR. Enter only integers separated by commas
a,1
ERROR. Enter only integers separated by commas
quit
connection closed
Connection closed by foreign host.
```

You can see that our server can handle the requests as we intended. Specifically, it can compute both the sum and the product of a given correctly formatted input string; it can appropriately switch the mode of calculation; and it can send error messages to its clients if the input strings are not correctly formatted. Again, this ever-running server can be stopped with a `KeyboardInterrupt` exception.

Building a non-blocking server

One thing that we will discover is that the server that we currently have is not non-blocking. In other words, it cannot handle multiple clients simultaneously. In this section, you will learn how to build on the current server to make it non-blocking, using Python keywords that facilitate concurrent programming, in addition to low-level functionalities from the `socket` module.

Analyzing the concurrency of the server

We will now illustrate that the server that we currently have cannot have multiple clients at the same time. First, execute the `Chapter18/example3.py` file to run the server again, as follows:

```
> python3 example3.py
Server up, running, and waiting for call on localhost 8080
```

Similar to what we did in the previous examples, let's now open another Terminal and use Telnet into the running server:

```
> telnet localhost 8080
Trying 127.0.0.1...
Connected to localhost.
Escape character is '^]'.
<welcome: starting in sum mode>
```

To create the second client for this server, open another Terminal and type in the same `telnet` command, as follows:

```
> telnet localhost 8080
Trying 127.0.0.1...
Connected to localhost.
Escape character is '^]'.
```

Here, we can already see that the server is not handling this second client correctly: it is not sending back the welcome message (`<welcome: starting in sum mode>`) to this client. If we look at the output of our server, we can also see that it is only registering one client—specifically, the first of the two:

```
> python3 example3.py
Server up, running, and waiting for call on localhost 8080
Received connection from ('127.0.0.1', 61099)
```

Next, we will try to enter input from each of the clients. We will see that the server is only successfully handling requests from the first client. Specifically, the following is my output from the first client, with various types of input:

```
> telnet localhost 8080
Trying 127.0.0.1...
Connected to localhost.
Escape character is '^]'.
<welcome: starting in sum mode>
hello
ERROR. Enter only integers separated by commas
1,5
Sum of input numbers: '6'
product
<switching to product mode>
6,7
Product of input numbers: '42'
```

Now, with the first client still maintaining the connection with the server, switch to the Terminal of the second client and try to enter its own input. You will see that unlike the first client, this client is not receiving any message back from the server:

```
> telnet localhost 8080
Trying 127.0.0.1...
Connected to localhost.
Escape character is '^]'.
hello
1,5
product
6,7
```

If we look at the server output, we will see that the server is only handling requests from the first client:

```
> python3 example3.py
Server up, running, and waiting for call on localhost 8080
Received connection from ('127.0.0.1', 61099)
('127.0.0.1', 61099) --> hello
('127.0.0.1', 61099) --> 1,5
('127.0.0.1', 61099) --> 6,7
```

The only way for the second client to be able to interact with the server is if the first client disconnects from the server—in other words, when we stop the connection between the first client and the server, as follows:

```
> telnet localhost 8080
Trying 127.0.0.1...
Connected to localhost.
Escape character is '^]'.
<welcome: starting in sum mode>
hello
ERROR. Enter only integers separated by commas
1,5
Sum of input numbers: '6'
product
<switching to product mode>
6,7
Product of input numbers: '42'
quit
connection closed
Connection closed by foreign host.
```

Now, if you switch to the Terminal of the second client, you will see that the client will be flushed with messages from the server that it should have been receiving earlier:

```
> telnet localhost 8080
Trying 127.0.0.1...
Connected to localhost.
Escape character is '^]'.
hello
1,5
product
6,7
<welcome: starting in sum mode>
ERROR. Enter only integers separated by commas
Sum of input numbers: '6'
<switching to product mode>
Product of input numbers: '42'
```

All of the appropriate replies from the server are now present, but they were sent all at once, and not after each of the input messages. The same surge of information is also illustrated in the output from our server Terminal, as follows:

```
> python3 example3.py
Server up, running, and waiting for call on localhost 8080
Received connection from ('127.0.0.1', 61099)
('127.0.0.1', 61099) --> hello
('127.0.0.1', 61099) --> 1,5
('127.0.0.1', 61099) --> 6,7
('127.0.0.1', 61099) quit
Received connection from ('127.0.0.1', 61100)
('127.0.0.1', 61100) --> hello
('127.0.0.1', 61100) --> 1,5
('127.0.0.1', 61100) --> 6,7
```

This output makes it seem as if the server only received the connection from the second client after the first client had quit, when in reality, we created the two clients and had them communicate with the server at the same time. This is because our current server is only able to handle one client at a time, and only after the current client has quit can it move on to the next client that has requested a communication channel. We call this a blocking server.

Generators in Python

In the next section, we will discuss how to convert the blocking server that we currently have to a non-blocking one, while keeping the calculating functionalities. In order to do that, we will first need to look into another concept in Python programming, called **generators**. Chances are you have already worked with Python generators, but to recap, we will go over the key features of generators in this section.

Generators are functions that return iterators and can be paused and resumed dynamically. Return values from generators are often compared to list objects, because generator iterators are **lazy** (https://en.wikipedia.org/wiki/Lazy_evaluation) and only produce results when explicitly asked. For this reason, generator iterators are more efficient in terms of memory management, and are therefore often preferred over lists when large amounts of data are involved.

Each generator is defined as a function, but instead of using the keyword `return` inside the function block, we use `yield`, which is to indicate that the return value is only temporary and the whole generator itself can still be resumed after the return value is obtained. Let's look at how Python generators work in an example, included in the `Chapter18/example4.py` file, as follows:

```
# Chapter18/example4.py

def read_data():
    for i in range(5):
        print('Inside the inner for loop...')
        yield i * 2

result = read_data()
for i in range(6):
    print('Inside the outer for loop...')
    print(next(result))

print('Finished.')
```

Here, we have a generator named `read_data()`, which returns multiples of 2, from 0 to 8, in a lazy manner. This is done with the keyword `yield`, which is placed in front of what would be the return value in an otherwise normal function: `i * 2`. Note that the `yield` keyword is placed in front of the **individual** elements in the iterator that should be sent back, which facilitates the lazy generation.

Now, in our main program, we are obtaining the whole iterator and storing it in the variable `result`. Then, we loop through that iterator six times, using the `next()` function (which, evidently, returns the next element in the iterator passed in). After executing the code, your output should be similar to the following:

```
> python3 example4.py
Inside the outer for loop...
Inside the inner for loop...
0
Inside the outer for loop...
Inside the inner for loop...
2
Inside the outer for loop...
Inside the inner for loop...
4
Inside the outer for loop...
Inside the inner for loop...
6
Inside the outer for loop...
Inside the inner for loop...
8
Inside the outer for loop...
Traceback (most recent call last):
  File "example4.py", line 11, in <module>
    print(next(result))
StopIteration
```

You can see that, even though the iterator was generated and returned from the `read_data()` generator before we looped through it, the actual instructions inside the generator were only executed as we tried to obtain more items from the iterator.

This is illustrated by the fact that the print statements in the output were alternatively placed with each other (one print statement from the outer `for` loop and one from the inner `for` loop, alternatively): the execution flow goes into the outer `for` loop first, tries to access the next item in the iterator, goes into the generator, and goes into its own `for` loop. As soon as the execution flow reaches the `yield` keyword, it goes back out to the main program. This process continues until one of the `for` loops terminates; in our case, the `for` loop in the generator stopped first, and we therefore encountered a `StopIteration` error at the end.

The laziness in the generation of the iterator comes from the fact that the generator stops executing when it reaches the `yield` keyword, and only continues its execution when asked by outside instructions (in this case, by the `next()` function). Again, this form of data generation is significantly more efficient in memory management than simply generating everything that might need to be iterated over (such as a list).

Asynchronous generators and the send method

How are generators relevant to our purposes of building an asynchronous server? The reason our current server cannot handle multiple clients is because the `readline()` function that we are using in the user business logic part, in order to obtain client data, is a blocking function that prevents the execution flow from going to other potential clients, as long as the current `file` object is still open. That is why, when the current client stops its connection with the server, the next client immediately receives the surge of information that we saw earlier.

If we could rewrite this function into an asynchronous one that allowed the execution flow to switch between different clients while those clients were all connecting to the server, that server would then become non-blocking. We will do this by using asynchronous generators to concurrently generate data from potentially multiple clients at the same time for our server.

To see the underlying structure of the asynchronous generator that we will use for our server, let's first consider the `Chapter18/example5.py` file, as follows:

```python
# Chapter18/example5.py

import types

@types.coroutine
def read_data():
    def inner(n):
        try:
            print(f'Printing from read_data(): {n}')
            callback = gen.send(n * 2)
        except StopIteration:
            pass

    data = yield inner
    return data

async def process():
    try:
        while True:
            data = await read_data()
            print(f'Printing from process(): {data}')
    finally:
        print('Processing done.')

gen = process()
callback = gen.send(None)
```

```
def main():
    for i in range(5):
        print(f'Printing from main(): {i}')
        callback(i)

if __name__ == '__main__':
    main()
```

We are still considering the task of printing out multiples of 2, between 0 and 8. The `process()` function is our asynchronous generator in this example. You can see that there is, in fact, no `yield` keyword inside the generator; this is because we are using the `await` keyword, instead. This asynchronous generator is responsible for printing out the multiples of 2, computed by another generator, `read_data()`.

The `@types.coroutine` decorator is used to convert the generator `read_data()` into a coroutine function that returns a generator-based coroutine, which can still be used as a regular generator but can also be awaited. This generator-based coroutine is the key to converting our blocking server to a non-blocking one. The coroutine performs the computation with the `send()` method, which is a way to provide a generator with input (in this case, we are providing the `process()` generator with multiples of 2).

This coroutine returns a callback, which can be called by our main program later. This is why, before looping through `range(5)` in the main program, we need to keep track of the `process()` generator itself (stored in the variable `gen`) and the callback that is returned (stored in the variable `callback`). The callback, specifically, is the return value of `gen.send(None)`, which is used to start the execution of the `process()` generator. Finally, we simply loop over the aforementioned `range` object and call the `callback` object with the appropriate input.

A lot has been said about the theory behind this method of using asynchronous generators. Now, let's see it in action. Execute the program, and you should get the following output:

```
> python3 example5.py
Printing from main(): 0
Printing from read_data(): 0
Printing from process(): 0
Printing from main(): 1
Printing from read_data(): 1
Printing from process(): 2
Printing from main(): 2
Printing from read_data(): 2
Printing from process(): 4
Printing from main(): 3
Printing from read_data(): 3
Printing from process(): 6
```

```
Printing from main(): 4
Printing from read_data(): 4
Printing from process(): 8
Processing done.
```

In the output (specifically, the print statements), we can still observe the task switching events that are quintessential for both the asynchronous programming that was discussed in earlier chapters and the generators that produce output lazily. Essentially, we have achieved the same goal as the previous example (printing multiples of 2), but here, we used asynchronous generators (with the `async` and `await` keywords) to facilitate task switching events, and we were also able to pass specific arguments to generators by using a callback. These techniques, when combined, form the basic structure that will be applied to our currently blocking server.

Making the server non-blocking

Finally, we will consider the problem of implementing a non-blocking server again. Here, we are applying the asynchronous generators discussed previously to facilitate the asynchronous reading and handling of data received from clients of the server. The actual code for the server is included in the `Chapter18/example6.py` file; we will be going through various parts of it, as it is a relatively long program. Let's turn our attention to the global variables that we will have in this program, as follows:

```
# Chapter18/example6.py

from collections import namedtuple

###########################################################################
# Reactor

Session = namedtuple('Session', ['address', 'file'])

sessions = {}          # { csocket : Session(address, file)}
callback = {}          # { csocket : callback(client, line) }
generators = {}        # { csocket : inline callback generator }
```

To be able to successfully facilitate services for multiple clients at the same time, we will allow the server to have multiple sessions (one for each client) at the same time, and therefore, we will need to keep track of multiple dictionaries, each of which will hold one specific piece of information about the current session.

Specifically, the `sessions` dictionary maps a client socket connection to a `Session` object, which is a Python `namedtuple` object that contains the address of the client and the `file` object associated with that client connection. The `callback` dictionary maps a client socket connection to a callback that is the return value of the asynchronous generator that we will implement later; each of these callbacks takes in its corresponding client socket connection and data read from that client as arguments. Finally, the `generators` dictionary maps a client socket connection to its corresponding asynchronous generator.

Now, let's take a look at the `reactor` function:

```python
# Chapter18/example6.py

import socket, select

# Main event loop
def reactor(host, port):
    sock = socket.socket()
    sock.bind((host, port))
    sock.listen(5)
    sock.setblocking(0) # Make asynchronous

    sessions[sock] = None
    print(f'Server up, running, and waiting for call on {host} {port}')

    try:
        while True:
            # Serve existing clients only if they already have data ready
            ready_to_read, _, _ = select.select(sessions, [], [], 0.1)
            for conn in ready_to_read:
                if conn is sock:
                    conn, cli_address = sock.accept()
                    connect(conn, cli_address)
                    continue

                line = sessions[conn].file.readline()
                if line:
                    callback[conn](conn, line.rstrip())
                else:
                    disconnect(conn)
    finally:
        sock.close()
```

Aside from what we already had from our previous blocking server, we are adding in a number of instructions: we use the `setblocking()` method from the `socket` module to potentially make our server asynchronous, or non-blocking; as we are starting a server, we also register that specific socket to the `sessions` dictionary, with a `None` value for now.

Inside our infinite `while` loop (the event loop) is part of the new non-blocking feature that we are trying to implement. First, we use the `select()` method from the `select` module to single out the sockets from the `sessions` dictionary that are ready to be read (in other words, the sockets that have available data). Since the first argument of the method is for the data to be read, the second is for the data to be written, and the third is for exception data, we are only passing in the `sessions` dictionary in the first argument. The fourth argument specifies the timeout period for the method (in seconds); if unspecified, the method will block infinitely, until at least one item in `sessions` becomes available, which is not suitable for our non-blocking server.

Next, for every client socket connection that is ready to be read, if the connection corresponds to our original server socket, we will accept that connection and call the `connect()` function (which we will look at soon). In this `for` loop, we will also handle the callback methodologies. Specifically, we will access the `file` attribute of the session of the current socket connection (recall that each session has an `address` attribute and a `file` attribute) and will read data from it using the `readline()` method. Now, if what we read is valid data, then we will pass it (along with the current client connection) to the corresponding callback; otherwise, we will end the connection.

Note that even though our server is made asynchronous by the socket being set to non-blocking, the preceding `readline()` method is still a blocking function. The `readline()` function returns when it gets to a carriage return in its input data (the `'\r'` character in ASCII). This means that if the data sent by a client somehow does not contain a carriage return, then the `readline()` function will fail to return. However, since the server is still non-blocking, an error exception will be raised so that other clients will not be blocked.

Now, let's look at our new helper functions:

```
# Chapter18/example6.py

def connect(conn, cli_address):
    sessions[conn] = Session(cli_address, conn.makefile())

    gen = process_request(conn)
    generators[conn] = gen
    callback[conn] = gen.send(None) # Start the generator
```

```
def disconnect(conn):
    gen = generators.pop(conn)
    gen.close()
    sessions[conn].file.close()
    conn.close()

    del sessions[conn]
    del callback[conn]
```

The `connect()` function, which is to be called when a client connection has data that is ready to read, will initiate starting instructions at the beginning of a valid connection with a client. First, it initializes the `namedtuple` object associated with that specific client connection (we are still using the `makefile()` method to create the `file` objects here). The rest of the function is what we saw in the usage pattern of asynchronous generators, which we discussed earlier: we pass the client connection to `process_request()`, which is now an asynchronous generator; register it in the `generators` dictionary; have it call `send(None)` to initiate the generator; and store the return value to the `callback` dictionary, so that it can be called later (specifically, in the last part of the event loop in the reactor that we just saw).

The `disconnect()` function, on the other hand, facilitates various cleaning instructions when a connection with a client stops. It removes the generator associated with the client connection from the `generators` dictionary and closes the generator, the `file` object stored in the `sessions` dictionary, as well as the client connection itself. Finally, it deletes the keys that correspond to the client connection from the remaining dictionaries.

Let's turn our attention to the new `process_request()` function, which is now an asynchronous generator:

```
# Chapter18/example6.py

from operator import mul
from functools import reduce

#####################################################################
# User's Business Logic

async def process_request(conn):
    print(f'Received connection from {sessions[conn].address}')
    mode = 'sum'

    try:
        conn.sendall(b'<welcome: starting in sum mode>\n')
        while True:
            line = await readline(conn)
```

```
            if line == 'quit':
                conn.sendall(b'connection closed\r\n')
                return
            if line == 'sum':
                conn.sendall(b'<switching to sum mode>\r\n')
                mode = 'sum'
                continue
            if line == 'product':
                conn.sendall(b'<switching to product mode>\r\n')
                mode = 'product'
                continue

            print(f'{sessions[conn].address} --> {line}')
            try:
                nums = list(map(int, line.split(',')))
            except ValueError:
                conn.sendall(
                    b'ERROR. Enter only integers separated by commas\n')
                continue

            if mode == 'sum':
                conn.sendall(b'Sum of input integers: %a\r\n'
                    % str(sum(nums)))
            else:
                conn.sendall(b'Product of input integers: %a\r\n'
                    % str(reduce(mul, nums, 1)))
    finally:
        print(f'{sessions[conn].address} quit')
```

The logic that handles client data and performs the computation remains the same, and the only differences with this new function are the `async` keyword (placed in front of the `def` keyword) and the `await` keyword used with the new `readline()` function. These differences, in essence, convert our `process_request()` function into a non-blocking one, with the condition that the new `readline()` function is also non-blocking:

```
# Chapter18/example6.py

import types

@types.coroutine
def readline(conn):
    def inner(conn, line):
        gen = generators[conn]
        try:
            callback[conn] = gen.send(line) # Continue the generator
        except StopIteration:
            disconnect(conn)
```

```
            line = yield inner
            return line
```

Similar to what we saw in the previous example, we are importing the `types` module from Python and using the `@types.coroutine` decorator to make the `readline()` function a generator-based coroutine, which is non-blocking. Each time a callback (which takes in a client connection and a line of data) is called, the execution flow will go into the `inner()` function inside this coroutine and execute the instructions.

Specifically, it sends the line of data to the generator, which will enable the instructions in `process_request()` to handle it asynchronously and store the return value to the appropriate callback—unless the end of the generator has been reached, in which case the `disconnect()` function will be called.

Our last task is to test whether this server is actually capable of handling multiple clients at the same time. To do this, execute the following script first:

```
> python3 example6.py
Server up, running, and waiting for call on localhost 8080
```

Similar to what you saw earlier, open two additional Terminals and use Telnet into this running server with both:

```
> telnet localhost 8080
Trying 127.0.0.1...
Connected to localhost.
Escape character is '^]'.
<welcome: starting in sum mode>
```

As you can see, both clients are being handled correctly: both are able to connect, and both receive the welcome message. This is also illustrated by the server output, as follows:

```
> python3 example6.py
Server up, running, and waiting for call on localhost 8080
Received connection from ('127.0.0.1', 63855)
Received connection from ('127.0.0.1', 63856)
```

Further tests could involve sending messages to the server at the same time, which it can still handle. The server can also keep track of individual modes of calculation that are unique to individual clients (in other words, assuming each client has a separate mode of calculation). We have successfully built a non-blocking, concurrent server from scratch.

Summary

More often than not, low-level network programming involves the manipulation and handling of sockets (defined as theoretical endpoints within the nodes of a specific computer network, responsible for receiving or sending data from the nodes that they are in). The architecture of server-side communication consists of multiple steps involving socket handling, such as bind, listen, accept, read, and write. The `socket` module provides an intuitive API that facilitates these steps.

To create a non-blocking server with the `socket` module, asynchronous generators need to be implemented, in order for the execution flow to switch between tasks and data. This process also involves using callbacks that can be run by the execution flow at a later time. These two elements allow for the server to read and handle the data coming in from multiple clients at the same time, allowing the server to become non-blocking.

We will conclude our book with the next chapter, with practical techniques for designing and implementing concurrent programs. Specifically, we will discuss how to test, debug, and schedule concurrent applications, methodically and effectively.

Questions

- What is a socket? How is it relevant to network programming?
- What is the procedure for server-side communication when a potential client makes a request to connect?
- What are some methods provided by the `socket` module to facilitate low-level network programming on the server-side?
- What are generators? What is their advantage over Python lists?
- What are asynchronous generators? How can they be applied to build a non-blocking server?

Further reading

For more information, you can refer to the following links:

- *Keynote on Concurrency*, PyBay 2017, Raymond Hettinger (`https://pybay.com/site_media/slides/raymond2017-keynote/async_examples.html`)
- *A simple Python webserver*, Stephen C. Phillips (`blog.scphillips.com/posts/2012/12/a-simple-python-webserver/`)
- *How to Work with TCP Sockets in Python*, Alexander Stepanov (`steelkiwi.com/blog/working-tcp-sockets/`)
- *Socket Programming in Python*, Nathan Jennings (`realpython.com/python-sockets/#multi-connection-client-and-server`)
- *Introduction to Python Generators* (`realpython.com/introduction-to-python-generators/`)

19
Testing, Debugging, and Scheduling Concurrent Applications

In this chapter, we will discuss the process of using concurrent Python programs on a higher level. First, you will learn about scheduling Python programs to be run concurrently at a later time—either once, or periodically. We will analyze APScheduler, a Python library that allows us to do this on a cross-platform basis. Furthermore, we will go over testing and debugging, which are essential yet are often overlooked components of programming. Given the complexities of concurrent programming, testing and debugging are even more difficult than in traditional applications. This chapter will cover a number of strategies for the effective testing and debugging of concurrent programs.

The following topics will be covered in this chapter:

- The APScheduler library and its usage in concurrently scheduling Python applications
- Different testing techniques for Python programs
- Debugging practices in Python programming, as well as concurrency-specific debugging techniques

Technical requirements

The following is a list of prerequisites for this chapter:

- Ensure that you have Python 3 installed on your computer
- Ensure that you have the `apscheduler` and `concurrencytest` libraries installed with your Python distribution

- Download the GitHub repository at `https://github.com/PacktPublishing/Mastering-Concurrency-in-Python`
- During this chapter, we will be working with the subfolder named `Chapter19`
- Check out the following video to see the Code in Action: `http://bit.ly/2OZdOZc`

Scheduling with APScheduler

APScheduler (short for **Advanced Python Scheduler**) is an external Python library that supports the scheduling of Python code to be executed later, either once or periodically. This library gives us high-level options to dynamically add/remove jobs to/from the job list so they can be scheduled and executed, as well as to decide how to distribute those jobs to different threads and processes.

Some might think of Celery (`http://www.celeryproject.org/`) as the go-to scheduling tool for Python. However, while Celery is a distributed task queue with basic scheduling capabilities, APScheduler is quite the opposite: a scheduler with basic task queuing options and advanced scheduling functionalities. Additionally, users of both tools have reported that APScheduler is easier to set up and implement.

Installing APScheduler

As with most common Python external libraries, APScheduler can be installed via the package manager, `pip`, by running the following command in your Terminal:

```
pip install apscheduler
```

Another way to install this library, if the `pip` command does not work, is to manually download the source code from PyPI, which can be found at `pypi.org/project/APScheduler/`. The downloaded file can then be extracted and installed by running the following command:

```
python setup.py install
```

As always, to test whether your APScheduler distribution has been correctly installed, open a Python interpreter and try to import the library, as follows:

```
>>> import apscheduler
```

If no errors are returned, it means that the library has been completely installed and is ready to be used.

Not a scheduling service

As the term scheduler can be quite misleading to specific groups of developers, let's clarify the functionalities that APScheduler provides, as well as what it does not provide. First and foremost, the library can be used as a cross-platform scheduler that is also application-specific, as opposed to more common schedulers that are platform-specific, such as the cron daemon (for Linux systems) or the Windows task scheduler.

It is important to note that APScheduler is not, in itself, a scheduling service that has a prebuilt GUI or command-line interface. It is still a Python library that has to be imported and utilized inside existing applications (that is why it is application-specific). However, as you will learn later on, APScheduler comes with numerous functionalities that can be leveraged to build an actual scheduling service.

For example, the ability to schedule jobs (specifically, background ones) is essential for web applications nowadays, as they can include different but important functionalities, such as sending emails or backing up and synchronizing data. In that context, APScheduler is arguably the most common tool to schedule tasks for cloud applications that involve Python instructions, such as Heroku and PythonAnywhere.

APScheduler functionalities

Let's explore some of the most common functionalities provided by the APScheduler library. Execution-wise, it offers three different scheduling mechanisms, so that one can choose the mechanism that is most suitable for one's applications (these mechanisms are also sometimes called event triggers):

- **Cron-style scheduling**: This mechanism allows jobs to have prespecified start and end times
- **Interval-based execution**: This mechanism runs jobs at even intervals (for example, every two minutes, every day), with optional start and end times
- **Delayed execution**: This mechanism allows the application to wait for a specific period of time before executing items in the job list

Furthermore, APScheduler allows us to store jobs to be executed in various backend systems, such as regular memory, MongoDB, Redis, RethinkDB, SPLAlchemy, or ZooKeeper. Whether it is a desktop program, a web application, or simply a Python script, APScheduler is most likely to be able to work with how scheduled jobs are stored.

In addition to that, the library can also work seamlessly with common Python concurrency frameworks, such as AsyncIO, Gevent, Tornado, and Twisted. This means that the low-level code included in the APScheduler library contains instructions that can cohesively schedule and execute functions and programs implemented in these frameworks, making the library even more dynamic.

Finally, APScheduler provides different options to actually execute the scheduled code, by specifying the appropriate executor(s). Specifically, one can simply execute jobs normally, in a blocking way or in the background. We also have the option to use a pool of threads or processes to distribute the work in a concurrent way. Later on, we will look at an example where we utilize a process pool to execute scheduled jobs.

The following diagram maps out all of the major classes and functionalities included in APScheduler:

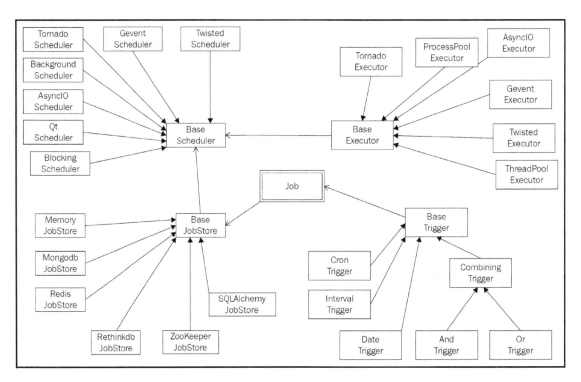

APScheduler—main classes and functionalities

APScheduler API

In this section, we will look at how to actually integrate APScheduler into existing Python programs, by analyzing the different classes and methods provided by the library. We will also look at how jobs are distributed across different threads and processes, when we utilize a concurrent executor to run our scheduled jobs.

Scheduler classes

First, let's look at the options available for our main scheduler, which is the most important component in the process of scheduling tasks to be executed at a later time:

- `BlockingScheduler`: This class should be used when the scheduler is intended to be the only task running in the process. As the name suggests, an instance of this class will block any other instructions in the same process.
- `BackgroundScheduler`: As opposed to `BlockingScheduler`, this class allows scheduled jobs to be executed in the background, inside an existing application.

In addition, there are also scheduler classes to be used if your application utilizes specific concurrency frameworks: `AsyncIOScheduler` for the `asyncio` module; `GeventScheduler` for Gevent; `TornadoScheduler` for Tornado applications; `TwistedScheduler` for Twisted applications; and so on.

Executor classes

Another important choice to be made during the process of scheduling jobs to be executed at a later time is: Which executor(s) should run the jobs? Generally, the default executor, `ThreadPoolExecutor`, which distributes the work across different threads in the same process, is recommended. However, as you have learned, if the scheduled jobs contain instructions that utilize CPU-intensive operations, then the workload should be distributed across multiple CPU cores, and `ProcessPoolExecutor` should be utilized.

It is important to note that these two executor classes interact with the `concurrent.futures` module that we discussed in earlier chapters, in order to facilitate concurrent execution. The default number of maximum workers for both executor classes is `10`, and can be changed upon initialization.

Trigger keywords

The last decision in the process of building a scheduler is how scheduled jobs should be executed in the future; this is the event-trigger option we mentioned earlier. APScheduler provides three different triggering mechanisms; the following keywords should be passed as an argument to the scheduler initializer, in order to specify the event trigger type:

- `'date'`: This keyword is used when the job is to be run once, at a specific point in the future.
- `'interval'`: This is keyword is used when the job is to be run at fixed intervals of time. We will be using this keyword in our examples later on.
- `'cron'`: This keyword is used when the job is to be periodically run at a certain time of day.

Additionally, it is possible to mix and match multiple types of trigger. We also have the option to have scheduled jobs executed either when all registered triggers so specify, or when at least one of them does.

Common scheduler methods

Finally, let's consider the methods that are commonly used when declaring a scheduler, in addition to the preceding classes and keywords. Specifically, the following methods are called by `scheduler` objects:

- `add_executor()`: This method is called to register an executor to run jobs in the future. Specifically, we typically pass the string `'processpool'` to this method to have the jobs be distributed across multiple processes. Otherwise, as mentioned, as thread pool will be used a the default executor. This method also returns an executor object that can be manipulated further.
- `remove_executor()`: This method is used on an executor object, to remove it from a scheduler.
- `add_job()`: This method can be used to add an additional job to the job list, to be executed later. The method first takes in a callable that is the new job in the job list, and various other arguments that are used to specify how the job should be scheduled and executed. Similar to `add_executor()`, this method can return a `job` object that can be manipulated outside the method.
- `remove_job()`: Similarly, this method can be used on a `job` object, to remove it from a scheduler.

- start(): This method starts scheduled jobs along with implemented executors, and begins to process the job list.
- shutdown(): This method stops the calling scheduler object, along with its job list and implemented executors. If it is called when there are current jobs running, those jobs will not be interrupted.

Examples in Python

In this subsection, we will look at how some of the APIs that we discussed are used in sample Python programs. Download the code for this book from the GitHub page, then go ahead and navigate to the Chapter19 folder.

Blocking scheduler

First, let's take a look at an example of a blocking scheduler in the Chapter19/example1.py file:

```
# Chapter19/example1.py

from datetime import datetime

from apscheduler.schedulers.background import BlockingScheduler

def tick():
    print(f'Tick! The time is: {datetime.now()}')

if __name__ == '__main__':
    scheduler = BlockingScheduler()
    scheduler.add_job(tick, 'interval', seconds=3)

    try:
        scheduler.start()
        print('Printing in the main thread.')
    except KeyboardInterrupt:
        pass

scheduler.shutdown()
```

In this example, we are implementing a scheduler for the `tick()` function specified in the preceding code, which simply prints out the current time at which it is executed. In our main function, we are using an instance from the `BlockingScheduler` class, imported from APScheduler, as our scheduler for this program. In addition to this, the aforementioned `add_job()` method is used to register `tick()` as a job to be executed later. Specifically, it should be executed periodically, at even intervals (specified by the `'interval'` string passed in)—particularly, every three seconds (specified by the argument `seconds=3`).

Recall that a blocking scheduler will block all other instructions in the same process that it runs in. To test this, we are also inserting a `print` statement, right after starting the scheduler, to see whether it will be executed. After running the script, your output should look similar to the following (except for the specific times that are being printed out):

```
> python3 example1.py
Tick! The time is: 2018-10-31 17:25:01.758714
Tick! The time is: 2018-10-31 17:25:04.760088
Tick! The time is: 2018-10-31 17:25:07.762981
```

Notice that this scheduler will run forever, unless it is stopped by a `KeyboardInterrupt` event or other potential exceptions, and the printing statement that we placed near the end of the main program will never be executed. For this reason, the `BlockingScheduler` class should only be used when it is intended to be the only task running in its process.

Background scheduler

In this example, we will look at whether the use of the `BackgroundScheduler` class would help if we wanted to execute our scheduler in the background, concurrent with other tasks. The code for this example is included in the `Chapter19/example2.py` file, as follows:

```
# Chapter19/example2.py

from datetime import datetime
import time

from apscheduler.schedulers.background import BackgroundScheduler

def tick():
    print(f'Tick! The time is: {datetime.now()}')

if __name__ == '__main__':
    scheduler = BackgroundScheduler()
    scheduler.add_job(tick, 'interval', seconds=3)
    scheduler.start()
```

```
    try:
        while True:
            time.sleep(2)
            print('Printing in the main thread.')
    except KeyboardInterrupt:
        pass

scheduler.shutdown()
```

The code in this example is almost identical to what we had previously. However, here, we are using the class for background schedulers, as well as printing out messages from the main program every two seconds, in an infinite `while` loop. Theoretically, if the `scheduler` object can indeed run the scheduled job in the background, our output will consist of a combination of print statements, in both the main program and the `tick()` function.

The following is my output, after executing the script:

```
> python3 example2.py
Printing in the main thread.
Tick! The time is: 2018-10-31 17:36:35.231531
Printing in the main thread.
Tick! The time is: 2018-10-31 17:36:38.231900
Printing in the main thread.
Printing in the main thread.
Tick! The time is: 2018-10-31 17:36:41.231846
Printing in the main thread.
```

Again, the scheduler will continue on forever, until an interruption from the keyboard is evoked. Here, we can see what we expected to see: print statements from the main program and the scheduled job are produced concurrently, indicating that the scheduler was indeed running in the background.

Executor pool

One additional functionality offered by APScheduler is the ability to distribute scheduled jobs to be executed across multiple CPU cores (or processes). In this example, you will learn how to do that with a background scheduler. Navigate to the `Chapter19/example3.py` file and inspect the included code, as follows:

```
# Chapter19/example3.py

from datetime import datetime
import time
import os
```

```
from apscheduler.schedulers.background import BackgroundScheduler

def task():
    print(f'From process {os.getpid()}: The time is {datetime.now()}')
    print(f'Starting job inside {os.getpid()}')
    time.sleep(4)
    print(f'Ending job inside {os.getpid()}')

if __name__ == '__main__':
    scheduler = BackgroundScheduler()
    scheduler.add_executor('processpool')
    scheduler.add_job(task, 'interval', seconds=3, max_instances=3)
    scheduler.start()

    try:
        while True:
            time.sleep(1)
    except KeyboardInterrupt:
        pass

scheduler.shutdown()
```

In this program, the job that we would like to schedule (the `task()` function) prints out the identifier of the process that is running it at each call (using the `os.getpid()` method) and is designed to last for around four seconds. In the main program, we are using the same background scheduler we used in the last example, but we are specifying that scheduled jobs should be executed in a pool of processes:

```
scheduler.add_executor('processpool')
```

Remember that the default value of the number of processes in this pool is 10, and can be changed to a different value. Next, as we add the job to the scheduler, we also have to specify that this job can be executed in more than one process instance (in this case, three instances); this allows our process pool executor to be utilized fully and efficiently:

```
scheduler.add_job(task, 'interval', seconds=3, max_instances=3)
```

The first few lines of my output, after running the program, are as follows:

```
> python3 example3.py
From process 1213: The time is 2018-11-01 10:18:00.559319
Starting job inside 1213
From process 1214: The time is 2018-11-01 10:18:03.563195
Starting job inside 1214
Ending job inside 1213
From process 1215: The time is 2018-11-01 10:18:06.531825
Starting job inside 1215
```

```
Ending job inside 1214
From process 1216: The time is 2018-11-01 10:18:09.531439
Starting job inside 1216
Ending job inside 1215
From process 1217: The time is 2018-11-01 10:18:12.531940
Starting job inside 1217
Ending job inside 1216
From process 1218: The time is 2018-11-01 10:18:15.533720
Starting job inside 1218
Ending job inside 1217
From process 1219: The time is 2018-11-01 10:18:18.532843
Starting job inside 1219
Ending job inside 1218
From process 1220: The time is 2018-11-01 10:18:21.533668
Starting job inside 1220
Ending job inside 1219
From process 1221: The time is 2018-11-01 10:18:24.535861
Starting job inside 1221
Ending job inside 1220
From process 1222: The time is 2018-11-01 10:18:27.531543
Starting job inside 1222
Ending job inside 1221
From process 1213: The time is 2018-11-01 10:18:30.532626
Starting job inside 1213
Ending job inside 1222
From process 1214: The time is 2018-11-01 10:18:33.534703
Starting job inside 1214
Ending job inside 1213
```

As you can see from the printed process identifiers, the scheduled job was being executed in different processes. You will also notice that the ID of the first process was `1213`, and, as soon as our scheduler started to use the process with the ID of `1222`, it then switched back to the `1213` process (notice the last few lines of the preceding output). This is because our process pool contains 10 workers, and the `1222` process was the last element of the pool.

Running on the cloud

Earlier, we mentioned that cloud services that host Python code, such as Heroku and PythonAnywhere, are some of the most common places to apply APScheduler's functionalities. In this subsection, we will look at one example from the user guide on the Heroku website, which can be found in the `Chapter19/example4.py` file:

```
# ch19/example4.py
# Copied from: http://devcenter.heroku.com/articles/clock-processes-python
```

```
from apscheduler.schedulers.blocking import BlockingScheduler

scheduler = BlockingScheduler()

@scheduler.scheduled_job('interval', minutes=3)
def timed_job():
    print('This job is run every three minutes.')

@scheduler.scheduled_job('cron', day_of_week='mon-fri', hour=17)
def scheduled_job():
    print('This job is run every weekday at 5pm.')

scheduler.start()
```

You can see that this program uses decorators to register scheduled jobs for the scheduler. Specifically, when the `scheduled_job()` method is called by a `scheduler` object, that whole instruction can be used as a decorator for a function, to convert it to a scheduler job for that scheduler. You can also see an example of a `cron` scheduled job in the preceding code, which can be executed at specific times of day (in this case, it is every weekday at 5:00 p.m.).

As a final note on APScheduler, we have seen that instructions utilizing the library API are also Python code, and not a separate service in itself. However, considering how flexible the library is in providing different scheduling options and how pluggable its programs are in terms of working with external services (such as cloud-based ones), APScheduler is a valuable tool for scheduling Python applications.

Testing and concurrency in Python

As mentioned previously, testing is an essential (yet often overlooked) component of software development specifically, and programming in general. The goal of testing is to evoke errors that would indicate the existence of bugs in our programs. This is to be contrasted with the process of debugging, which is used to identify the bugs themselves; we will discuss the topic of debugging in the next section.

In the most general sense, testing is about determining whether specific functions and methods can perform and produce results that we intend them to; this is typically done by comparing the results that are produced. In other words, testing is collecting evidence as to the correctness of our programs.

However, testing cannot ensure that all potential defects and bugs in the program under consideration will be identified. Additionally, the test results are only as good as the tests themselves, and if the tests do not cover some specific potential bugs, then those bugs will most likely not be detected during the testing process.

Testing concurrent programs

In this chapter, we will consider two distinct topics of testing, with regard to concurrency: **testing concurrent programs** and **testing programs concurrently**. When it comes to testing concurrent programs, the general consensus is that it is extremely demanding and difficult to get right. As you saw in previous chapters, bugs such as deadlocks or race conditions can be quite subtle in a concurrent program, and can manifest themselves in many ways.

Furthermore, one distinct feature of concurrency is nondeterminism, which means that it is possible for a concurrency bug to be detected in one run of the test and become invisible in another. This is because a major component of concurrent programming is the scheduling of tasks, and, like the order in which different tasks are executed in a concurrent program, concurrency bugs can show and hide themselves in an unpredictable way. We call these tests non-reproducible, to indicate that we cannot reliably pass or fail a program with these tests in a consistent way.

With that said, there are some general strategies that can help us to navigate through the process of testing concurrent programs. In the following section, we will explore the various tools that can assist us with specific strategies for testing concurrent programs.

Unit testing

The first strategy that we will consider is unit testing. The term indicates a method that tests for individual units of the program under consideration, where a unit is the smallest testable part of the program. For this reason, unit testing is not meant for testing a complete concurrent system. Specifically, it is recommended that you do not test a concurrent program as a whole, but that you break the program down into smaller components and test them separately.

As usual, Python provides libraries that offer intuitive APIs to solve most common problems in programming; in this case, it is the `unittest` module. The module was originally inspired by the unit testing framework for the Java programming language JUnit; it also provides common unit testing functionalities in other languages. Let's consider a quick example of how we can use `unittest` to test a Python function in the `Chapter19/example5.py` file:

```
# Chapter19/example5.py

import unittest

def fib(i):
    if i in [0, 1]:
        return i

    return fib(i - 1) + fib(i - 2)

class FibTest(unittest.TestCase):
    def test_start_values(self):
        self.assertEqual(fib(0), 0)
        self.assertEqual(fib(1), 1)

    def test_other_values(self):
        self.assertEqual(fib(10), 55)

if __name__ == '__main__':
    unittest.main()
```

In this example, we would like to test the `fib()` function that generates specific elements in the Fibonacci sequence (where an element is the sum of its two previous elements), whose starting values are 0 and 1, respectively.

Now, let's focus our attention on the `FibTest` class, which extends the `TestCase` class from the `unittest` module. This class contains different methods that test for specific cases of the results returned by the `fib()` function. Specifically, we have a method that looks at edge cases for this function, which are the first two elements of the sequence, and another method that tests for an arbitrary value in the sequence.

After running the preceding script, your output should be similar to the following:

```
> python3 unit_test.py
. .
----------------------------------------------------------------------
Ran 2 tests in 0.000s

OK
```

The output indicates that our tests passed without any errors. Additionally, as suggested by the class name, this class is an individual test case, which is a unit of testing. You can expand different test cases into a **test suite**, which is defined as a collection of test cases, test suites, or both. Test suites are generally used to combine tests that you would like to run together.

Static code analysis

Another viable method to identify potential errors and bugs in your concurrent programs is to perform static code analysis. This method looks for patterns in the code itself, as opposed to executing some (or all) parts of the code. In other words, static code analysis inspects a program by visually looking at its structure, the use of variables and instructions, and how different parts of the program interact with each other.

The main advantage of using static code analysis is that we are not relying on just the execution of our programs and the results produced during that process (in other words, dynamic testing) to determine whether the programs are correctly designed. This method can detect errors and bugs that do not manifest themselves (easily, or at all) in implemented tests. For this reason, static code analysis should be combined with other testing methods, such as unit testing, to create a comprehensive testing process.

Static code analysis is often used to identify subtle errors or bugs, such as unused variables, empty catch blocks, or even unnecessary object creation. In terms of concurrent programming, the method can be used to analyze synchronization techniques used in a program. Specifically, static code analysis can look for the atomicity of shared resources in a program, then reveal any uncoordinated usage of non-atomic resources that could produce detrimental race conditions.

Various tools are available to facilitate static code analysis for Python programs, with one of the more common ones being PMD (`https://github.com/pmd/pmd`). With that said, the specific use of these tools is beyond the scope of this book, and we will not go into them further.

Testing programs concurrently

Another aspect of combining testing and concurrent programming is performing tests in a concurrent way. This aspect of testing is more straightforward and intuitive than testing concurrent programs themselves. In this subsection, we will explore a library that can help us facilitate this process, `concurrencytest`, which can work seamlessly with test cases implemented with the preceding `unittest` module.

concurrencytest is designed as a testtools extension that implements concurrency in running test suites. It can be installed from PyPI, using pip, as follows:

```
pip install concurrencytest
```

Additionally, concurrencytest is dependent on the testtools (pypi.org/project/testtools/) and python-subunit (pypi.org/project/python-subunit/) libraries, which are a test extension framework and a streamlining protocol for test results, respectively. These libraries can also be installed via pip, as follows:

```
pip install testtools
pip install python-subunit
```

As always, to verify your installation, try to import the library in a Python interpreter:

```
>>> import concurrencytest
```

Receiving no printed errors means that the library and its dependencies were installed successfully. Now, let's look at how this library can help us to achieve better speed for our tests. Navigate to the Chapter19/example6.py file and consider the following code:

```python
# Chapter19/example6.py

import unittest

def fib(i):
    if i in [0, 1]:
        return i

    a, b = 0, 1
    n = 1
    while n < i:
        a, b = b, a + b
        n += 1

    return b

class FibTest(unittest.TestCase):
    def __init__(self, *args, **kwargs):
        super(FibTest, self).__init__(*args, **kwargs)
        self.mod = 10 ** 10

    def test_start_values(self):
        self.assertEqual(fib(0), 0)
        self.assertEqual(fib(1), 1)
```

```
    def test_big_value_v1(self):
        self.assertEqual(fib(499990) % self.mod, 9998843695)

    def test_big_value_v2(self):
        self.assertEqual(fib(499995) % self.mod, 1798328130)

    def test_big_value_v3(self):
        self.assertEqual(fib(500000) % self.mod, 9780453125)

if __name__ == '__main__':
    unittest.main()
```

The main goal of the examples in this section is testing the function that produces numbers in the Fibonacci sequence, specifically numbers with large indices. The `fib()` function that we have is similar to that of the previous example, although this one performs the calculation iteratively, without using recursion.

In our test case, aside from the two starting values, we are now testing numbers at indices 499,990, 499,995, and 500,000. Since the resulting numbers are significantly large, we are only testing the last ten digits for each number (this is done via the `mod` attribute of the test class, specified in the initialization method). This testing process will be executed in one process, in a sequential way.

Run the program, and your output should be similar to the following:

```
> python3 example6.py
....
----------------------------------------------------------------------
Ran 4 tests in 8.809s

OK
```

Again, the time specified in the output can vary from system to system. With that said, remember the amount of time that the program took, so that you can compare it with the speed of other programs that we will consider later on.

Now, let's look at how we can distribute the testing workload across multiple processes, with `concurrencytest`. Consider the `Chapter19/example7.py` file, as follows:

```
# Chapter19/example7.py

import unittest
from concurrencytest import ConcurrentTestSuite, fork_for_tests

def fib(i):
    if i in [0, 1]:
        return i
```

```
            a, b = 0, 1
            n = 1
            while n < i:
                a, b = b, a + b
                n += 1

            return b

    class FibTest(unittest.TestCase):
        def __init__(self, *args, **kwargs):
            super(FibTest, self).__init__(*args, **kwargs)
            self.mod = 10 ** 10

        def test_start_values(self):
            self.assertEqual(fib(0), 0)
            self.assertEqual(fib(1), 1)

        def test_big_value_v1(self):
            self.assertEqual(fib(499990) % self.mod, 9998843695)

        def test_big_value_v2(self):
            self.assertEqual(fib(499995) % self.mod, 1798328130)

        def test_big_value_v3(self):
            self.assertEqual(fib(500000) % self.mod, 9780453125)

    if __name__ == '__main__':
        suite = unittest.TestLoader().loadTestsFromTestCase(FibTest)
        concurrent_suite = ConcurrentTestSuite(suite, fork_for_tests(4))
        runner.run(concurrent_suite)
```

This version of the program is examining the same `fib()` function, using the same test case. However, in the main program, we are initializing an instance of the `ConcurrentTestSuite` class, from the `concurrencytest` library. This instance takes in a test suite, which was created using the `TestLoader()` API from the `unittest` module, and the `fork_for_tests()` function, with the parameter 4, to specify that we want to utilize four separate processes to distribute the testing procedure.

Now, let's run this program and compare its speed with that of our previous tests:

```
> python3 example7.py
....
-------------------------------------------------------------------
Ran 4 tests in 4.363s

OK
```

You can see that a significant improvement in speed was achieved by this method of multiprocessing. However, this improvement does not fall around perfect scalability (discussed in `Chapter 16`, *Designing Lock-Based and Mutex-Free Concurrent Data Structures*); that is because there is significant overhead in creating concurrent test suites that can be executed across multiple processes.

One more thing that we should mention is that it is quite possible to achieve the same multiprocessing setup that we implemented here by using the traditional concurrent programming tools that we discussed in previous chapters, such as `concurrent.futures` or `multiprocessing`. With that said, the `concurrencytest` library, as we have seen, is able to eliminate significant boilerplate code, and thus provides an easy and fast API.

Debugging concurrent programs

In this last section, we will discuss the various advanced debugging strategies that can be used individually, or in combination with each other, to detect and pinpoint bugs in our programs. In general, the term **debugging** is used to denote the process in which programmers attempt to identify and resolve problems or defects that would otherwise cause the computer applications they reside in to produce incorrect results, or even stop functioning.

The strategies that we will discuss include general debugging strategies, as well as particular techniques used in debugging concurrent applications. A systematic application of these strategies would improve your debugging process, in terms of both effectiveness and speed.

Debugging tools and techniques

First, let's briefly look at some of the most common techniques and tools that can facilitate the debugging process in Python:

- **Print debugging**: This is perhaps the most elementary and intuitive method of debugging. This method involves inserting print statements for the values of variables, or the states of functions, at various points in the execution of the considered program. Doing this allows us to keep track of how these values and states interact and change throughout the program, giving us insight into how particular errors or exceptions are raised.

- **Logging**: In the field of computer science, logging is the process of recording various events that take place during the execution of a particular program. In essence, logging can be quite similar to print debugging; however, the former typically writes to a log file that can be viewed later on. Python offers excellent logging functionalities, included in the built-in `logging` module. Users can specify the level of importance for the logging process; for example, normally, one can log only important events and operations, but during debugging everything will be logged.

- **Tracing**: This is another form of keeping track of program execution. Tracing follows the actual low-level details of the program execution, as opposed to only changes in variables and functions. Tracing functionalities can be implemented via the `sys.settrace()` method in Python.

- **Using a debugger**: Sometimes, the most powerful debugging options can be achieved via an automated debugger. The most popular debugger in the Python language is the Python debugger: `pdb`. This module provides an interactive debugging environment that implements useful functionalities, such as breakpoints, stepping through the source code, or inspecting the stack.

Again, the preceding strategies are applicable to both traditional and concurrent programs, and a combination of more than one of them can help programmers to obtain valuable information during the debugging process.

Debugging and concurrency

Similar to the problem of testing concurrent programs, debugging, when applied to concurrency, can become increasingly complex and difficult. Again, this is due to the fact that shared resources can interact with (and be altered by) multiple agents, simultaneously. With that said, there are still strategies that can make the process of debugging concurrent programs more straightforward. These include the following:

- **Minimization**: Concurrent applications are typically implemented in complex and interconnected systems. Debugging a whole system when an error occurs can be quite intimidating, and is not very feasible. The strategy is to isolate different parts of the system into individual, smaller programs, and identify the one that fails in the same way as for large systems. Here, we want to divide a large program into smaller and smaller parts, until they cannot be broken apart anymore. The original error can then be easily identified and efficiently fixed.

- **Single-threading and processing**: This method is similar to minimization, but focuses on only one aspect of concurrent programming: the interaction between different threads/processes. By eliminating the biggest aspect of concurrency in your concurrent programming, you can isolate errors to either the program logic itself (which can cause errors, even when running sequentially) or the interaction between threads/processes (which can result from the common concurrency bugs that we discussed in previous chapters).
- **Manipulating scheduling to amplify potential bugs**: We have actually seen the application of this method in previous chapters. Some concurrency bugs do not manifest themselves often, if the threads/processes implemented in our program are not scheduled to execute in a specific way. For example, an existing race condition may not affect a shared resource if the interactions between it and other agents happen so fast that they do not overlap each other often. This leads to the fact that testing might not reveal a race condition, even though it actually exists in the program.

Various methods can be implemented in Python so that incorrect values and operations resulting from concurrency bugs can be amplified. Two of the most common are fuzzing, achieved by inserting sleep functions between commands in thread/process instructions, and minimizing the system thread switching interval, achieved by using the `sys.setcheckinterval()` method (discussed in `Chapter 17`, *Memory Models and Operations on Atomic Types*). These methods disrupt the regular scheduling protocols of thread and process execution in Python in different ways, and can effectively reveal hidden concurrency bugs.

Summary

In this chapter, we provided a high-level analysis of concurrent programs in Python, via scheduling, testing, and debugging. Scheduling can be done in Python via the APScheduler module, which provides powerful and flexible functionalities to specify how scheduled jobs should be executed later on in the future. Furthermore, the module allows scheduled jobs to be distributed and executed across different threads and processes, offering a concurrency improvement in testing speed.

Concurrency also introduces complex problems in terms of testing and debugging, resulting from simultaneous and parallel interactions between the agents in a program. However, these problems can be approached effectively, with methodical solutions and the appropriate tools.

This topic marks the end of our journey through *Mastering Concurrency in Python*. Throughout this book, we have considered and analyzed various elements of concurrent programming with the Python language in depth, such as threading, multiprocessing, and asynchronous programming. Powerful applications involving concurrency, such as context management, reduction operations, image processing, and network programming, were also discussed, in addition to the common problems faced by programmers working with concurrency in Python.

In the most general sense, this book serves as a guide to some of the more advanced concepts of concurrency; it is my hope that, through reading this book, you have had the chance to become well versed in the topic of concurrent programming.

Questions

- What is APScheduler? Why isn't it a scheduling service?
- What are the main scheduling functionalities of APScheduler?
- What are the differences between APScheduler and another scheduling tool in Python, Celery?
- What is the purpose of testing in programming? How is it different in concurrent programming?
- What methods of testing were discussed in this chapter?
- What is the purpose of debugging in programming? How is it different in concurrent programming?
- What methods of debugging were discussed in this chapter?

Further reading

For more information, you can refer to the following links:

- *Advanced Python Scheduler* (`apscheduler.readthedocs.io/en/latest/index`)
- *Scheduled Jobs with Custom Clock Processes in Python with APScheduler* (`devcenter.heroku.com/articles/clock-processes-python`)
- *The Architecture of APScheduler*, Ju Lin (`enqueuezero.com/apscheduler`)
- , Alex. *APScheduler 3.0 released*, Alex Grönholm (`alextechrants.blogspot.com/2014/08/apscheduler-30-released`)
- *Testing Your Code* (*The Hitchhiker's Guide to Python*), Kenneth Reitz
- *Python – concurrencytest: Running Concurrent Tests*, Corey Goldberg (`coreygoldberg.blogspot.com/2013/06/python-concurrencytest-running`)
- *Getting Started With Testing in Python*, Anthony Shaw (`realpython.com/python-testing/`)
- *Tracing python code*, Andrew Dalke (`dalkescientific.com/writings/diary/archive/2005/04/20/tracing_python_code`)

Assessments

Chapter 1

What is the idea behind concurrency, and why is it useful?

Concurrency is about designing and structuring program commands and instructions so that different sections of the program can be executed in an efficient order, while sharing the same resources.

What are the differences between concurrent programming and sequential programming?

In sequential programming, the commands and instructions are executed one at the time, in a sequential order. In concurrent programming, some sections might be executed in an efficient way for better execution time.

What are the differences between concurrent programming and parallel programming?

In parallel programming, the separate sections of a program are independent of one another; they do not interact with one another, and therefore, they can be executed simultaneously. In concurrent programming, the separate tasks share the same resources, and some form of coordination between them is therefore required.

Can every program be made concurrent or parallel?

No.

What are embarrassingly parallel tasks?

Embarrassingly parallel tasks can be divided into separate, independent sections, with little or no effort.

What are inherently sequential tasks?

Tasks wherein the order of execution of individual sections is crucial to the results of the tasks, which cannot be made concurrent or parallel to obtain better execution time, are called inherently sequential.

What does I/O bound mean?

This is a condition in which the time it takes to complete a computation is determined mainly by the time spent waiting for input/output operations to be completed.

How is concurrent processing currently being used in the real world?

Concurrency can be found almost everywhere: desktop and mobile applications, video games, web and internet development, artificial intelligence, and so on.

Chapter 2

What is Amdahl's law? What problem does Amdahl's law look to solve?

Amdahl's law provides an estimate of the theoretical speedup in latency of the execution of a task at fixed workload that can be expected of a system whose resources are improved.

Explain the formula of Amdahl's Law, along with its components.

The formula for Amdahl's Law is as follows:

$$S = \frac{1}{B + \frac{1-B}{j}}$$

In the preceding formula, the following applies:

- S is the theoretical speedup in consideration.
- B is the portion of the whole task that is inherently sequential.
- j is the number of processors being utilized.

According to Amdahl's Law, would speedup increase indefinitely as resources in the system improved?

No; as the number of processors becomes larger, the efficiency gained through the improvement decreases.

What is the relationship between Amdahl's Law and the law of diminishing returns?

You have seen that in specific situations (namely, when only the number of processors increases), Amdahl's Law resembles the law of diminishing returns. Specifically, as the number of processors becomes larger, the efficiency gained through the improvement decreases, and the speedup curve flattens out.

Chapter 3

What is a thread? What are the core differences between a thread and a process?

A thread of execution is the smallest unit of programming commands. More than one thread can be implemented within a same process, usually executing concurrently and accessing/sharing the same resources, such as memory, while separate processes do not do this.

What are the API options provided by the `thread` module in Python?

The main feature of the `thread` module is its fast and efficient method of creating new threads to execute functions: the `thread.start_new_thread()` function. Aside from this, the module only supports a number of low-level ways of working with multithreaded primitives and sharing their global data space. Additionally, simple lock objects (for example, mutexes and semaphores) are provided for synchronization purposes.

What are the API options provided by the `threading` module in Python?

In addition to all of the functionalities for working with threads that the `thread` module provides, the `threading` module also supports a number of extra methods, as follows:

- `threading.activeCount()`: This function returns the number of currently active thread objects in the program.
- `threading.currentThread()`: This function returns the number of thread objects in the current thread control from the caller.
- `threading.enumerate()`: This function returns a list of all of the currently active thread objects in the program.

What are the processes of creating new threads via the `thread` and `threading` modules?

The processes for creating new threads using the `thread` and `threading` module is as follows:

- In the `thread` module, new threads are created to execute functions concurrently. The way to do this is by using the `thread.start_new_thread()` function: `thread.start_new_thread(function, args[, kwargs])`.

- To create and customize a new thread using the `threading` module, there are specific steps that need to be followed:
    1. Define a subclass of the `threading.Thread` class in our program
    2. Override the default `__init__(self [,args])` method inside the subclass to add custom arguments for the class
    3. Override the default `run(self [,args])` method inside the subclass to customize the behavior of the thread class when a new thread is initialized and started

What is the idea behind thread synchronization using locks?

In a given program, when a thread is accessing/executing the critical section of the program, any other threads need to wait until that thread finishes executing. The typical goal of thread synchronization is to avoid any potential data discrepancies when multiple threads access their shared resource; allowing only one thread to execute the critical section at a time guarantees that no data conflicts can occur in our multithreaded applications. One of the most common ways to apply thread synchronization is through the implementation of a locking mechanism.

What is the process of implementing thread synchronization using locks in Python?

In our `threading` module, the `threading.Lock` class provides a simple and intuitive approach to creating and working with locks. Its main usage includes the following methods:

- `threading.Lock()`: This method initializes and returns a new lock object.
- `acquire(blocking)`: When this method is called, all threads will run synchronously (that is, only one thread can execute the critical section at a time).
- `release()`: When this method is called, the lock is released.

What is the idea behind the queue data structure?

A queue is an abstract data structure that is a collection of different elements maintained in a specific order; these elements can be other objects in a program.

What is the main application of queuing in concurrent programming?

The concept of a queue is even more prevalent in the subfield of concurrent programming, as the order of elements maintained inside a queue plays an important role when a multithreaded program handles and manipulates its shared resources.

What are the core differences between a regular queue and a priority queue?

The priority queue abstract data structure is similar to the queue data structure, but each of the elements of a priority queue, as the name suggests, has a priority associated with it; in other words, when an element is added to a priority queue, its priority needs to be specified. Unlike in regular queues, the dequeuing principle of a priority queue relies on the priority of the elements: the elements with higher priority are processed before those with lower priority.

Chapter 4

What is a file descriptor, and in what ways can it be handled in Python?

A file descriptor is used as a handle on an opened external file in a program. In Python, a file descriptor is handled by either using `open()` and `close()` functions or using the `with` statement; for example:

- `f = open(filename, 'r'); ... ; f.close()`
- `with open(filename, 'r') as f: ...`

What problem arises when file descriptors are not handled carefully?

Systems can only handle a certain number of opened external files in one running process. When that limit is passed, the handles on the opened files will be compromised and file descriptor leakage will occur.

What is a lock, and in what ways can it be handled in Python?

A lock is a mechanism in concurrent and parallel programming that performs thread synchronization. In Python, a `threading.Lock` object can be handled by either using the `acquire()` and `release()` methods or using the `with` statement; for example:

- `my_lock.acquire(); ... ; my_lock.release()`
- `with my_lock: ...`

What problem arises when locks are not handled carefully?

When an exception occurs while a lock is acquired, the lock can never be released and acquired again if it is not handled carefully, causing a common problem in concurrent and parallel programming called deadlock.

What is the idea behind context managers?

Context managers are in charge of the context of resources within a program; they define and handle the interaction of other entities with those resources, and perform cleanup tasks after the program exits the context.

What options does the `with` statement in Python provide, in terms of context management?

The `with` statement in Python offers an intuitive and convenient way to manage resources while ensuring that errors and exceptions are handled correctly. Aside from better error handling and guaranteed cleanup tasks, the `with` statement also provides extra readability from your programs, which is one of the strongest features that Python offers to its developers.

Chapter 5

What is HTML?

HTML stands for **Hypertext Markup Language**, which is the standard and most common markup language for developing web pages and web applications.

What are HTTP requests?

Most of the communication done via the internet (more specifically, the World Wide Web) utilizes HTTP. In HTTP, request methods are used to convey information on what data is being requested and should be sent back from a server.

What are HTTP response status codes?

HTTP response status codes are three-digit numbers that signify the state of communication between a server and its client. They are sorted into five categories, each indicating a specific state of communication.

How does the `requests` module help with making web requests?

The `requests` module manages the communication between a Python program and a web server through HTTP requests.

What is a ping test and how is one typically designed?

A ping test is a tool typically used by web administrators to make sure that their sites are still available to clients. A ping test does this by making requests to the websites under consideration and analyzes the returned response status codes

Why is concurrency applicable in making web requests?

Both the process of making different requests to a web server and the process of parsing and processing downloaded HTML source code are independent across separate requests.

What are the considerations that need to be made when developing web scraping applications?

The following considerations should be made when developing applications that make concurrent web requests:

- The terms of service and data-collecting policies
- Error handling
- Updating your program regularly
- Avoiding over-scraping

Chapter 6

What is a process? What are the core differences between a process and a thread?

A process is an instance of a specific computer program or software that is being executed by the operating system. A process contains both the program code and its current activities and interactions with other entities. More than one thread can be implemented within the same process to access and share memory or other resources, while different processes do not interact in this way.

What is multiprocessing? What are the core differences between multiprocessing and multithreading?

Multiprocessing refers to the execution of multiple concurrent processes from an operating system, in which each process is executed on a separate CPU, as opposed to a single process at any given time. Multithreading, on the other hand, is the execution of multiple threads, which can be within the same process.

What are the API options provided by the multiprocessing module?

The `multiprocessing` module provides APIs to the `Process` class, which contains the implementation of a process while offering methods to spawn and interact with processes using an API similar to the `threading` module. The module also provides the `Pool` class, which is mainly used to implement a pool of processes, each of which will carry out the tasks submitted.

What are the core differences between the `Process` class and the `Pool` class from the multiprocessing module?

The `Pool` class implements a pool of processes, each of which will carry out tasks submitted to a `Pool` object. Generally, the `Pool` class is more convenient than the `Process` class, especially if the results returned from your concurrent application should be ordered.

What are the options to determine the current process in a Python program?

The `multiprocessing` module provides the `current_process()` method, which will return the `Process` object that is currently running at any point of a program. Another way to keep track of running processes in your program is to look at the individual process IDs through the `os` module.

What are daemon processes? What are their purposes, in terms of waiting for processes in a multiprocessing program?

Daemon processes run in the background and do not block the main program from exiting. This specification is common when there is not an easy way for the main program to tell if it is appropriate to interrupt the process at any given time, or when exiting the main program without completing the worker does not affect the end result.

How can you terminate a process? Why is it sometimes acceptable to terminate processes?

The `terminate()` method from the `multiprocessing.Process` class offers a way to quickly terminate a process. If the processes in your program never interact with the shared resources, the `terminate()` method is considerably useful, especially if a process appears to be unresponsive or deadlocked.

What are the ways to facilitate interprocess communication in Python?

While locks are one of the most common synchronization primitives used for communication among threads, pipes and queues are the main way to communicate between different processes. Specifically, they provide message passing options to facilitate communication between processes: pipes for connections between two processes, and queues for multiple producers and consumers.

Chapter 7

What is a reduction operator? What conditions must be satisfied so that an operator can be a reduction operator?

An operator is a reduction operator if it satisfies the following conditions:

- The operator can reduce an array of elements into one scalar value
- The end result (the scalar value) is obtained through creating and computing partial tasks

What properties do reduction operators have that are equivalent to the required conditions?

The communicative and associative properties are considered to be equivalent to the requirements for a reduction operator.

What is the connection between reduction operators and concurrent programming?

Reduction operators require communicative and associative properties. Consequently, their sub-tasks have to be able to be processed independently, which makes concurrency and parallelism applicable.

What are some of the considerations that must be made when working with multiprocessing programs that facilitate interprocess communication in Python?

Some considerations include implementing the poison-pill technique, so that sub-tasks are distributed across all consumer processes; calling `task_done()` on the task queue each time the `get()` function is called, to ensure that the `join()` function will not block indefinitely; and avoiding using the `qsize()` method, which is unreliable and is not implemented on Unix operating systems.

What are some real-life applications of concurrent reduction operators?

Some real-life applications include heavy number-crunching operators and complex programs that utilize logic operators.

Chapter 8

What is an image processing task?

Image processing is the task of analyzing and manipulating digital image files to create new versions of the images, or to extract important data from them.

What is the smallest unit of digital imaging? How is it represented in computers?

The smallest unit of digital imaging is a pixel, which typically contains an RGB value: a tuple of integers between 0 and 255.

What is grayscaling? What purpose does the technique serve?

Grayscaling is the process of converting an image to gray colors by considering only the intensity information of each pixel, represented by the amount of light available. It reduces the dimensionality of the image pixel matrix by mapping traditional three-dimensional color data to one-dimensional gray data.

What is thresholding? What purpose does the technique serve?

Thresholding replaces each pixel in an image with a white pixel if the pixel's intensity is greater than a previously specified threshold, and with a black pixel if the pixel's intensity is less than that threshold. After performing thresholding on an image, each pixel of that image can only hold two possible values, significantly reducing the complexity of image data.

Why should image processing be made concurrent?

Heavy computational number-crunching processes are typically involved when it comes to image processing, as each image is a matrix of integer tuples. However, these processes can be executed independently, which suggests that the whole task should be made concurrent.

What are some good practices for concurrent image processing?

Some good practices for concurrent image processing are as follows:

- Choosing the correct method (out of many)
- Spawning an appropriate amount of processes
- Processing input/output concurrently

Chapter 9

What is the idea behind asynchronous programming?

Asynchronous programming is a model of programming that focuses on coordinating different tasks in an application with the goal that the application will use the least amount of time to finish executing those tasks. An asynchronous program switches from one task to another when it is appropriate to create overlap between the waiting and processing time, and therefore shorten the total time taken to finish the whole program.

How is asynchronous programming different from synchronous programming?

In synchronous programming, the instructions of a program are executed sequentially: a task has to finished executing before the next task in the program starts processing. With asynchronous programming, if the current task takes a significant amount of time to finish, you have the option to specify at one time during the task to switch the execution to another task.

How is asynchronous programming different from threading and multiprocessing?

Asynchronous programming keeps all of the instructions of a program in the same thread and process. The main idea behind asynchronous programming is to have a single executor switch from one task to another if it is more efficient (in terms of execution time) to simply wait for the first task for a while, while processing the second.

Chapter 10

What is asynchronous programming? What advantages does it provide?

Asynchronous programming is a model of programming that takes advantage of coordinating computing tasks to overlap the waiting and processing times. If successfully implemented, asynchronous programming provides both responsiveness and an improvement in speed, as compared to synchronous programming.

What are the main elements in an asynchronous program? How do they interact with each other?

There are three main components of an asynchronous program: the event loop, the coroutines, and the futures. The event loop is in charge of scheduling and managing coroutines by using its task queue; the coroutines are computing tasks that are to be executed asynchronously, and each coroutine has to specify, inside its function, exactly where it will give the execution flow back to the event loop (that is, the task-switching event); the futures are placeholder objects that contain the results obtained from the coroutines.

What are the `async` **and** `await` **keywords? What purposes do they serve?**

The `async` and `await` keywords are provided by the Python language as a way to implement asynchronous programming on a low level. The `async` keyword is placed in front of a function, in order to declare it as a coroutine, while the `await` keyword specifies the task-switching events.

What options does the `asyncio` **module provide, in terms of the implementation of asynchronous programming?**

The `asyncio` module provides an easy-to-use API and an intuitive framework to implement asynchronous programs; additionally, this framework makes the asynchronous code just as readable as synchronous code, which is generally quite rare in asynchronous programming.

What are the improvements, in regards to asynchronous programming, provided in Python 3.7?

Python 3.7 comes with improvements in the API that initiates and runs the main event loop of asynchronous programs, while reserving `async` and `await` as official Python keywords.

What are blocking functions? Why do they pose a problem for traditional asynchronous programming?

Blocking functions have non-stop execution, and therefore, they prevent any attempts to cooperatively switch tasks in an asynchronous program. If forced to release the execution flow back to the event loop, blocking functions will simply halt their execution until it is their turn to run again. While still achieving better responsiveness, in this case, asynchronous programming fails to improve the speed of the program; in fact, the asynchronous version of the program takes longer to finish executing than the synchronous version, most of the time, due to various overheads.

How does `concurrent.futures` **provide a solution to blocking functions for asynchronous programming? What options does it provide?**

The `concurrent.futures` module implements threading and multiprocessing for the execution of coroutines in an asynchronous program. It provides the `ThreadPoolExecutor` and `ProcessPoolExecutor` for asynchronous programming in separate threads and separate processes, respectively.

Chapter 11

What is a communication channel? What is its connection to asynchronous programming?

Communication channels are used to denote both the physical wiring connection between different systems and the logical communication of data that facilitates computer networks. The latter is related to computing, and is more relevant to the idea of asynchronous programming. Asynchronous programming can provide functionalities that complement the process of facilitating communication channels efficiently.

What are the two main parts of the Open Systems Interconnection (OSI) model protocol layers? What purposes do each of them serve?

The media layers contain fairly low-level operations that interact with the underlying process of the communication channel, while the host layers deals with high-level data communication and manipulation.

What is the transport layer? Why is it crucial to communication channels?

The transport layer is often viewed as the conceptual transition between the media layers and the host layers, responsible for sending data along end-to-end connections between different systems.

How does `asyncio` **facilitate the implementation of server-side communication channels?**

Server-wise, the `asyncio` module combines the abstraction of transport with the implementation of an asynchronous program. Specifically, via its `BaseTransport` and `BaseProtocol` classes, `asyncio` provides different ways to customize the underlying architecture of a communication channel.

How does `asyncio` **facilitate the implementation of client-side communication channels?**

Together with the `aiohttp` module and, specifically, `aiohttp.ClientSession`, `asyncio` also offers efficiency and flexibility regarding client-side communication processes, via asynchronously making requests and reading the returned responses.

What is `aiofiles`**?**

The `aiofiles` module, which can work in conjunction with `asyncio` and `aiohttp`, helps to facilitate asynchronous file reading/writing.

Chapter 12

What can lead to a deadlock situation, and why is it undesirable?

A lack of (or mishandled) coordination between different lock objects can cause deadlock, in which no progress can be made and the program is locked in its current state.

How is the dining philosophers problem related to the problem of deadlock?

In the dining philosophers problem, as each philosopher is holding only one fork with their left hand, they cannot proceed to eat or put down the fork they are holding. The only way a philosopher gets to eat their food is for their neighbor philosopher to put their fork down, which is only possible if they can eat their own food; this creates a never-ending circle of conditions that can never be satisfied. This situation is, in essence, the nature of a deadlock, in which all elements of a system are stuck in place and no progress can be made.

What are the four Coffman conditions?

Deadlock is also defined by the necessary conditions that a concurrent program needs to have at the same time, in order for deadlock to occur. These conditions were first proposed by the computer scientist Edward G. Coffman, Jr., and are therefore known as the Coffman conditions. The conditions are as follows:

- At least one resource has to be in a non-shareable state. This means that that resource is being held by an individual process (or thread) and cannot be accessed by others; the resource can only be accessed and held by a single process (or thread) at any given time. This condition is also known as **mutual exclusion**.

- There exists one process (or thread) that is simultaneously accessing a resource and waiting for another held by other processes (or threads). In other words, this process (or thread) needs access to two resources in order to execute its instructions, one of which it is already holding, and the other of which it is waiting for from other processes (or threads). This condition is called **hold and wait**.

- Resources can only be released by a process (or a thread) holding them if there are specific instructions for the process (or thread) to do so. This is to say that unless the process (or thread) voluntarily and actively releases the resource, that resource remains in a non-shareable state. This is the **no preemption** condition.

- The final condition is called **circular wait**. As suggested by the name, this condition specifies that there exists a set of processes (or threads) such that the first process (or thread) in the set is in a waiting state for a resource to be released by the second process (or thread), which, in turn, needs to be waiting for the third process (or thread); finally, the last process (or thread) in the set is waiting for the first one.

How can resource ranking solve the problem of deadlock? What other problems occur when this is implemented?

Instead of accessing the resources arbitrarily, if the processes (or threads) are to access them in a predetermined, static order, the circular nature of the way that they acquire and wait for the resources will be eliminated. However, if you place enough locks on the resources of your concurrent program, it will become entirely sequential in its execution, and, combined with the overhead of concurrent programming functionalities, it will have an even worse speed than the purely sequential version of the program.

How can ignoring locks solve the problem of deadlock? What other problems can occur when this is implemented?

By ignoring locks, our program resources effectively become shareable among different processes/threads in a concurrent program, thus eliminating the first of the four Coffman conditions, **mutual exclusion**. Doing this, however, can be seen as misunderstanding the problem completely. We know that locks are utilized so that processes and threads can access the shared resources in a program in a systematic, coordinated way, to avoid mishandling the data. Removing any locking mechanisms in a concurrent program means that the likelihood of the shared resources, which are now free from accessing limitations, being manipulated in an uncoordinated way (and therefore becoming corrupted) increases significantly.

How is livelock related to deadlock?

In a livelock situation, the processes (or threads) in the concurrent program are able to switch their states, yet they simply switch back and forth infinitely, and no progress can be made.

Chapter 13

What is starvation, and why is it undesirable in a concurrent program?

Starvation is a problem in concurrent systems in which a process (or a thread) cannot gain access to the necessary resources to proceed with its execution, and therefore, cannot make any progress.

What are the underlying causes of starvation? What are the common superficial causes of starvation that can manifest from the underlying cause?

Most of the time, a poorly coordinated set of scheduling instructions is the main cause of starvation. Some high-level causes for starvation might include the following:

- Processes (or threads) with high priorities dominate the execution flow in the CPU, and thus, low-priority processes (or threads) are not given the opportunity to execute their own instructions.
- Processes (or threads) with high priorities dominate the usage of non-shareable resources, and thus, low-priority processes (or threads) are not given the opportunity to execute their own instructions. This situation is similar to the first one, but addresses the priority of accessing resources, instead of the priority of execution itself.
- Processes (or threads) with low priorities are waiting for resources to execute their instructions, but as soon as the resources become available, other processes (or threads) with higher priorities are immediately given access to them, so the low-priority processes (or threads) wait infinitely.

What is the connection between deadlock and starvation?

Deadlock situations can also lead to starvation, as the definition of starvation states that if there exists a process (or a thread) that is unable to make any progress because it cannot gain access to the necessary process, the process (or thread) is experiencing starvation. This is also illustrated in the dining philosophers problem.

What is the readers-writers problem?

The readers-writers problem asks for a scheduling algorithm so that readers and writers can access the text file appropriately and efficiently, without mishandling/corrupting the data included.

What is the first approach to the readers-writers problem? Why does starvation arise in that situation?

The first approach allows for multiple readers to access the text file simultaneously, since readers simply read in the text file and do not alter the data in it. The problem with the first approach is that when a reader is accessing the text file and a writer is waiting for the file to be unlocked, if another reader starts its execution and wants to access the file, it will be given priority over the writer that has already been waiting. Additionally, if more and more readers keep requesting access to the file, the writer will be waiting infinitely.

What is the second approach to the readers-writers problem? Why does starvation arise in that situation?

This approach implements the specification that once a writer makes a request to access the file, no reader should be able to jump in line and access the file before that writer. As opposed to what we see in the first solution to the readers-writers problem, this solution is giving priority to writers and, as a consequence, the readers are starved.

What is the third approach to the readers-writers problem? Why does it successfully address starvation?

This approach implements a lock on both readers and writers. All threads will then be subject to the constants of the lock, and equal priority will thus be achieved among separate threads.

What are some common solutions to starvation?

Some common solutions to starvation include the following:

- Increasing the priority of low-priority threads
- Implementing a first-in-first-out thread queue
- A priority queue that also gives gradually increasing priority to threads that have been waiting in the queue for a long time
- Or if a thread has been able to access the shared resource for many times, it will be given less priority

Chapter 14

What is a critical section?

Critical sections indicate shared resources that are accessed by multiple processes or threads in a concurrent application, which can lead to unexpected, and even erroneous, behaviors.

What is a race condition, and why is it undesirable in a concurrent program?

A race condition occurs when two or more threads/processes access and alter a shared resource simultaneously, resulting in mishandled and corrupted data.

What is the underlying cause of a race condition?

The root cause of a race condition is multiple threads/process reading in and altering a shared resource simultaneously; and, when all of the threads/processes finish their execution, only the result of the last thread/process is registered.

How can locks solve the problem of a race condition?

Since the race conditions arise when multiple threads or processes access and write to a shared resource simultaneously, the solution is to isolate the execution of different threads/processes, especially when interacting with the shared resource. With locks, we can turn a shared resource in a concurrent program into a critical section, whose integrity of data is guaranteed to be protected.

Why are locks sometimes undesirable in a concurrent program?

There are a number of disadvantages to using locks: with enough locks implemented in a concurrent program, the whole program might become entirely sequential; locks don't lock anything.

What are the problems race conditions raise in real-life systems and applications?

The problems race conditions raise in real-life systems and applications are as follows:

- **Security**: A race condition can be both exploited as a security vulnerability (to give external agents illegal access to a system) and used as random key generation, for security processes.

- **Operating systems**: A race condition occurring when two agents (users and applications) interact with the same memory space can lead to unpredictable behaviors.
- **Networking**: In networking, a race condition can lead to giving multiple users powerful privileges in a network.

Chapter 15

What is the difference in memory management between Python and C++?

C++ associates a variable to its value by simply writing the value to the memory location of the variable; Python has its variables reference point to the memory location of the values that they hold. For this reason, Python needs to maintain a reference count for every value in its memory space.

What problem does the GIL solve for Python?

To avoid race conditions, and consequently, the corruption of value reference counts, the GIL is implemented so that only one thread can access and mutate the counts at any given time.

What problem does the GIL create for Python?

The GIL effectively prevents multiple threads from taking advantage of the CPU and executing CPU-bound instructions at the same time. This means that if multiple threads that are meant to be executed concurrently are CPU-bound, they will actually be executed sequentially.

What are some of the approaches to circumventing the GIL in Python programs?

There are a few ways to deal with the GIL in your Python applications; namely, implementing multiprocessing instead of multithreading, and utilizing other, alternative Python interpreters.

Chapter 16

What is the main approach to solving the problem that locks don't lock anything?

The main approach is to have the locks internally implemented within the data structure's class attributes and methods, so that external functions and programs cannot bypass those locks and access a shared concurrent object simultaneously.

Describe the concept of scalability, in the context of concurrent programming.

By the scalability of a program, we mean the changes in performance when the amount of tasks to be processed by the program increases. Andre B. Bondi defines the term scalability as, *"the capability of a system, network, or process to handle a growing amount of work, or its potential to be enlarged to accommodate that growth."*

How does a naive locking mechanism affect the scalability of a concurrent program?

The scalability of a simple lock-based data structure is highly undesirable: as more threads are added to the program to execute more tasks, the performance of the program decreases somewhat linearly. Since only one thread can access and increment the shared counter at any given time, the more increments the program has to execute, the longer it will take to finish all of the incremented tasks.

What are approximate counters, and how do they help with the problem of scalability in concurrent programming?

The basic idea behind approximate counters is to distribute the work (incrementing the shared global counter) across other low-level counters. When an active thread executes and wants to increment the global counter; first, it has to increment its corresponding local counter. With one separate counter object for each thread, the threads can update their corresponding local counters independently and simultaneously, creating overlaps that will result in a better performance in speed for the programs.

Are lock-free data structures possible in Python? Why, or why not?

The characteristic of being lock-free is impossible to implement in CPython, due to the existence of the **Global Interpreter Lock (GIL)**, which prevents more than one thread from executing in the CPU at any given time.

What is a mutex-free concurrent data structure, and how is it different from a concurrent lock-based one?

The term mutex-free concurrent data structures indicates a lack of a locking mechanism and the use of other synchronization mechanisms to protect the data.

What is the RCU technique, and what problem does it solve for mutex-free concurrent data structures?

To protect the integrity of concurrent data structures, the RCU technique creates and maintains another version of the data structure when a thread or process is requesting reading or writing access to it. By isolating the interaction between the data structure and the threads/processes within a separate copy, RCU ensures that no conflicting data can occur.

Chapter 17

What are the main components of the Python memory manager?

The main components of the Python memory manager are as follows:

- The raw memory allocator handles the allocation of memory at a low level by interacting with the memory manager of the operating system.
- Object-specific memory allocators interact with the private heap of objects and values in Python. These allocators execute memory operations that are specific to given data and object types.
- The system allocators from the standard C library are responsible for helping the raw memory allocator interact with the memory manager of the operating system.

How does the Python memory model resemble a labeled directed graph?

The memory model keeps track of its data and variables via nothing but pointers: the value of every variable is a pointer, and this point can be pointing to a symbol, a number, or a subroutine. So, these pointers are the directed edges in the object graph, and the actual values (symbols, numbers, and subroutines) are the nodes in the graph.

What are the advantages and disadvantages of the Python memory model, in terms of developing concurrent applications in Python?

Reasoning about the behaviors of a concurrent program can be significantly easier than doing the same in another programming language. However, the ease of understanding and debugging concurrent programs in Python also comes with a decrease in performance.

What is an atomic operation, and why is it desirable in concurrent programming?

Atomic operations are instructions that cannot be interrupted during their execution. Atomicity is a desirable characteristic of concurrent operations, as it guarantees the safety of data shared across different threads.

Give three examples of innately atomic operations in Python.

Some examples are as follows:

- Appending a predefined object to a list
- Extending a list with another list
- Fetching an element from a list
- Popping from a list
- Sorting a list
- Assigning a variable to another variable
- Assigning a variable to an attribute of an object
- Creating a new entry for a dictionary
- Updating a dictionary with another dictionary

Chapter 18

What is a socket? How is it relevant in network programming?

Low-level network programming, more often than not, involves the manipulation and handling of sockets, which are defined as theoretical endpoints within the nodes of a specific computer network, responsible for receiving or sending data from the nodes that they are in.

What is the procedure of server-side communication when a potential client makes a request to connect?

To open a communication channel from the server side, a network programmer must first create a socket and bind it to a specific address. The server then begins to listen to any potential communication requests created by the clients in the network. Upon receiving a request to connect from a potential client, the server can now decide whether to accept that request. A connection is then established between the two systems in the network, which means that they can start to communicate and share data with each other. As the client sends a message to the server via the communication channel, the server then processes the message, and eventually sends a response back to the client through the same channel; this process continues until the connection between them ends, either by one of them quitting the connection channel or through some external factors.

What are some methods provided by the socket module to facilitate low-level network programming on the server side?

Some of the important methods are as follows:

- `socket.bind()` binds the calling socket to the address that is passed to the method
- `socket.listen()` allows the server that we create to accept connections from potential clients
- `socket.accept()` accepts a specific connection that the calling socket object has
- `socket.makefile()` returns a file object that is associated with the calling socket object
- `socket.sendall()` sends the data passed as a parameter to the calling socket object
- `socket.close()` marks the calling socket object as closed

What are generators? What is their advantage over Python lists?

Generators are functions that return iterators and are able to be paused and resumed dynamically. Generator iterators are lazy, and only produce results when specifically asked. For this reason, generator iterators are more efficient in terms of memory management, and are therefore often preferred over lists when large amounts of data are involved.

What are asynchronous generators? How can they be applied in order to build a non-blocking server?

Asynchronous generators allow for the execution flow to switch between generating tasks. Combined with using callbacks that can be run at a later time, a server can read and handle data coming in from multiple clients at the same time.

Chapter 19

What is APScheduler? Why isn't it a scheduling service?

APScheduler is an external Python library that supports scheduling Python code to be executed later. APScheduler is not, in itself, a scheduling service that has a built-in GUI or command-line interface. It is still a Python library that has to be imported and utilized inside existing applications. However, APScheduler comes with numerous functionalities that can be leveraged in order to build an actual scheduling service.

What are the main scheduling functionalities of APScheduler?

It offers three different scheduling mechanisms: cron-style scheduling, interval-based execution, and delayed execution. Furthermore, APScheduler allows for storing the jobs to be executed in various backend systems, and working with common Python concurrency frameworks, such as AsyncIO, Gevent, Tornado, and Twisted. Finally, APScheduler provides different options to actually execute the scheduled code, by specifying the appropriate executor(s).

What are the differences between APScheduler and another scheduling tool in Python, Celery?

While Celery is a distributed task queue with basic scheduling capabilities, APScheduler is quite the opposite: a scheduler with basic task queuing options and advanced scheduling functionalities. Users have reported that APScheduler is easier to set up and implement than Celery.

What is the purpose of testing in programming? How is it different in concurrent programming?

Testing evokes errors that indicate the existence of bugs in our programs. Testing concurrent programs is typically difficult, as non-determinism allows for a concurrency bug to be detected in one run of the test and become invisible in another. We call the concurrency bugs that might become invisible from test to test non-reproducible, and they are the main reason why we cannot reply on testing to detect all concurrency bugs consistently.

What are the methods of testing that were discussed in this chapter?

Unit testing is applied to individual units of the program under consideration, where a unit is the smallest testable part of the program. Static code analysis, on the other hand, looks at the actual code itself without executing it. Static code analysis scans for visual errors in the code structure and usage of variables and functions.

What is the purpose of debugging in programming? How is it different in concurrent programming?

Debugging is the process by which programmers attempt to identify and resolve problems or defects that would otherwise cause the computer applications that they reside in to produce incorrect results, or even stop functioning. Similar to the problem of testing concurrent programs, debugging, when applied to concurrency, can become increasingly complex and difficult, as shared resources can interact with (and be altered by) multiple agents simultaneously.

What are the methods of debugging that were discussed in this chapter?

General debugging methods include print debugging, logging, tracing, and using a debugger. The process of debugging concurrent programs can utilize minimization, single-threading/processing, and manipulating scheduling in order to amplify potential bugs.

Other Books You May Enjoy

If you enjoyed this book, you may be interested in these other books by Packt:

Learn Python Programming - Second Edition
Fabrizio Romano

ISBN: 978-1-78899-666-2

- Get Python up and running on Windows, Mac, and Linux
- Explore fundamental concepts of coding using data structures and control flow
- Write elegant, reusable, and efficient code in any situation
- Understand when to use the functional or OOP approach
- Cover the basics of security and concurrent/asynchronous programming
- Create bulletproof, reliable software by writing tests
- Build a simple website in Django
- Fetch, clean, and manipulate data

Clean Code in Python
Mariano Anaya

ISBN: 978-1-78883-583-1

- Set up tools to effectively work in a development environment
- Explore how the magic methods of Python can help us write better code
- Examine the traits of Python to create advanced object-oriented design
- Understand removal of duplicated code using decorators and descriptors
- Effectively refactor code with the help of unit tests
- Learn to implement the SOLID principles in Python

Leave a review - let other readers know what you think

Please share your thoughts on this book with others by leaving a review on the site that you bought it from. If you purchased the book from Amazon, please leave us an honest review on this book's Amazon page. This is vital so that other potential readers can see and use your unbiased opinion to make purchasing decisions, we can understand what our customers think about our products, and our authors can see your feedback on the title that they have worked with Packt to create. It will only take a few minutes of your time, but is valuable to other potential customers, our authors, and Packt. Thank you!

Index

www.ingramcontent.com/pod-product-compliance
Lightning Source LLC
Chambersburg PA
CBHW060647060326
40690CB00020B/4542